COMPUTER CULTURE
The Scientific, Intellectual, and Social Impact of the Computer

ANNALS OF THE NEW YORK ACADEMY OF SCIENCES
Volume 426

COMPUTER CULTURE
The Scientific, Intellectual, and Social Impact of the Computer

Edited by Heinz R. Pagels

The New York Academy of Sciences
New York, New York
1984

Library of Congress Cataloging in Publication Data

Main entry under title:

Computer culture.

(Annals of the New York Academy of Sciences; v. 426)
Papers presented at a symposium sponsored by the New York Academy of Sciences, held Apr. 5–8, 1983.
Bibliography: p.
Includes indexes.
1. Computers—Congresses.   I. Pagels, Heinz R., 1939–   . II. New York Academy of Sciences.
III. Title: Computer culture.   IV. Series.
Q11.N5   vol. 426   500 s   84-22638
[QA75.5]   [001.64]

SP
Printed in the United States of America
ISBN 0-89766-244-X (Cloth)
ISBN 0-89766-245-8 (Paper)
ISSN 0077-8923

ANNALS OF THE NEW YORK ACADEMY OF SCIENCES
Volume 426
November 1, 1984

COMPUTER CULTURE[a]
The Scientific, Intellectual, and Social Impact of the Computer

Editor and Conference Organizer
HEINZ R. PAGELS

Organizing Committee
SIDNEY BOROWITZ, BONNIE BROWNSTEIN, ROLF LANDAUER, ARTHUR MELMED, MARVIN MINSKY, SEYMOUR PAPERT, RAJ REDDY, JACOB SCHWARTZ, GEORGE SOROS, DONALD STRAUS, JOSEPH TRAUB, JOHN THOMAS, SHERRY TURKLE, and HAO WANG

CONTENTS

[a]This volume is the result of a symposium entitled Computer Culture: The Scientific Intellectual, and Social Impact of the Computer held on April 5-8, 1983 and sponsored by The New York Academy of Sciences.

Part XII. Panel Discussion
Donald B. Straus, *Moderator*

Part XIII. How Computers Change the Way We Think about Ourselves
Donald B. Straus, *Chair*

Financial assistance was received from:
- INTERNATIONAL BUSINESS MACHINES CORPORATION
- RICHARD LOUNSBERY FOUNDATION

Introduction

HEINZ R. PAGELS

The New York Academy of Sciences
New York, New York 10021

Last year, *Time* magazine chose not a man of the year but a machine of the year, the computer, a selection that confirmed what many people knew—computers and their impact on society were major news. Unlike political figures, no one voted for the creation of computers. Like radio, television, the jet airplane, they are not part of a political movement. Yet their impact on our lives is as great as a political movement and is becoming greater every day. Somehow, the order of nature allows for the invention of computers, human enterprise has brought them into existence, and now it is our task to comprehend what they mean for our lives.

New technologies alter our perceptions, the way we think about social, political, and material realities. No one living in a modern society is isolated from technology, its promises, its terrors, and the subtle ways it changes our perceptions. Like other technological inventions, computers will find their place in our civilization. What place that will be remains an open question but we will hear more about that during this symposium.

There is an ancient Chinese curse (some say it is a blessing) that says, "May you live in interesting times." We live in such "interesting times" as witnesses to one of the great technological revolutions of all times, a revolution that promises to bring forth a new world, even while the old one is dying.

We should acknowledge that computers are not just another product of industrial society. They are not like automobiles, cameras, or telephones, which represent extensions of human physical or sensory capabilities. Computers are information processing systems. They manipulate symbols, and thus resemble us more closely in what we see as our essential being: a thinking person. In computers we see the first flickerings of what we recognize as man-made intelligence, a new kind of intelligence different from ours, in some ways more powerful and in others much more limited. Computers, in an extreme view, can be seen as alien beings which we are striving to exploit for human purposes.

Much work by people we might call "computer diplomats" tries to relate the world of computers to that of humans and focuses on making computers less alien and more friendly to their users. The unfriendliness of computers, their complexity as perceived by many people, is the outstanding barrier in the way of even greater acceptance of this new technology. But once that barrier is down (and it is falling, especially among young people), the integration of human culture and computer culture will become a fact of our lives.

A few years ago as I was reflecting upon the growing impact of computers, I realized that this would be an ideal subject for a Science Week Symposium of The New York Academy of Sciences. I had been to computer conferences before, but they were for experts and technicians. But a technological revolution is too important to be left to the technologists. The computer revolution is not just new hardware and software in the home and office but is also changing our world view. Even as the classical world view is disappearing around us, new metaphors for an invisible reality are being created. Yet many intellectually aware and educated people are ignorant of this, dismissing these new intellectual developments and failing to grasp the dimensions of the change. I am reminded of the many philosophers and social theorists of the early nineteenth century who failed to see the coming impact of the industrial revolution.

Supporting the computer revolution is a new outlook on the universe and the place of humanity in it. I thought that a symposium that could bring this outlook to interested people would be exciting.

With the generous help of the organizing committee I tried to identify the leaders of the computer revolution, and here I ran into a problem. Unlike many fields of science, for example, physics or biology, the computer revolution had no universally agreed upon leaders. Of course, there were leaders in special areas, but there was no small group that everyone agreed on. The Isaac Newton or Charles Darwin of computer science has not been identified. Put simply, the architectonic of the computer sciences was not yet defined, and this made it difficult to design a conference program.

The computer revolution is just beginning; what may be important today may be forgotten tomorrow. Still, in spite of the disagreements about where the computer revolution was headed, who was leading it, and what is important, I thought the idea of a symposium, if it brought forth the sense of intellectual excitement, the tumultuousness of different viewpoints, would serve the interest of communicating science. The committee had to be selective, and as a consequence, some areas in computer culture are not covered in this symposium. Yet, I am sure they will be touched upon in the lectures and discussions.

Watching the development of computer culture is like watching a child grow up, with all of its associated precosity and unpredictable changes. Who could have predicted the popularity of personal computers in the grand area of the main frames? Who can tell where we will be 10 years from now or 100 years from now? We are on the threshold of tomorrow, sensitive to the realization that we are glimpsing a domain we cannot see clearly.

We did not ask for this new world. But it is the opportunity of our generation to seize the computer revolution, make it ours, and bring it forth for the good of all humanity. It is a task that instills a sense of responsibility, excitement, promise, and hope.

The Social Impact of the Computer

ROBERT W. LUCKY

Bell Telephone Laboratories
Holmdel, New Jersey 07733

Sometimes I am proud of us. I mean all of mankind. I wonder if there is some intelligence in the universe that applauds our accomplishments. We have split the atom and spliced genes, walked on the moon, and probed the reaches of the solar system. But of it all, I think the most miraculous is the microcomputer. We have breathed life into a fingernail-sized slice of silicon, and given it the capacity to change the fabric of our existence. Indeed, who among us has not already been touched by the computer revolution? And yet—we have just begun.

I am an optimist and a technologist. My viewpoint is unavoidably cluttered with visions of the thrills of technological accomplishment. I see no limit to what we can do in the current fertile technological environment. In such a euphoria it is easy to forget the sociology of our product. To technologists, the pace of the social sciences seems so slow in comparison to our own kaleidoscopic whirl. Too often, also, the individual engineer is caught up inside this kaleidoscope and, like one sliver of colored glass, has very little insight into the pattern being formed by the ensemble of his neighbors.

I believe that computers will provide life enrichment for mankind. However, I am not such an optimist that I believe this can be done without strife and temptation. The strife I shall speak of later in connection with our work life, while the potential for temptation will exist in our homelife. At best, computers can pull us up the evolutionary ladder, freeing us to do meaningful, intellectual work. They can increase our productivity, enabling us to create more wealth with less work, and fill our expanded, discretionary time with alternative forms of education and entertainment. At worst they will steal our jobs, and offer us in return a vicarious existence in the form of an electronic nirvana.

As computer technology progresses, will computers be our servants or our masters? Will they be our competitors, or our friends? To these questions I answer yes. I believe that computers will be servants to those of us who would be masters, they will be competitors to those of us who would be servants, and they will be friends to none.

WHAT COMPUTERS CAN DO

Obviously computers can compute. Everyone also knows that they can store information. Moreover, they can manipulate and process information according to stored algorithms. Recently the capacity of using

1

synthesized speech has been added. Computer speech, while perhaps not as pleasing as we might wish, is reasonably intelligible, and can even be derived by rule from text. Computers can also now recognize isolated spoken commands.

Computers have an embryonic capability to understand natural language sentences (from text input), and to reply in like form. We are perhaps only a few years away from being able to acquire specific information from a computer by speaking to it—albeit using simple speech and sticking strictly to the topic of an information base that the computer knows about.

Given television eyes and robotic arms, computers can recognize simple objects, pick them up, and place them in desired locations and orientations.

WHAT COMPUTERS CANNOT DO

Computers cannot recognize fluent speech. Neither can they recognize complex objects in a picture. As one of my associates pointed out, while we have been able to construct computer programs that can play world-class chess, no one has been able to build a computer that can walk into a room and find the chess board! The irony of this from a human standpoint is obvious, and though the quote somewhat overstates the case, the fact is that there is a set of abilities that seem very simple to humans, but are extremely hard for machines. Many of these hard problems derive from the pattern-recognition ability that we humans have evolved so well. Giving computers the ability to recognize patterns in fluent speech, objects in pictures, and relevant facts in a knowledge base will undoubtedly use up all the capacity that hardware designers are able to design into computers for many years to come.

Computer scientists have been largely unsuccessful in constructing machines that can write their own programs. Automatic programming is thought to be very high on a scale of inherent difficulty, and is not seriously anticipated by scientists at the present time. Since we are becoming more and more dependent upon large and complex programs, and there is a general belief that the productivity of programmers has not significantly increased in the last decade, this is a matter for much deeper philosophical and scientific consideration than we can even allude to in this context.

Finally I should say that I do not believe that a computer will be able to "think," in the context of the famous Turing test, in my lifetime. This means that I do not believe that a machine can pose as a human in answering questions designed to distinguish men from machines. However, neither this shortcoming nor those mentioned above will stop computers from interacting in a very effective fashion with us to do things that will change our lives profoundly.

COMPUTER LITERACY AND THE TWO CULTURES

Who in our society shall benefit from computers? Much has been written in the past few years about the need for computer literacy in our population. Some will be able to participate in the computer revolution, while others—disadvantaged by a lack of familiarity or literacy with computers and their languages—will not. I used to subscribe to this notion myself, but events have changed my opinion. No longer will we need to seek the friendship of computers; they will figuratively walk up and introduce themselves to us. They will meet us on our own terms, and beg our friendship. It will be very hard to avoid their overtures, as they will use a most skillful guile.

I see evidence of C. P. Snow's two cultures about me everywhere, though the infiltration of computer technology into the social sciences has helped close the gap between the cultures. However, I do not feel that this dichotomy will seriously affect the ability of the nontechnologists to make use of computer capabilities. Once I asked my wife if it bothered her that she did not know how a television set worked. It was a stupid question, and I got the answer I deserved. "You turn this knob to the right," she replied absently. She was absolutely correct, and she makes just as effective use of that television set as I do. Indeed, I haven't the foggiest notion of how the automatic transmission in my car works, yet I seem to commute effectively to work each day.

Now in the old days—some four or five years ago—you had to know a lot about computers to use them. Relatively speaking, I did, and secretly I enjoyed membership in the exclusive club. Nonmembers were kept away from the altar of computational power. Journals devoted to computer science were filled with the esoteric jargon and acronyms of the high priests. It was fun! But there was a powerful force afoot—the desire to make money. The easier computers were to use, the friendlier the software, the less complicated the instructions, the more computers could be sold. To the horror of the computer scientists, BASIC swept the land. Screen editors replaced line editors. Menus replaced command vocabularies, and along came electronic spreadsheet programs. Instead of writing complicated computer programs, it was only necessary to answer a series of simple questions in order to customize one's own application. Then along came ikons, mice, and bitpads. Speech synthesis was introduced, and speech recognition was on the verge. Through it all computer sales skyrocketed.

And still, we have just begun to explore the human interface with computers. This problem is attracting a large crowd. Every day new entrepreneurial companies attack the marketplace. The local bookstores have large sections devoted to computer books, the magazine racks are filled with computer magazines, and the colleges are inundated with a disproportionate number of applicants for computer-related studies. In the early years of my career, as a communications theorist I often reflected upon a conjecture that there were only about a hundred people like myself in this field in the world, most of whom I knew personally. Most scientific fields are like this today. But how many people are working on computers and computer applications? There are millions, I am sure. Never before has a particular scientific specialization attracted such a following. All this activity is being fed by the powerful financial incentive of bringing computers to the untouched masses who care nothing for technology. Thus I do not believe that computer illiteracy will protect even the diehards from being personally and decisively affected by the computer revolution.

THE FRIENDLY COMPUTER

Assuming that everyone will have access to computers, the question remains. To whom will computers owe their allegiance? In the preceding section I followed the current vogue with the generous use of the adjective "friendly." This is usually a code word used to indicate a simple, approachable, human interface. For a paper on the social impact of computers, I think it appropriate to take the matter of computer friendship quite literally. Can a computer be a friend to a human?

To begin with we should establish what we mean by "friend." To me the essence of friendship is someone (or something) that has my best interest at heart, cares for me, and has a certain sympathetic understanding. I do not know what goes on in another's mind, so I can only gauge friendship by past actions. Has the other entity always acted in such a way as to reflect a concern for my best interests? Do I have confidence that in a future situation it will act thusly? My dog satisfies this criterion. My neighbor's cat does not. (This is a simpler test than that of thinking— my poor dog would not last a minute in a Turing test.)

The question is, if a computer has always acted as if it had my best interests at heart, is it a friend? After giving the computer all the benefit of a rational argument to this point, I answer with an emotional no. The fact is put simply—I do not trust the computer to continue to act in this way. I confess this is partly emotional, but there is also a scientific basis for this distrust. Complexity has advanced well beyond the single-programmer machine. How can I be sure that those programs that I did not author will act on my behalf? In fact, how can I even be sure that those I did write will behave as I intended? Proving the correctness of all but the most simple programs has turned out to be an essentially impossible problem. Furthermore, the experience of most people who work with computers is to learn a certain wary distrust for them. It is not a question of malevolence, but rather an overwhelming complexity that cannot be completely and predictably controlled. I do not believe that people will feel that computers can really be counted on to be their friends. Even the most infrequent users will collect anecdotal evidence that machines will not always act in the ways we would expect from a friend.

Computers in Our Work Life

Earlier I said that I believed that computers would pull us up the evolutionary ladder. It is almost as if they were the way to get to the next rung. In the office place, however, it may seem more a matter of computers pushing us from behind, always crouching on the rung behind us. I think of the famous quote of Satchel Paige, "Don't look behind you; something may be gaining on you." We may sometimes feel that computers are after our jobs. Of course, it is not the computers themselves but those people who would exploit computers for business purposes that should draw our concern. Computers, in themselves, will not change the age-old roles of the exploiter and the exploited, but they will certainly make new forms of exploitation possible. It is my belief that the computer will enrich our jobs, free us from disagreeable labor, and increase our productivity. Along the way to these accomplishments, we should expect job displacements in various forms and, probably, rebellions against technology.

Computers in business have started on the clerical level. Primarily, they have been "keepers of the information." Actually, we have a long way to go yet in this capacity, since the flow of information in the office is as yet imperfectly understood. In this role they have been a work facilitator, and have not seriously impacted the labor market. A good example of man-machine interaction on this level is word processing for secretaries. Remember the days of multiple carbon copies, when a secretary spent most of his time typing with meticulous care? Recent polls have shown that secretaries are overwhelmingly happy in having computers to help them with document preparation and distribution. They are freed to do more meaningful work. My company recently reevaluated secretarial jobs from the standpoint that, more and more, secretaries are doing tasks and making decisions formerly the exclusive province of executives.

Computers have had a large part in guiding us into the so-called information age. We have recognized that information is a commodity with value, which can be bought, sold, and manipulated. Today most of us can be classed as information workers. Each day we sift through information, combining this piece with that, in the process creating new information and adding value. Through it all the computers have been our acolytes, preserving and guarding the precious information, serving it up on demand, and quizzically raising their electronic eyebrows when the information served does not match the desired purpose.

Having created a large new category of jobs—people who work in front of computer displays—computers could now be gearing up to jeopardize these very jobs they have created. Computer communication networks can disperse these jobs geographically, opening them up to competition in a wider labor market. For example, lawyers in the Midwest, where the cost of living is moderate, handle New York cases via telecommunications links; word processing is electronically placed into cheap labor markets on offshore islands. The word that has been recently coined is "telescabbing." The information worker is being freed from geographic constraints, but at a cost of increased competition. Furthermore, computers themselves may soon compete for these jobs. Currently a flurry of activity in computer science centers around what are called "expert systems," in which a knowledge base in a particular field is made easily accessible to a naive computer user. There are many jobs today in which people access information from a terminal and relay the information to other people (presumably lacking the magical knowledge or authorizations needed to access it themselves). Computers should be able to handle these jobs themselves. It can only be a matter of a little time before computers compete in earnest for information-type jobs in which there is little value added by the workers themselves.

Can computers reach up the corporate ladder? I think not. To stress the point I would like to relate a small incident. The president of my company expressed a desire to use experimentally some office automation system equipment. At the time I had in my laboratory a small group that did research on office automation systems. I asked them to report back to me in two weeks with some recommendations for appropriate equipment for the president's office. At the end of the two-week interval, I met with the research group to receive their recommendations. There was a lot of silence around the table. Finally, one of the group started out with, "We've got this problem—." It was, as they say, an inauspicious beginning. I impatiently asked them what their problem was. The researcher blurted out plaintively, "We don't know what presidents do!"

That simple response is rather profound. It is easy to design computer systems to aid the structured jobs of lower- and middle-echelon information workers, but not so for the higher executives. They have eclectic jobs, are aided by efficient human secretaries and assistants, and have very little time and patience for manipulating unforgiving keyboards in search of elusive, hard-to-categorize information. Yet, and sometimes unfortunately, they are so often the ones who command the attention and resources to possess expensive terminals, computer systems, and support personnel. In spite of a great deal of publicity, management information systems have not yet been an overwhelming success. Much, much harder yet is the actual automation of this job function itself.

Instead, computers will strike downwards in the company hierarchy. At risk will be the blue-collar workers with jobs involving repetitive, manual tasks. When I visit electronic assembly plants and see acres of workers stuffing the same little parts into the same circuit boards hour after hour, I wonder how far we have come from the infamous factories of the industrial revolution era. These jobs can be automated. There has been a recent explosion of interest in the robotics field. Robotic arms give computers manipulative capability, television cameras give them vision, and tactile sensors add touch. Here too there is great economic incentive. The electronic assembly plants I mentioned are not competitive in the United States when matched in the marketplace with their counterparts elsewhere in the world. In order to retain much of its industry, the United States will have to automate low-skill jobs. I do not think it is a question of computers taking these jobs from our people. Other people will take the jobs if the computers do not. Furthermore, the replacement by robots will probably not go as fast as some fear. Robots and advanced technology are not inexpensive. People will be able to compete in the labor market with machines for a long time to come. I, for one, feel that this competition is demeaning to humankind. I do not believe that man was born to toil over either machinery or computer terminals.

WHAT JOBS ARE LEFT?

To the extent to which a job is routine, it is susceptible ultimately to automation. This should tend to eliminate repetitive, boring tasks, and leave intellectually challenging jobs filled with variety. I feel that this is for the betterment of mankind, but I would not expect everyone to agree with this. There will undoubtedly be a cry for a return to simplicity and honest labor, for the jobs remaining for people will be more complex and fraught with uncertainties and pressures. I sometimes wonder as I walk the streets of our large cities how many people on this earth are privileged to have jobs in which they are allowed to think and exercise free will. Very few, I think. What could mankind accomplish if one percent of the world's population was freed to work on intellectual pursuits?

I think there is a kind of application of the second law of thermodynamics to the workplace. The automation of repetitive jobs will tend to eliminate the routine and accentuate the complex. This is a progression in the direction of increasing entropy, or uncertainty. Modern executives have already felt this. Instant worldwide communication, increased competition, the tangled web of law, and the pace of technology have created jobs that seem frantic, pressured, and complex. I believe that the management of complexity, both in technology and sociology, is one of the key philosophical problems of our time. Those who benefit from the computer revolution may well be those who are most comfortable with complexity and uncertainty, whether they be scientists or businessmen. It is a way of life.

COMPUTERS IN OUR HOMELIFE

A few million of us already have computers in our homes. Quite a few years ago I prided myself in the building of an early home-brew computer. People always asked me what it was good for. They still do. I have consistently answered that it is not good for anything. It does not control the heating of my house, nor does it balance my checkbook. It does not keep the inventory of our kitchen supplies or the names on our Christmas card list. No, I just like having it. I like to make it work, to write systems and applications programs that serve no purpose whatsoever. I do not even play games on it. Why, I wonder, do computer owners have to rationalize their hobby? People do not ask stamp collectors what stamp collecting is good for. Sometimes it just feels good.

Now it is true that there are numerous useful tasks that a computer can do in the average home. Many of these will be accomplished by special-purpose processors built into appliances and controls, while I believe a lesser number will remain the province of the general-purpose home computer. Thus far the most profound social impact of computers in the home has been as a hobby occupying tens of millions of hours of their owners' leisure time, while in the process interesting and training a substantial fraction of our population in the computer art.

Computers will help bring information into the home too. In some cases this information will permit people to transplant their office to the home—more I believe as a part-time adjunct to the regular office environment than as a substitute for it. Other information sources will serve the home environment directly. Systems such as Prestel in England, Telidon in Canada, and Viewtron in the United States bring news, weather, stocks, shopping, banking, entertainment and travel schedules, sports scores, and a wealth of other information onto the home television screen. Soon these sources will be augmented by selective frame freeze of CATV-transmitted material. Some nominal household chores, such as shopping and banking activities, can be partially displaced by the new technology, while others will only be mildly facilitated.

Education is another large area of opportunity in the home market. Already some interactive courses are available on computer disks and through videotex services. However, I think nothing that has been mentioned so far has had or will have a profound effect on our homelife. In the home, entertainment is king, and like it or not, the one application of computer technology that has had such a profound impact is video games. I have heard it persuasively argued that more computing cycles (or instructions) are spent playing games than for all other purposes combined. The top-selling programs of all times are all games. There are scores of game cartridges that have sold in the millions of copies, versus perhaps half a million copies of the best-selling nongame programs. How much of the adolescence of our country's youth has been spent in pursuit of moving, colored blobs on video display screens?

Some say that the video game craze is a passing fancy. Frankly, I doubt it. There is a lot of technology that can yet be applied to games. Look how far computer graphics have come in the last few years from ponglike games to the present genre of arcade games. The computer-generated graphic sequences in the movie *Tron* give us a preview of coming attractions in the computer graphics technology. Increasingly the graphics will be more realistic representations of both lifelike and fantasy scenarios. Wide-screen projection television will improve and become the norm. Three-dimensional display techniques will become commercially attractive, and video disk players will be interfaced with home computers to provide interactive, high-quality animation sequences. An early example of this is the Aspen disk done by Nicholas Negroponte at the Massachusetts Institute of Technology, which enables a user to drive a car at his own direction along any street in Aspen, Colorado.

Telecommunications will add dramatic new possibilities to computer-mediated games. There will soon be networks that enable us to dial into game pools. For example, we will be able to be matched instantly with suitable partners and opponents for a game of bridge. We see the bidding and play as it progresses on our television screen. After each hand, the computer network informs us about our play relative to others in the country, and updates our national ranking percentile. Ladders and tournaments in this and other games should be possible on a local, regional, or national basis. In a similar vein, a retired woman in Vermont once called me with her precious idea for what the phone company should implement. Tentatively she whispered one word over the phone. The word was "bingo."

As we move further into future technological capabilities, home terminals will animate on a custom basis our own viewpoint on interactive game scenarios. For example, we could drive a race car in a grand prix race against other drivers around the country. Our television display becomes our own window onto the world of the game. We see the view of the instrument panels and controls of our racer, and through our windscreen we see the other cars in the race. The car in front of us, driven by another participant, reacts in our view as it is controlled from afar. That driver, in turn, sees our car react in his rearview mirror as we steer it through the course of the race. One could dream of games involving many people throughout the country, each interacting in his own way through game scenarios with other players.

In Ray Bradbury's *Fahrenheit 451* the fireman's wife participated in a daily soap opera by reading her lines in a room surrounded by walls that were television screens. Other participants, acting their parts from their own homes, appeared each day on her walls. This world became more real to her than the physical world around her. With such possibilities in mind, some might say that computers will take our jobs away from us, and give us in return an electronic, vicarious nirvana in our homes. Perhaps, like drugs, there will come a time when such alternatives have to be regulated for the good of society.

Robotics also has social implications for our homelife. Of course it is conceivable that we will have robot housekeepers and gardeners for our homes, but I imagine such devices would only be possible for the rich, who already have alternative ways of freeing themselves from such drudgery. Robots will also create new entertainment possibilities. I think we could now make a robot tennis player that would scurry about the court, catching our shots and returning (perhaps via a gunlike arrangement) realistic tennis hits. I imagine having a cartridge I could insert that programs the robot to simulate the play of such as John McEnroe (possibly even occasionally protesting a line call). Could I get a point from it, I wonder, or would I have to insert a different cartridge?

Another socially significant application that could at least be partially implemented today would be a robotics extension for a human, known as telepresence. Our vision could be remoted through television to a robot's eyes, our hearing through microphones in its ears, our movements and touch through sensory detection and manipulative ability, until it is perhaps philosophically arguable that we ourselves are remotely located. Maybe I could temporarily rent a robot to walk down the beach in Tahiti. How depressing it would be if the person walking towards me there also turns out to be a robotic extension!

WHAT DOES IT ALL MEAN?

In these meanderings I have been acutely conscious of my shortcomings as a technologist looking at the social world we sometimes consider only a marketplace. Technologists also have a proven track record of not being able to predict the future of technology itself. It is not so much that anyone else does any better, but simply the case that the extrapolation of the present does not yield the future, and doing otherwise is extremely difficult.

I have made a few disjointed observations about the evolving roles of computers in various aspects of our lives. For those of us in the field (and there are many of us), it is a time of excitement. We know that it will be possible to build computers a million times more powerful than those we have today. What will we do with such power? Few of us really have visionary answers to that question. Nonetheless, we feel that we hold the magical power to alter our environment for the better. Applications of the new technology seem boundless. We feel like laying down a challenge to society. "Name something," we say, "we'll do it." But not that much really gets named. What does society want? If I could come back in a century, I could say. Right now, if you will excuse me, I will take my leave. I cannot tell you.

Coping with Complexity

J. F. TRAUB

Department of Computer Science and
Department of Mathematics
Columbia University
New York, New York 10027

A common complaint about modern life is its complexity. I am sure the word complex brings varied associations to your minds; I will give you a few of mine:

- Designing a jet aircraft.
- Managing a large organization such as a city, a corporation, a university, or even a country.
- Sending a man to the moon.
- Deciding where to drill for oil.
- Investing in the stock or commodity markets.
- Designing and maintaining a national communication system.
- Trying to understand the mind of man.
- Controlling the national money supply to achieve certain goals.
- Designing a safe nuclear power plant.

In a recent talk, Bob Lucky stated that the *management of complexity* is a key problem. As examples of complexity he cited million-word programs written by a hundred programmers and the design of chips with tens of thousands of transistors. He pointed out that we will, one day, have a billion transistors on a chip.

What are some of the features that make a problem or system complex?

Size

Arranging a schedule for an airline that flies four planes between New York and Washington can be done on the back of an envelope. On the other hand, preparing the schedule for an airline with hundreds of planes and scores of cities is a complex task. Size often leads to complexity.

Interconnections

If a system can be decomposed into subsystems, then those smaller subsystems can be independently analyzed. If, on the other hand, a system or problem has many interconnections, we must tackle it whole. If we jiggle it a bit here, there may be major unforseen consequences there.

Limited and Inexact Information

For most systems and problems the available information is limited and inexact. I will use weather prediction as an example. Thousands of weather stations make measurements at various altitudes. In addition, planes, ships, and satellites also make measurements.

Inevitably these measurements, as all measurements, will be contaminated with errors. Furthermore, since there are only a certain number of measurements the information is limited. Hence we do not know the worldwide weather at any moment.

Why is that significant? If we do not exactly know the worldwide weather at any time, this severely limits the extent to which we can do long-term prediction.

In general, making predictions or decisions under conditions of limited and inexact information adds enormously to complexity.

When people say a situation is complex they often mean they must proceed with insufficient information. We return to this theme later.

As you know, computers are widely used by corporations, governments at all levels, the military, and many professions such as medicine, law, journalism, engineering, sociology; the list goes on and on. We use computers to control complexity because of certain characteristics. They have great speed, high reliability, and large memories. If the plans for the fifth generation are successful, we will have machines that draw inferences as fast as today's computers perform arithmetic. A major benefit will be to help us deal with complexity.

Although computers are used to control complexity, they are also its cause. For example, the design of a large computer or of a microprocessor on a chip is among the most complex tasks performed by man. Indeed, it is so complex that we use computers to design computers.

So far, I have discussed complexity in vague everyday language. If we are going to get a scientific handle on complexity, we have to be more precise. There is a major area within computer science devoted to the study of complexity. I want to tell you about a number of the most challenging problems and opportunities facing the field.

I will start by describing a famous problem. You are given a set of cities and the distances between them. Determine the order in which the cities should be visited so that each city is visited exactly once, the tour ends in the starting city, and the distance traveled is as small as possible.

For obvious reasons this is called the traveling salesman problem and is an abstraction of many scheduling and layout problems that arise in practice.

Say the number of cities is six: New York, San Francisco, St. Louis,

Miami, Fargo, and Santa Fe. Then the problem could be solved at sight or with a little pencil and paper work.

What if the number of cities is 50 or 100 rather than 6. Then how long will it take to find the shortest tour of the cities?

Many people have puzzled over this for decades. No matter what procedures they devised for finding the shortest tour, and no matter how clever they were, they discovered that the time required to carry out the procedures took hundreds of centuries on the fastest available computers. Since computers were only invented some 40 years ago, no one has computed for hundreds of centuries. What I mean is that analysis reveals that if the procedures were implemented, that is how long they would take.

One way around that seems clear—build faster computers. But that does not help significantly. The number of operations required by these procedures is so large that even the coming generation of supercomputers, computers capable of performing billions of operations per second, would not make a big difference.

I have been using the word procedure to denote a method for solving a problem. From now on, I will use the word used in computer science instead of procedure—the word is algorithm.

If people keep devising algorithms to solve the traveling salesman problem and all these algorithms take centuries, a natural question arises—Is there any algorithm for solving the problem faster or is the problem inherently intractable? You can see what an important question that is. If we know the problem is intractable, then we can stop looking for algorithms to solve it faster.

I am now going to introduce the basic idea of intrinsic problem difficulty. A measure of intrinsic difficulty is called the computational complexity or, for brevity, the complexity.

Let me stress a point that is often misunderstood. The complexity depends on the problem, not on any particular algorithm for solving it.

If the complexity is large, in a sense I could make technically precise, we say the problem is hard. Is the traveling salesman problem hard? On April 5, 1983, no one on earth knows.

Computer scientists have however made a remarkable discovery. There exist numerous problems, some of them extremely important, that are all equivalent from the complexity viewpoint. They are all hard or they are all easy. The common belief among experts is that they are all hard, but no one knows.

These problems are said to be NP-complete. Pioneers in this work are Professor Steven Cook at the University of Toronto and Professor Richard Karp at the University of California, Berkeley.

Determining whether NP-complete problems are hard or easy is one of the great questions to be decided in the future. If you want to read more, an excellent account is given by Garey and Johnson.[1]

In the traveling salesman problem we concerned ourselves with the time taken to find the shortest tour. But time is only one measure of cost. A second is the amount of memory required, and a third is area. Since it is harder to produce a large VSLI chip than a small one, we are interested in the area required to solve a problem. Interesting tradeoffs have been discovered between the time and the area required to solve a problem.[2]

You may think, from the examples I have provided, that complexity is bad. Complexity may indeed be desirable. For example, modern techniques for encrypting communications are based on the belief that problems such as factoring large integers have high complexity.

I have discussed at some length the traveling salesman problem and the great open question of the complexity of NP-complete problems. I now turn to an area where we are still, relatively, near the beginning but for which I expect major progress over the next decade.

Interest in this area is motivated by the fact that for most problems, information is limited and inexact. We therefore cannot find the exact answer, that is, we must live with uncertainty.

At this point you might appreciate an example. The examples are everywhere. In almost every discipline or subject—physical science, biological science, engineering, control, prediction, decision theory, tomography, economics, design of experiments, seismology, sociology, medicine—one deals with limited and contaminated information and therefore one must be content with uncertainty in the answer.

Typically the larger the system the more likely that one does not have exact information, especially if the system is changing with time. Therefore one has to settle for knowing a certain outcome is probable but one cannot be sure.

The areas I have mentioned above look very different from each other. Are there laws regarding how well they can be solved that apply to all of them?

We believe the answer to be yes, and a number of my colleagues and I at Columbia, as well as co-workers around the world, are trying to discover these laws and apply them to the solution of problems in many disciplines. For a moment I want to step back and take a broad view of science. Science has been called the study of invariants, seeking laws that are valid in varied domains. An archetypal example is provided by Newtonian mechanics. Before Newton, any "reasonable" person believed that apples and planets were very different objects obeying different laws. For some characteristics this is true, as you can verify by biting into an apple and a planet. But if you consider the correct quantities, which are force, mass, and acceleration, then there are laws that apply equally to apples and planets as well as to carriages, water-wheels, and buildings.

For most problems we have only limited or inexact information and consequently such problems can only be solved with uncertainty. Such problems are as different from each other as apples and planets. For such seemingly unrelated problems we believe that we have identified the basic quantities and a fundamental invariant, which we call the radius of information.

The radius of information measures the intrinsic uncertainty in the solution of a problem due to the available information. It not only tells us how well a problem can be solved, but also leads to the best algorithm and the best information. For emphasis we state the

INFORMATION PRINCIPLE There exists a quantity called the radius of information which measures the intrinsic uncertainty of solving a problem if certain information is known

Because of the emphasis on information we call this the information-centered approach. Currently the algorithm-based approach is in wide-spread use. In this approach, an algorithm is created and analyzed. Then another algorithm is proposed and analyzed, and so on. One never knows how much better one might be.

We contrast this with the information-centered approach. In this approach, one merely states what problem one wants solved and indicates the type of information available. The theory then tells one the best information, the best algorithm, and the complexity.

I hope I have convinced you that if information is limited or inexact you *cannot* solve a problem exactly. Sometimes you have complete and exact information and *choose* not to solve exactly. The use of artificial intelligence techniques in chess provides us with an example.

Assume you are white and wish to find a winning strategy (if it exists) against all possible moves by black. The information is complete and exact. Therefore there exists an algorithm with no uncertainty. Indeed, we have the following gedanken—algorithm. Consider all possible first moves for white and for each of these consider all possible moves for black. Continue this process for the second, third, etc., moves. If there exist one or more winning strategies against all moves by black, choose one of these strategies.

Such a "brute-force" approach would be far too expensive, and we use a heuristic approach instead. We live with the uncertainty of the heuristics to decrease complexity.

Chess is an example of a common phenomenon. We *choose to* live with uncertainty to decrease complexity.

I have mentioned that the information-centered approach gives you the best algorithm and the computational complexity. What else can it provide? It can, for example, tell you whether a problem can be decomposed for solution on a parallel computer or, more generally, on a distributed network.

I will use the game of twenty questions, with which you are all familiar, for illustration. I will describe a simplified version of twenty questions. You tell me you are thinking of an integer between 1 and 16. I ask questions concerning your integer, to which you respond yes or no. If you are thinking of 15, the sequence of questions and answers might be as follows:

Is the number between 1 and 8?	No.
Is the number between 9 and 12?	No.
Is the number between 13 and 14?	No.
Is the number 15?	Yes.

I obtained your number with four questions, and it is well known that one of 16 possibilities can always be identified with four questions with yes or no answers.

The questions I asked were adaptive because I waited for your answer to each question and then adapted my next question to your answer. This is an example of *adaptive* information.

What if I asked all my questions simultaneously? That means I have no opportunity to adapt my questions to your answers. This is an example of *nonadaptive* information.

We saw that four adaptive questions are sufficient. This is the best adaptive information in that fewer than four questions are not enough. How many nonadaptive questions are required?

It turns out that four nonadaptive questions are also enough. I will leave it for you to see what nonadaptive questions should be asked.

Thus for this problem nonadaptive information is just as powerful as adaptive information.

Why is this result of interest? During the 1980s and 1990s, parallel computation, that is, computation on a machine with many processors capable of simultaneous operation, will be increasingly important. If the information is nonadaptive, we have a natural decomposition for parallel computation. Various components of the information can be simultaneously and independently obtained.

We saw in the twenty questions example that nonadaptive information can be as good as the best adaptive information. But that is just a toy example. What about real problems?

Almost everyone believes that "usually" adaptation helps. However, almost everyone is mistaken. Although there are problems where adaptation helps, the information-based approach enables us to show there are many important problems for which adaptation cannot help.

Although much has been accomplished in the information-centered approach, a vast amount remains to be done before we can say we have established a general theory for dealing optimally with limited and inexact information. Of special interest is the application of the information-centered approach to areas as diverse as distributed computation, control, seismology, design of experiments, and signal processing. We can provide interesting research for many people over many years.

An introduction to the information-centered theory may be found in a recent expository paper.[3] The general theory is presented in two research monographs.[4,5]

In closing I want to recapitulate. Coping with complexity is a central issue for us individually and collectively. I started this talk with examples of complex problems ranging from managing a large organization to putting a man on the moon. I then indicated some of the results of the new field called computational complexity.

I am hopeful that computational complexity will eventually provide us a general scientific framework for coping with complexity in the everyday sense of the word.

REFERENCES

1. GAREY, M. R. & D. S. JOHNSON. 1979. Computers and Intractability W. H. Freeman and Company. San Francisco, Calif.
2. THOMPSON, C. D. 1980. A Complexity Theory for VLSI. Computer Science Department Report. Carnegie-Mellon University. Pittsburgh, Pa.
3. TRAUB, J. F. & H. WOŹNIAKOWSKI. 1984. Information and computation. In Advances in Computers. M. Yovits, Ed. **23**. Academic Press. New York, N.Y. (In press.)
4. TRAUB, J. F. & H. WOŹNIAKOWSKI. 1980. A General Theory of Optimal Algorithms. Academic Press. New York, N.Y.
5. TRAUB, J. F., G. W. WASILKOWSKI & H. WOŹNIAKOWSKI. 1983. Information, Uncertainty, Complexity. Addison-Wesley. Reading, Mass.

DISCUSSION OF THE PAPER

QUESTION: Why have you chosen an abstract framework?

J. F. TRAUB: This is typical in science. One realizes that many problems can be included in a unified framework. One draws conclusions in this general setting that apply both to the problems that motivated the abstraction and to new problems.

QUESTION: Do you believe that the new information mechanics, the type of systems you're talking about, will change the basic approaches to discovery in physical sciences?

J. F. TRAUB: Information mechanics is being used to designate a different field. There was a major meeting at MIT about a year ago to talk about a possible new field called either digital physics or information mechanics. The phrase I'd like to use to describe our work is information theory, but I can't do that because the term has already been used. (Recall that Shannon and Weaver called what they did the mathematical theory of communication, which is very descriptive of their work.) To answer the nub of your question, it's my intention to talk to physicists and chemists, to see what kind of overlap there might be. I can't answer your question yet.

QUESTION: What is the relation between information and algorithm?

J. F. TRAUB: We regard information as a basic concept and algorithm as a secondary concept. In principle, the theory gives you the optimal algorithm. I say "in principle" since applying the general theory to specific problems can be very hard. But again, that's typical of science. For example, quantum mechanics gives a general formulation and that's very valuable. To apply this formulation to specific problems can be difficult.

I've emphasized formulation, but we're keenly interested in applying this idea to many different disciplines. Towards this end we've been looking at disciplines and areas as diverse as statistics, distributed computation, economics, seismology, prediction, numerical analysis, and decision theory.

QUESTION: What can you contribute to international diplomacy?

J. F. TRAUB: We deal with problems that can be mathematically formulated. I don't think we have such a formulation for international diplomacy at this stage.

QUESTION: Would you give an example of an application of your work?

J. F. TRAUB: I'll give you one that's just a little bit technical. There is a widely used technique for numerical quadrature called Gauss integration. We've recently shown that you can pay an exponential penalty for using Gauss information rather than optimal information. That's one example, and I would be happy to give you additional examples after this session.

QUESTION: The four-color problem was recently "solved," using the computer. I'm sure there are lots of other problems, number theory and elsewhere, that could be solved perhaps using an algorithmic approach. What do you see as the nature of mathematical proof in the future?

J. F. TRAUB: The mathematicians at Illinois who cracked the four-color conjecture were using an algorithmic approach. However, I believe there has been no formal verification of that program to prove that it's correct. We have not investigated theorem proving from our viewpoint. One interesting problem, and I don't think anyone has looked at this, is what if I don't have to be sure I've got a correct theorem? What if I am willing to accept 95% probability it's correct? Then our ideas might be applied because you are now trading uncertainty for complexity.

QUESTION: In your initial statement about complexity, you said that it had three causes and then you said nothing further about that during your talk. Would you comment on that?

J. F. TRAUB: Speaking informally, three of the causes of complexity are size, interconnections, and limited and inexact information. That's not a complete list. I discussed size in the traveling salesman problem. When nonadaptive information is optimal it provides a natural decomposition, which means you don't have to worry about interconnections. I devoted a considerable portion of my remarks to limited and inexact information.

The Information Revolution
Developments and Consequences by 2000 A.D.

MICHAEL L. DERTOUZOS

Laboratory for Computer Science
Massachusetts Institute of Technology
Cambridge, Massachusetts 02139

INTRODUCTION

We have already begun to experience the information revolution, a movement that I believe will affect humanity more profoundly than the industrial revolution. After all, the industrial revolution replaced our muscles with engines, while the information revolution aims a bit higher than our muscles!

This talk tries to substantiate the potential primacy of the information revolution by looking at expected technological developments as well as their uses and consequences by the end of the twentieth century. While it is based in part on a recent book[1] and on the cutting edge of current computer science research, this talk is ultimately the product of the author's imagination and personal bias.

THE RELENTLESS HARDWARE FORCE

The primary force that propels the information revolution stems from *silicon typography*, in other words, our technological capability to "print" microscopic silicon-based integrated circuits or chips. Silicon typography has been responsible for a steady improvement of some 30% per year in performance/cost and size/cost of primary solid-state memories and processor components. This improvement, which has been going on for some 15 years, is expected to continue well into the 1980s and early 1990s. By the end of this century, this trend is likely to yield at least a 100-fold improvement relative to today, leading for example to an automated personal information base containing the equivalent of 100 books and costing as much as an automobile. By the year 2000, the more ambitious undertaking of storing and accessing the world's written knowledge would still be very expensive but not prohibitive at about two or three billion dollars per LOC.*

These expected hardware improvements are so huge that were they to

---

*The LOC (for Library of Congress) unit of memory was established half jokingly, half seriously by the author to represent large amounts of information. (1 LOC = 10^{14} characters).

19

happen in the field of personal transportation, they would promise by analogy a future price of $10 for today's cars or a future fuel efficiency of 5,000 miles/gallon at today's car prices. Imagine the huge societal impact of such a transportation revolution! By analogy, the information revolution will have an even greater impact, since it is expected to affect a substantially broader sector of the economy and of our lives.

The Lawless World of Programming

Unlike the physical world with its conservation laws, the virtual world of computer programming has almost no laws, and few predictive powers. Suppose that I ask several civil engineers if a one-mile-long wooden bridge can be built. My expectation is that they will arrive at a common answer in reasonable time. Suppose however that I ask several computer scientists if they can construct an 80% automated airline office, i.e., a program that responds at least as well as a conventional airline office to 80% of the queries typed in English by prospective travelers. The computer scientists will generally disagree as to the feasibility of this project because they have no adequate science to predict whether it can or cannot be done. Like the alchemist predecessors of today's chemists, we must first try to do this task before we can determine if we can do it!

To be sure, much progress has taken place in computer science theory, but in the cutting edge of sophisticated programming, the field is still as devoid of laws as the above example suggests. To cope with this lawlessness, good programmers realize the importance of establishing their own set of laws before undertaking the development of a big program. This lawlessness also explains why young programmers become very good in their profession—the excess baggage of experience normally possessed by older people may actually impede the creation of and adherence to new laws in the course of programming.

Looking toward the year 2000 and barring any surprising breakthroughs, there is unfortunately little hope in today's research horizon that the programming process will become much less costly. Even if programming productivity improves at the optimistic rate of 2-5% per year, it will still continue to fall short of the 30% yearly improvement of the hardware base, thereby shifting costs and human efforts progressively further in the direction of programming.

There are, however, two bright lights in this otherwise cloudy horizon which indirectly offset some of these programming problems—they are *hidden computers* and *expert systems* discussed in the next two sections.

Hidden Computers

Programming is a consequence of an historic relic—the effective utilization of a scarce and expensive resource. In the early days of the field, when computers cost a great deal of money, it was natural that different users should prepare their programs and wait in line for hours, if not days, to get a few minutes of the computer's precious time. Later, when time sharing came into widespread use, programmers still had to program in order to time share the still expensive central resource. With future computer costs converging to zero, cost sharing is *no longer a valid reason for programming*. Instead, a program could be developed at the factory and sold in large quantities with the computer thrown in at little or no extra cost. Such systems dedicated to individual applications will no longer be viewed as computers to be programmed but rather as appliances that perform specific tasks—hence the name *hidden computers*. Such hidden computers will offer an economic solution to the high cost of programming since that cost will be spread over a large number of users.

By the year 2000, we are likely to see such appliances as the personal memo pad, the dentist's machine, the drugstore machine, and the automobile safety, convenience, maintenance, and fuel-control units— all disguised by the functions that they perform, in the same sense that today's electric motors are disguised by the appliances that contain them.

We must, however, keep this future development in proper perspective: hidden computers will not eradicate programming from the face of this earth, since *user flexibility* and *new uses* will continue to be possible only through individual programming efforts on general-purpose programmable computers.

Expert Systems

Today's research programs that are characterized as intelligent exhibit expertise in such diverse fields as clinical decision making, mathematics, circuit design, and oil exploration. Take for example a program developed at the MIT Laboratory for Computer Science, which tries to behave like an expert physician in the administration of the drug digitalis.[2] Given the patient's history and symptoms, this program recommends appropriate dosage amounts. The program contains within it a good deal of knowledge about digitalis, much like a book on that subject. Unlike a book, however, the program can respond to a nonspecialist-physician's questions. Matching human queries to machine explanations is one of several features that distinguish such *expert programs* from specialist texts.

Expert systems such as this are characterized by a large size (usually over 500,000 characters), a lack of a common structure that can be transported from one domain to another, and a very experimental development approach. In a way, computer science research seems to be chipping away at problems from both the mundane and the expert extremes toward the difficult middle of common sense.

Programs like the above, along with ongoing improvements, suggest that by the turn of this century expert systems will lead toward the automation of educational, legal, recreational, financial, governmental, business, and other services. The automation of certain services by computer further suggests as a major potential advantage the tailoring of these services to individual needs.

ROBOTICS

In applications of *control and instrumentation* it is already evident that inexpensive microcomputers are displacing traditional systems because of their flexibility to follow different strategies, their ability to communicate with other processors, and their low cost. Such systems have already appeared in automobiles, in aircraft and ships (navigation computers), and in factories (process control). Many others are now at the design stage.

Beyond traditional control and instrumentation lies the science fiction writers' workhorse—the robot. General-purpose robots that can be programmed to perform any number of different tasks have been in existence for some time in the welding of automobile frames and in limited assembly operations. Such robots, however, behave like tape recorders, in that they mimic exactly a present motion. Of far greater interest are robots capable of sensing their environment especially through vision, and of planning their activities. Early research experiments have established the not so surprising conclusion that the greatest technical difficulty in robot development lies in perception, that is, in a computer's ability to understand a scene sufficiently in order to act upon the work pictured in that scene. Accordingly, for dramatic progress to take place in programmable general-purpose robots, a correspondingly dramatic progress will have to take place in sensory computing—a topic that is discussed in the following section.

Regardless, however, of whether such a dramatic development takes place, we will undoubtedly see by the year 2000 advanced applications of computers to factory automation through less sophisticated (tactile-sensing) techniques, and through the use of special-purpose assembly-line computers. The latter will monitor and control the manufacturing process and, by communicating with each other and with higher-level planning computers, will lead to manufacturing productivity increases.

A very exciting societal consequence in this area is the potential for tailor fitting products to individual needs. The computer is eminently suited to such *mass individualized production,* as for example in the manufacture of apparel, furniture, and other products whose size or function is adaptable to varying human needs. In this way, the information revolution may lead us back to the preindustrial era of artisans and craftsmen, while retaining the postindustrial economies of mass production.

COMPUTATION BY THE YARD AND SENSORY COMPUTING

The stage is set for a major computer breakthrough—the utilization of hundreds and thousands of processors, all dedicated to a single task. These *multiprocessor* structures are currently the topic of a good deal of research, stimulated by the decreasing hardware costs. For example, 1000 processors each costing $100 would give rise to a computing system whose combined computing power of 1000 MIPS (million instructions per second) would exceed by a factor of 10 today's most powerful machine, at 1/100th the cost of such a single processor supercomputer. There is a catch, of course, to this development: discovering effective ways for interconnecting and programming such *scalable* multiprocessor aggregates to carry out single tasks satisfactorily in the presence of *local failures*. Scalability, here, means the ability of a machine architecture to utilize as many processors as are necessary for a given task, hence the notion of computation by the yard. Local failures of individual processors will always be present in a machine that employs several thousand processors; yet the overall task must be carried out effectively in spite of such failures.

While multiprocessor approaches are currently in the research stage, a whole set of new applications are waiting impatiently for these underlying system developments to mature. These applications include some old number-crunching problems like weather forecasting but, more significantly, the exciting new prospects for *sensory computing* and *cognitive functions*. By sensory computing, I mean speech comprehension and machine vision. These applications, if realized, would have an unprecedented impact on our use of computers because they would enable us to communicate naturally with all sorts of programs and they would bring computer capabilities closer to human capabilities through sensory augmentation. By cognitive functions I mean a whole spectrum of activities characterized by progressively higher levels of deduction or inference. Finally, in addition to sensory computing and logical inference, I also expect effective application of these large machines to *complex graphics, dynamic simulation, signal processing,* and *intelligent data bases.*

GEOGRAPHICALLY DISTRIBUTED SYSTEMS

A time-shared computer system today is a centralized hardware and software structure which knows all that it must about different users, different programs, and different data stores. Such a centralized system, because of inherent complexity limitations, has an upper bound on the number of people in the community that it can serve. Today, this bound is somewhere in the vicinity of 50 to 100 users and can be explained by analogy to a human being's inability to cope simultaneously with more than a few tasks.

With the ever decreasing hardware costs and communications advances, it is now possible to interconnect many different machines so that, in effect, data are communicated among several centralized installations over satellite or local terrestrial networks. I expect this trend toward decentralization to extend quite rapidly to the extreme where each computer serves one user and all such computers are interconnected. The Xerox Palo Alto Research Center has already demonstrated this principle with some 700 interconnected single-user computers.

The information marketplace that is discussed in the following sections will utilize a mixture of predominantly single-user as well as multiple-user computers, all interconnected through a variety of paths, as in today's worldwide telephone network. The reasons leading to such interconnections are economic. First, large corporations with distributed plants and offices have begun and will continue to seek such interconnections among their own locations in order to make their business more efficient. Later, perhaps in the early 1990s, different businesses will seek connections with each other to improve the effectiveness of automatically handling interorganizational transactions. Somewhere in this time frame, individuals will seek interconnections to certain organizations for the purpose of buying and selling information and informational services. However, while the future evolution of intra- and interorganizational interconnections appears certain today, the interpersonal development is not as clear at this time. It will succeed if it exhibits an avalanche effect, as was the case in citizens band radio—if enough people and organizations are interconnected then the resultant information marketplace will be more useful, leading to more people seeking to benefit from the interconnected aggregate.

In summary, the technological base of the information marketplace lies in geographically distributed and decentralized systems, which by the year 2000 will evolve in this way because technology permits it and because people—and hence the collection, processing, and use of information—are geographically distributed in the first place.

COMPUTER TRIBES AND THE INFORMATION MARKETPLACE

Unlike the multiprocessor systems, which carry out a single task like vision, the geographically distributed systems forecast above will constitute what we might call *loosely connected computer tribes.* I expect these tribes to be analogous to today's human societies: the constituent computers will be autonomous, as are today's people and organizations, and they will communicate with each other sparsely as do today's people and organizations. Carrying this analogy further, there will not be a single chief computer or central program any more than there is a single individual or organization running today's society. Instead, I expect that the participants of this information marketplace will puchase and sell data and informational services on a free-market basis as we do today for traditional goods and services.

In the work environment, the information marketplace will involve office automation in its broadest sense, i.e., (in order of increasing difficulty) (1) word processing and text management; (2) intercommunication of memos, mail, and messages (data, voice, and images); (3) intraorganizational office procedures; (4) interorganizational transactions; and (5) new activities such as automated filing and retrieval of information, based on understanding of its content.

In addition, the information marketplace will involve a collection of *data entrepreneurs* who will sell information and processes against the public's needs, i.e., by offering medical, legal, educational, financial, travel, and other services. Once again, an important benefit of these developments lies in *tailoring* typically available information to individual users' needs.

Finally, the information marketplace will make possible new work modes such as working from rural or other remote areas, selling one's work for a few hours a day (parents with children at home), or employing the physically handicapped, who can interact with a computer input-output device.

In the house environment of the year 2000, I expect office work from the home and use of recreational, educational, and medical information services. In addition, and to the extent that the information marketplace grows to a large size, we are likely to see *common-interest groups* and *information clubs* that will explore their common pursuits over the worldwide networks.

FOR BETTER OR FOR WORSE?

Some commonly cited negative effects of computers on our society are as follows:

1. *Human displacement.* Continuing progress in office, service, and factory automation will result in the displacement of human labor from the corresponding economic sectors.

Such displacement is likely, yet at a slow rate and over a period of several generations. We should feel no more and no less threatened by such events than by the earlier displacement of people from certain jobs as a consequence of the industrial revolution. If such a transition is slow, if it replaces lower-level functions and if it spans several human generations, as seems to be the case with the information revolution, then the human labor force will be gradually displaced toward more challenging and less mundane activities.

2. *Mental atrophy.* This is a likely consequence of the information revolution in the same sense that the industrial revolution decreased the need for and capability of human and animal muscle power.

I have no doubt that some mental atrophy will accompany the information revolution as and if expert programs become more capable. It has already started in arithmetic with the advent of the inexpensive calculator. This is clearly an area that we should watch with caution and try to anticipate through control of our educational system and even through some conscious mental jogging.

3. *Responsibility and liability.* Large programs developed by many authors tend to diffuse responsibility of authorship. Who is responsible when such programs malfunction and cause us harm?

I cannot conceive of a hospital or a physician who will install and use a program on digitalis therapy without comprehending how the program works and without identifying a human organization that is accountable for the program's actions. In short, liability and responsibility must rest, as they do today, with the humans or organization exploiting the sale of an informational service. The often advanced excuse that large programs are too complex and incomprehensible because they were put together by many people is plain baloney! A jumbo aircraft is equally complex, yet we make sure that it is comprehensible and that we know whom to prosecute if it crashes.

4. *Undue trust of machines.* People may be intimidated into courses of action they do not understand, because of undue trust of computer-generated plans and advice.

Undue trust is placed on machines by some people who are either unaware of a machine's capabilities or who purposefully wish to deflect the opinions of others. While such cases will undoubtedly arise, it is my belief that they will be infrequent, since people will seek to comprehend and question the results of computing machines as they have done for other human artifacts. Toward that end, it is important that the public be kept aware of the capabilities and limitations of computers—a responsibility that falls equally on the public, the computer professionals, and the media.

5. *Dehumanization.* Increased computer acculturation of our society will cause progressive suppression of traditional values and will promote a narrower technologically based thinking mode.

We often hear about our potential dehumanization, without stopping to consider that we have been already considerably dehumanized through the industrial revolution. Gone are the artisans and craftsmen of the preindustrial era with their tailor-fitting products and services. The low-cost, mass-produced goods and services of today have reduced us to affordable uniformity and impersonal numerical identities. And traditional human values have been already subjected to a variety of pressures. To my thinking, the much feared computerization of our society may balance, instead of exaggerate, some of these dehumanizing trends—in particular, it may make possible through factory, service, and office automation the tailoring of goods and services to the most variable of demand centers, ourselves, at affordable costs, and it may increase human-to-human communication through computer networks.

6. *Reduced privacy and computer crimes.* Aggregation of information about humans in machine form and intercommunication of sensitive information among computer systems offers many possibilities for abuse.

Stealing data, altering data, and misrepresenting the signatory of a message are typical violations that I fear will take place on the large computer tribes of tomorrow. Even though it is possible to use computers to help carry out such crimes, the technology for safeguarding information among interconnected computers is progressing well. It is therefore likely that by the turn of this century, if we plan carefully, we will be able to provide adequate safeguards for interconnected computer systems. Meanwhile, we have an obligation to insure that before any information systems become linked to one another, enough privacy safeguards are introduced to make the prospect of potential violations tolerable. In the absence of such demonstrable safeguards, our responsibility is clearly in slowing down or arresting, probably through regulatory means, such interconnections.

Ultimately, of course, computer crimes are, and will be, perpetrated by *people* and not by machines. To my thinking, it is important that we pursue major and comprehensive information-related legislation soon since by the time such legislation becomes unavoidable, we may be well into the information revolution era with a sizable and irreversible technoeconomic investment behind us. Some issues for consideration by such legislation beyond privacy violations and financial computer crimes include (1) the extent to which information should be treated like or unlike real property; (2) the extent to which programs should be protected from unauthorized duplication and misuse; (3) the regulation of computer-to-computer interconnections; (4) the desirability for mandatory audit trails whenever sensitive information is read or changed by anyone; (5) the desirability for mandatory destruction of machine-stored information after a certain time has elapsed or other conditions are met; (6) the development of criteria for determining what kinds of information may not be stored in machine-accessible form; (7) the handling of authentication violations (when the purported signatory of a computer message is an imposter); (8) the regulation of unauthorized expeditions (typically aided by other computers) over data bases; and (9) the purposeful confusion of "mistakes" with planned computer crimes in badly organized machine installations.

7. *Global consequences.* The information revolution by virtue of its importance is likely to lead to geopolitical changes.

First I expect that East-West governmental uses of computers will differ considerably because the totalitarian regimes of the East can better utilize and impose massive centralized computerization upon their societies. Next and along the north-south direction, I expect the gap between rich and poor countries to increase. The reason for this lies in my belief that *the value of information* is inextricably linked to the economic value of tangible goods and other human desires that become more easily acquired as a result of such information. Thus the countries that already have a great deal of material wealth will also value and use information more than will the poorer countries. Partially offsetting this negative trend is the possible beneficial use of information technology by developing countries in such fields as medicine, agriculture, and education.

Finally, in the same sense that northern Europe and the United States acquired a great deal of power as a result of their control of the industrial revolution, it is likely that the countries that control the information revolution will exert a comparable influence upon the postindustrial world. Thus, Japan, which is equipped for and is putting great emphasis on controlling the information revolution, may end up dominating the United States in this new form of global power.

8. *Superior machine intelligence.* Expert programs become so intelligent as to be comparable or superior, and threatening to humans.

We have no scientific basis today to establish that this will or will not happen. Instead, we are at the mercy of either technoromantic or humanoromantic dogma. However, we can focus philosophically on the fundamental difference between our biological basis and the silicon basis of computers. Since these bases differ, it follows that there will also be differences at the higher-level human functions that rest on these bases—even if machines some day reach or surpass us from a *logical* point of view. Thus, the linkage of higher-level human functions (e.g., love) to basal functions (e.g., glandular secretions) can at best be *logically simulated* and not *duplicated* by machines. In that sense, we can conclude that by the year 2000 or beyond, while true identity cannot be reached, logical equivalence may or may not be reached depending on future progress.

We summarize next the potential benefits of the information revolution as follows:

1. Increased productivity through automation of services and through factory and office automation.

2. Reduced energy dependence through replacement of current energy-consuming activities such as transportation of people by the less energy demanding transportation of data.

3. Tailor fitting of products and services. We have already discussed the prospects for mass-individualized products such as apparel, or services like individualized newspapers and advertising, at mass production costs.

4. Information filtering. This refers to the selection, by machine, of information important to us, and the screening away of the ever increasing amounts of informational junk that bombard us. In effect, the machine becomes our personal butler, which aids and protects us.

5. Improving our way of life through increased convenience, through the availability of useful services, and through the liberation of minds that currently tackle uninteresting, repetitive, and mundane tasks.

6. Augmenting the labor force by making possible through the infor-

mation marketplace the employment in information services of rural people, of handicapped individuals, of caretakers of small children, and in general of people who cannot physically leave their home.

These benefits need not be further discussed here, as was done with the earlier negative factors, since as is by now clear this is the write-up of a technological optimist who does not plan to argue against his own position.

Let us finally observe that information, unlike food, shelter, health, or energy, is not a primary factor to human survival. It is, however, necessary immediately next to these basic factors, for it helps us plan and carry out actions aimed at satisfying our most basic necessities. It is my view that in this role, as a very important but nonvital necessity, information and its management by the information revolution will contribute to human progress, and will find its proper balance within human endeavor as did its precursor, the industrial revolution.

REFERENCES

1. DERTOUZOS, M. L. & J. MOSES. 1979. The Computer Age: A Twenty-Year View. MIT Press. Cambridge, Mass.
2. GORRY, G. A., S. G. PAUKER & H. SILVERMAN. 1978. Computing clinical expertise that considers clinical responses to digitalis. Am. J. Med. **64:** 452–460.
3. WEIZENBAUM, J. 1976. Computer Power and Human Reason. W. H. Freeman. San Francisco, Calif.

DISCUSSION OF THE PAPER

QUESTION: I can't possibly see how you can relate a shoemaker—to whom I can go and complain—to a computer. There are so many layers in between. There's a responsibility; there are the lawyers who we have to reach, and all this. I think even the comparison insults our intelligence.

M. L. DERTOUZOS: Thank you sir. I think you heard what you wanted to hear. You heard me say that the shoemaker is going to be replaced by a computer that will do everything that a shoemaker does. I didn't say that of the economy; I put up the possibility of automating a certain sector, and then I told you that we have already lost the human shoemaker from our economy. We don't have cobblers any more. Maybe you have them in New York City. But the rest of the country does not have cobblers. It has supermarkets where you buy plastic shoes sir. I am talking about recapturing some of the lost artisanship in tailor fitting products to the individual. I'm not trying to replace the cobbler. He has been replaced. Thank you.

QUESTION: What will happen to the world if everyone becomes a programmer? What kind of computer literacy should everyone have?

M. L. DERTOUZOS: There is no question in my mind that we need general computer literacy in the same sense that up to now we have needed literacy in calculus and in freshman physics. Beyond that, I think there must be a balance. I don't think everybody is going to go around programming. Some people are very bored by programming. I think programming will find its own level like every other human invention. It will be used for good and for bad, and it will eventually find its balance.

QUESTION: Will computers essentially create a new elite class of those that know how to use them?

M. L. DERTOUZOS: Well, I don't think we really know. I tried to give you my thoughts on how computers will be used in intra- and interorganizational transactions. Do you call that elite? Do you call the companies of the world elite? If you do, fine, that's where it stops. How about the third world? We know today of computer uses in Senegal and in other developing countries that pursue medical, agricultural, and educational applications and help accelerate the growth of these nations. Is that elite? I don't think we know sir.

QUESTION: You indicated the need for regulation in the computer field. What do you have in mind?

M. L. DERTOUZOS: I'm thinking of something like this: no two data bases having information about you and me and other individuals should be interconnected unless it can be demonstrated to the regulatory agency that certain safeguards are met to protect each data base from the path that is thus formed between them. That's the same kind of thing that we do in aircraft regulation. For example, we demand a minimal protection before we let aircraft land or take off at airports.

QUESTION: May I raise a regulation question? In the field of biomedical ethics—I am relating it to regulation that is evolving now in the field of biomedical ethics. The evolution of that came through a private center, interdisciplinary center, of research scientists who started to focus on the public policy and responsibility issues. I wonder if some interdisciplinary effort to get a kind of ethical baseline for development has already begun, and if not, shouldn't there be one?

M. L. DERTOUZOS: I think your question is excellent. I think there definitely should be action in this area. Some activity has already started throughout our universities. People are meeting! It's informal and it's not yet a big movement. But they're meeting, they're asking precisely these questions, and they are trying to do exactly what you say in the case of biotechnology.

COMMENT: May I mention that in the civic and political area, the public organizations are very concerned about this. I have been working with them to suggest to Congress that the bicentennial constitutional observance—I mean in 1987—be used as a way to get a think-tank operation on the instituting of computers and telecommunications. And I would like everyone here to give that some thought as a personal citizen responsibility to carry forward. Thank you.

Experimental Computer Science

HERBERT SCHORR

International Business Machines Corporation
Thomas J. Watson Research Center
Yorktown Heights, New York 10598

This paper will focus on experimental computer science, why it is of current importance, its links to other disciplines, and some examples of the work being done at IBM's Research Division and elsewhere. It will also touch on the future of computer science and how private industry can best support this emerging discipline.

What makes experimental computer science distinct is the positing of hypotheses and the rigorous testing of these hypotheses under controlled conditions. Its goal is to acquire new knowledge about computers and computing. The questions posed and testing methods vary widely. But, in each case there must be an explicit underlying conceptual model that is tested by an experimental device with features approximating the model being questioned. Techniques like simulation and prototyping are essential elements of the experimental apparatus. As in the empirical sciences much effort must be devoted to developing "better microscopes" to capture, in greater detail, experimental results. Additionally, the data must be carefully interpreted within the context of the model.

In the future, experimental computer science will increase in importance. What may have been a luxury for a small number of institutions will become a necessity for many if this science is to advance beyond the *ad hoc* methods of the past. I hope to see a strong collaboration between industry and academia. From this relationship a sharing of expertise that will maintain the vitality of computer research in both sectors will emerge.

One example of experimental computer science is the work on comparing microprocessor architectures at the University of Massachusetts,[1] which is similar to the comparative analysis of architectures for military applications at Carnegie-Mellon University[2] and work done at Stanford University.[3,4] It was hypothesized that architectures could be meaningfully distinguished by their efficiency independent of the technology of their embodiments. However, in the past, debating the merits of different architectures often took on the flavor of a religious schism. An experiment was designed in which a set of equivalent tasks were programmed on implementations of the VAX-11/780, Z-8000, HP-300, LSI-11, Motorola 6801, and Intel 8080 architectures. Restrictions on the style of coding such as that all kernels except the input/output (I/O) had to be reentrant were made to focus on the basic aspects of the instruction set.

Five measures of efficiency were used: the number of bytes of program storage; the number of instructions executed; the number of data bytes transferred during execution; the number of instruction bytes transferred during execution; and the total number of bytes transferred during execution.

Each of the 10 programmers in the experiment coded three different kernels on each of the six machines. The kernels were selected to exercise all basic machine features. Each of the submitted kernels was tested to verify that it worked correctly and then subjected to hand analysis from which the numerical data were derived.

The design of the experiment, the execution of the experiment, the analysis of the data, and the interpretation of the data as to what architectural features affected the outcome are all crucial parts of the work. Based on these studies conclusions about the efficiencies of different architectures were reached. More importantly, a piece of evidence was made available to computer science, and the body of knowledge was enlarged.

There are a number of reasons why experimental computer science has become so important. There are four factors that are sparking its growth.

1. Systems have grown larger and faster. They contain more functions and greater degrees of concurrency. These factors have increased the difficulty and expense of modeling and simulating, tools whose strengths are limited to understood areas. These tools require that data reflecting the environment are available, and that second-order effects are accurately represented. They require that the model can be created, calibrated, and run in a timely fashion.

Software modeling for logic verification has become tremendously time consuming. For example 1,800 hours of an IBM System/370 Model 168 CPU time were required to verify the logic design of ¼ of a medium-range System/370 CPU. Problems of this kind, which steeply increase their time requirements with complexity, have kindled the experimental work in special-purpose machines. It has been hypothesized that the parallel nature of underlying algorithms can be embodied in hardware, thus providing great gains in performance.

The Yorktown Simulation Engine (YSE)[5] is a special-purpose, highly parallel programmable machine for gate-level simulation of logic, which was built to test this hypothesis. The YSE is an array of parallel processors each capable of simulating 4,096 gates (where each gate computes an arbitrary 4-input function on 4-valued logic). Two million gates can be simulated at a rate exceeding 3 billion gate computations per second. The YSE uses a unique interprocessor communication scheme, which has low hardware cost and introduces essentially no communication overhead.

The key components of the YSE are logic processors, hard-wired special-purpose gate-simulation machines; array processors, logic to simulate RAMs and ROMs; an interprocessor switch, provides communication among up to 256 logic and array processors during simulation; and

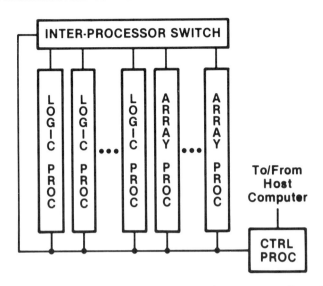

FIGURE 1. Key components of the Yorktown Simulation Engine. (Reproduced from Reference 5 with permission. Copyright 1982 IEEE.)

a control processor, which performs YSE-host communications (FIGURE 1).

By building this system we were able to address profound problems such as intrasystem and intersystem communications without oversimplification. At this time it seems beyond the scope of analytic modeling to accurately attack system problems like these. It may be that only by creating special-purpose machines that the viability of new ideas in fields such as design automation and artificial intelligence can be tested. The newness of these areas and the size of the problems attacked readily support this case. One hopes that through experimentation a solid theoretical outlook will evolve.

2. We continue to experience an explosive growth in new technologies and at the same time see computers pervading our world. We need to explore and integrate these innovations into an existing environment. Ideas must be evaluated with respect to their value to the whole system. An example is the use of fiber optics for I/O interconnections.[6] The features of fiber optics such as freedom from electromagnetic interference, smaller lighter cables, high bandwidth, and low attenuation indicate that this technology has great promise. However, investigations into its architectural implications are necessary for its successful implementation.

The performance of current parallel S/370 I/O architecture is limited by the skew associated with data transmission on a parallel bus. This problem as well as the cable and connector bulk can be relieved by serializing the data transfer. Experiments in serializing the channel with fiber optics have been demonstrated by Sperry Univac and Fujitsu. However, serialization of the existing channel does not result in an enhanced data rate due to protocol limitations. Currently, an acknowledgment is required for every eight bits of data. If the full benefits of fiber optics are to be achieved, new interface protocols designed around high-speed serial transmission must be designed and integrated into existing systems. But because of the complexity of systems, experiments to determine the best protocols must be performed before designs are chosen.

3. Computers are moving out of the "glass house" and encountering users with many different levels of expertise and expectation. The burden of understanding is shifting from the user to the machine. The human factors of all components have become paramount to their success. Work in speech recognition, signature verification, natural text analysis, and alternatives to keyboards as input devices rely heavily on experimental results.

In designing the cognitive interface of a computing system, the basic problem is to fit the informational aspects of the system to the mental characteristics of the user. Due to our limited understanding of mental machinery to which systems must be fit, we must rely on an empirical approach in which an interface is designed, a mock-up devised and tested with users, the design modified based on observed difficulties, and the process repeated.

An effective technique for discovering why a given design feature is good or bad is the "thinking aloud" method used in cognitive psychology.[7] This is a form of detailed observation in which the participant is asked to keep a running commentary of his or her thoughts while working. This method is being used to study how new users learn text-processing systems. Computer-naive learners find this a particularly difficult task. Using office temporaries in the laboratory, subjects are asked to verbalize as they work, describing what questions, plans, strategies, inferences, or knowledge they are currently aware of.

The method does not produce a small number of numerically dependent measures that can be easily summarized with statistical techniques nor does it lend itself to strictly quantitative criteria. But it is valuable in investigations where specific information about design features and how they work or fail to work is needed.

4. Computer science is maturing. There are greater attempts at applying theory to practical problems. The limited application of "scientific method" to the study of systems in the past has left us deficient in applicable theories. In many ways computer science in the past was more engineering art than science. Pursuing the path of "empirical sciences" from observation to theory to application will lead to a decreased dependence on intuition and *ad hoc* solutions.

Maintaining large software systems has been the subject of work that captures some of this process. Preventative service helps users to the extent that it avoids costly operational problems, but costs them the resources required to prepare, disseminate, and install fixes (which themselves can introduce errors). The benefit from removing a given defect in a program depends on how many problems it would otherwise cause.

Estimating the benefits of preventative service requires a model of the potential occurrence of problems and of the service to forestall the problems. A model of the distribution in time of the occurrence of "defect-originating problems" within a population of users of a piece of software was created at IBM.[8] This model was calibrated and evaluated using data obtained from IBM's service organization. Based on this work it is possible to evaluate and optimize a service plan. It was found that most of the benefit to be realized by preventative service comes from removing a relatively small number of high-rate defects that are found early in the service life of the code. Corrective service where problems are fixed only where they have occurred is preferable as a way of dealing with most defects found after the code has cumulatively some hundreds of usage months of service.

The situation is similar to medical treatment. There are many hostile organisms in the body. A small dangerous set can cause a large number of symptoms and is sufficiently virulent that vaccinating the general population is warranted. Some other organisms may require treatment as they affect specific individuals. Many others may be of potential hazard but are not treated until symptoms appear.

These four reasons give a flavor of the future direction I see for computers and computer science and explain why experimental work has and will become more important.

The Computer Science Department within the Research Division of IBM has two primary missions. The first is to advance science; the second is to apply this knowledge to influence products. There is no product responsibility or direct development in research. Rather technologies are transferred to the development divisions for application in products. Ideas generated both in academia and research are tested and evaluated, and those of greatest promise are transferred to the product-developing units in the corporation. Research helps bridge the gap between new ideas and new products.

As the computer industry matures the process of technology transfer requires an increased understanding of the characteristics of current systems. New ideas must be integrated into the systems of today. Growing design costs imply the need for strong evidence to alter existing paths. The quantification of value added to a system is essential to precipitate change.

The increase in development time and cost and the decrease in market life of products have made early design decisions much more critical. How do we tell good from bad? We have developed sophisticated timers and other models that can answer this question in a few well-understood areas, like the performance of different machine organizations for a fixed architecture. But when we ask this question about how to compare DECNET, SNA, ARPANET, CHAOSNET, etc., for large, busy networks, we cannot give a satisfactory answer. Benchmarks and quantitative measures beyond our current modeling capabilities are needed.

In 1977 the Systems Laboratory was created at Yorktown Heights for the sole purpose of experimentation. Here an assemblage of experts in a broad range of computer-related disciplines brings a diversity of talents to bear on the theory, analysis, and creation of computer systems via the experimental orientation typical of the "hard sciences." We started with three IBM System/370 Model 168's to be used as we saw fit. Groups that wish to use the system schedule time and have complete control. The machines are entirely dedicated to their experiments. Our system continues to grow and now includes IBM System/370 Models 3081 and 4341. Our main areas of concentration have been in systems software design, machine organization and architecture, office systems, networking, systems analysis tools and techniques, design automation, and new applications such as speech recognition.

A key purpose in creating this laboratory was to attempt to find basic design principles, to enable a coherent systematic approach to design, rather than a succession of *ad hoc* improvements. The ability to closely observe, measure, alter, revise, and observe again a complex environment has paid large dividends in our knowledge of working systems. It has enabled the discovery of new problems and provided insights for solutions.

The laboratory has enhanced research in numerous ways beyond the answers to specific questions. Most work has been carried out in close cooperation with development groups. This has allowed researchers to be exposed to the rationale for past decisions, while developers have been permitted a view free of business considerations. The cross-fertilization between the laboratory work and other disciplines has increased awareness of related problems and techniques in many fields.

Often finding a solution is considerably easier than designing the experiment and proving that it works. It is challenging to make people understand and to motivate them to work in this environment. Science tends to glorify individuals rather than groups. At IBM research, dealing with groups of outstanding professionals, we have succeeded in part because of the continuing commitment and recognition of all levels of management.

Let me give two examples of work that utilized the Systems Laboratory. I hope they will give insight into the role of the laboratory in both the advancing of computer science and the understanding of existing systems.

The first example pertains to the problem of increasing the performance of a computer system through parallelism at the expense of delay across an interface. Specifically, what is the effect on performance if I/O supervisor functions are separated from an operating system and executed on an auxiliary processor?

It might be expected that, on the one hand, the CPU would have less to do and therefore would provide greater throughput. On the other hand, extra code would be executed since the CPU must dispatch the task to the auxiliary processor. That creates a delay attributable to the second processor. The interprocessor interference and the possible global effects clearly reduce the advantage of the parallelism to some extent. Given the complexity of this problem, accurate estimates of the overall systems improvement were not possible without experimentation.

A controlled experiment was designed to test the performance variations. In the base configuration (FIGURE 2), a data-base system running under the operating system MVS on one of the Model 168 processors with 6 megabytes of memory was used. In the modified configuration (FIGURE 3), an asynchronous interface was created between two Model 168's. The portions of MVS that handle the I/O requests were moved into the auxiliary 168 processor. When an I/O request was encountered by the primary processor, it was queued for the auxiliary processor and then, upon completion, notification was passed back.

A controllable transaction work load was presented to the data-base system by a terminal simulation program executing a script in the same processor at a specific rate. The work load was synthesized from a large variety of transaction types. By adjusting the distribution of transaction types, the system could be made to exhibit the characteristics of different applications and industries. Thus, it was possible to generate transactions invoking real-life programs accessing real-life data bases in a controlled environment and thereby provide a test vehicle for performing repeatable experiments.

Both hardware and software monitors were used to measure system performance. The transaction rate and the transaction response time were chosen as the major criteria for evaluating the merit of this special

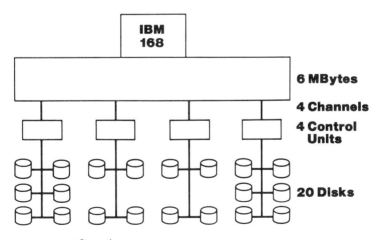

FIGURE 2. Base configuration.

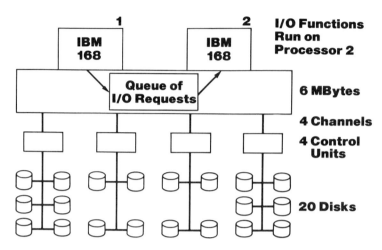

FIGURE 3. Modified configuration.

form of distributed processing. The goal of the data analysis then was to characterize and compare the response time distribution, as a function of throughput, of the two alternative systems. Given the complexity of the system and the work load it was necessary to observe the transactions for a long period before data representing "steady-state" conditions could be gathered. The many sources of random fluctuation such as I/O device access time, randomization of transaction types, and arrival rate fluctuations made it necessary to use special statistical techniques to ascertain the accuracy of estimates. It was discovered that the data-analysis problem faced here was parallel to that experienced by an experimenter analyzing the output of discrete event simulation models.

During the experiment, a constant interchange between the people primarily involved with system performance and our statisticians enhanced the quality of this research project. Sophisticated data analysis is, of course, common in many other sciences. In passing, let me point out that I think we need to place, in our educational institutions, a greater emphasis on such techniques and their application to computer systems analysis.

From this experiment we found that there is a significant performance improvement to be gained by this kind of "offloading" in practical situations. We also developed an idea of the cost in hardware and software to achieve the performance gain. Here, part of the experiment was measuring the experimental process.

As a second example I will talk about the recent work on the fractal nature of software-cache interaction. Fractal geometry is a mathematical theory developed by Benoit Mandelbrot, an IBM Fellow, which provides a model for irregularity and fragmentation in nature.[9] Suppose one attempts, for example, to measure a stretch of rugged coastline in a piecewise linear fashion using a fixed measuring stick. Each measuring step consists of moving from one point on the coast to another point lying at a distance of the measuring stick. We take the length to be the number of steps multiplied by the length of the stick. Now suppose a shorter stick is used in an attempt to gain a more accurate measurement. If the coast is rugged the length will increase. The number of steps will increase proportionately more than the length of the stick decreases. If the coast is sufficiently irregular then as the measuring stick continues to decrease in size, the estimated length of the coastline grows without bound.

Examining empirical data, it has been observed that the variation in length of the coastline is relatively stable within certain ranges of measuring stick lengths. Plotting the measuring stick length against the coastline length on a double logarithmic scale, the points fall near a straight line of negative slope for each coastline. This slope is an indication of the nature of the irregularity of the coast, and from it we can derive a fractional dimension. An intuitive way of looking at this dimension, which has been called fractal, is to recognize the difficulty in considering the outline of the coast as a one-dimensional curve. In the sense that as a curve becomes more complex and irregular it approaches a space-filling curve (a two-dimensional object), fractal geometry assigns a dimension between 1 and 2 to such a curve. This fractional dimension reflects the irregularity.

A necessary condition for applying the techniques of fractal geometry is self-similarity. Naively, this means that successively closer views of the curve maintain the same structure as the whole curve. In the example of the coastline we see bays and peninsulas which are made up of subbays and subpeninsulas which in turn are made up of subsubbays and subsubpeninsulas.

In analyzing computer programs we refer to the set of unique memory references within a given time window as "the working set over the defined window." This is used as a measure of reference locality. However, by varying the window size one finds different working sets. In other words as the size of the window changes, what we see changes.

At IBM we have been examining the patterns of memory lines not found during demand fetches in caches or cache misses. These have been discovered to occur in "bursts," i.e., clusters of misses over some time interval. One can think of these bursts as periods during which a working set is developed and the gaps between bursts as when work is done inside the working set. Demand fetching exploits the statistical property of program reference patterns. Cache misses are a direct reflection of changes in locality of references.

There appear to be certain analogies between finding a working set in software and the coastline measuring problem. The hierarchical structure of modern software with modules composed of submodules and the observation that bursts of cache misses are composed of subbursts have led to the conjecture that these data are statistically self-similar. One senses that the degree to which these phenomena are captured by a fractal model in turn implies that they belong to a larger class of natural processes.

In the Experimental Systems Laboratory, we took three program traces each representing a different computing environment: one of data-base interactive, one of time sharing, and one of scientific.[10] These traces were used to drive a simulation model of a 64K cache which produced the pattern of cache misses for each of these benchmarks. The probability that the intermiss distance exceeded a given value was calculated for each of the three environments. FIGURES 4, 5, and 6 show the cumulative probability distribution resulting from these simulations. All three graphs are presented in log-log coordinates. By inspection it appears that the data approximate a straight line over a large range of intermiss distances.

This work has led to a new definition of a working set as the number of cache lines in a gap burst pair. The notion of dimension appears to be an effective measure of software complexity, where complexity is meant to reflect the structure and dynamics of the program rather than the computational complexity. It proposes a theory that can measure with a single number—the slope of the curve—the complexity of a benchmark.

We are, of course, fortunate to have the skill mix at our laboratory to describe the interrelationship of the cache problem and the applicability of the relatively new theory of fractals.

The decreasing cost and the standardization of hardware have made more experimentation possible. The availability of microprocessors and support components makes prototyping of many experimental apparatuses within the budgets of small organizations. However cost continues to play a major role in limiting the scope and selection of experimental endeavors. Pressing questions in networking, supercomputers, distributed systems, VLSI, and new technologies require very costly investments for apparatuses with which to experiment. Ways must be found through the pooling of strengths to support this kind of work. Both the private and public sectors have come to recognize the importance of experimental computer science. Industry, academia, and government need to find means to promote this work and share its fruits.

Experimentation is a springboard for innovation. The understanding of problems within a realistic context is the moment before invention. Students need to be exposed to and gain experience with not only the apparatus but the methodology and discipline of computer science. Private industry has a responsibility to support and encourage these valuable efforts. The new joint project between IBM and Carnegie-Mellon University, exploring networking and distributed processing, I see as a promising step in this direction. It will bring "real world" problems onto the campus and add vitality to computer science.

These kinds of ventures are new. There is a great deal to be gained by both sectors. Flexibility and understanding must be used to allow this interaction to take form. We are seeing the beginnings of a new era in computer science. It requires an openness to new relationships by all parties if its potential is to be fulfilled.

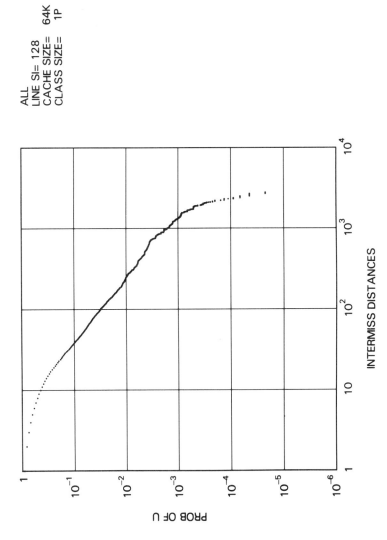

ALL
LINE SI= 128
CACHE SIZE=   64K
CLASS SIZE=   1P

FIGURE 4. Probability data for data-base interactive. (FIGURES 4–6 are reproduced from Reference 10 with permission. Copyright 1983 by International Business Machines Corporation.)

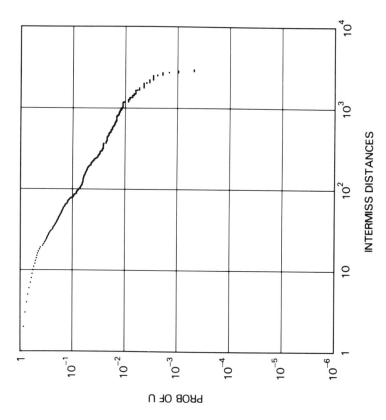

ALL
LINE SI= 128
CACHE SIZE= 64K
CLASS SIZE= 1P

FIGURE 5. Probability data for scientific environments.

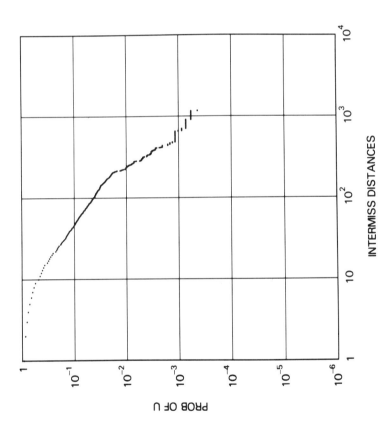

FIGURE 6. Probability data for time sharing.

REFERENCES

1. STONE, H. S. & M. SUTHERLAND. 1981. Interim Final Report—Studies in Microprocessors: Results of Statistical Analyses. University of Massachusetts. Boston, Mass.
2. DIETZ, W. & L. SZEWERENKO. 1979. Architectural efficiency measures: an overview of three studies. Computer 12(4): 26–34.
3. NEUHAUSER, C. J. 1975. An Emulation Oriented, Dynamic Microprogrammable Processor. Technical Note No. 65. Computer Systems Laboratory. Stanford University. Stanford, Calif.
4. HUCK, J. 1982. Comparative analysis of computer architecture. Doctoral Dissertation. Stanford University. Stanford, Calif.
5. PFISTER, G. F. 1982. The Yorktown Simulation Engine: introduction. In 19th Design Automation Conference. Institute of Electrical and Electronics Engineers. New York, N.Y.
6. CROW, J. D. & M. W. SACHS. 1980. Optical fibers for computer systems. Proc. IEEE 68(10).
7. LEWIS, C. 1982. Using the "Thinking-Aloud" Method in Cognitive Interface Design. Report No. RC9265. IBM Thomas J. Watson Research Center. Yorktown Heights, N.Y.
8. HEIDELBERGER, P., P. WELCH & P. C. YUE. 1981. Statistical analysis of data base systems measurements. In Performance '81. North-Holland Publishing Company. New York, N.Y.
9. MANDELBROT, B. B. 1982. The Fractal Geometry of Nature. W. H. Freeman and Company. San Francisco, Calif.
10. VOLDMAN, J., B. MANDELBROT, L. W. HOEVEL, J. KNIGHT & P. ROSENFELD. 1983. Fractal nature of software-cache interaction. IBM J. Res. Dev. 27(2): 166.

DISCUSSION OF THE PAPER

QUESTION: You talk about the high cost of putting computers in anywhere, including particular universities. We realize you have this ambitious program with Carnegie-Mellon. We also realize you have a $50 million grant program. But these things are so little. We're talking about 200 to 300 engineering schools in the country. How do you propose to take care of the financial aspect of pushing CAD and computer-oriented engineering in engineering schools in the country?

H. SCHORR: We're trying to do more than we've done in the past. I think there's a growing realization in this and other countries that it's an important area of research. Computers, as Dr. Dertouzos said, are probably the most important revolution that we've seen in our lifetime. And I think there will be more support from all segments of society. We have been working a great deal more with different universities than we have in the past. There have been an awful lot of cooperative efforts involving IBM—for example, some of our resources were made available to MIT to run an experiment that it didn't have the facilities for. To the extent of our ability, we'll do those sort of things.

QUESTION: My present income comes from programming IBM computers. I've found that a substantial part of my time programming on both IBM machines and on other machines comes in either programming around obscure features or trying to isolate and then program around bugs in systems software of various kinds. You said earlier that you're not committed to trying to produce programs that are completely bug free. Bugs that are sufficiently obscure will be left in the program, and I see an analogy between this and the attitude of the American semiconductor industry, which got burned several years ago when it was discovered that Japanese-produced chips, notably 64 kilobit random access memory chips, were of substantially higher quality than the American chips. The consequence was that a number of companies started to buy Japanese and U.S. industry lost something like 60% of the market for these chips. Do you see the same kind of thing happening with software and software quality? And if so, what do you intend to do about it?

H. SCHORR: I guess I've miscommunicated the point. To the extent that a bug is important to a particular customer or user of a program—and is an obstacle—that bug will be eliminated or fixed. The problem is that if you go to the entire set of customers and fix every known bug, unfortunately, you introduce other bugs. So basically once the program gets past a certain working point, the strategy is not to fix the bugs in a customer's environment unless there's a specific need. I'm not saying we're not going to fix problems. It's just that we don't want to fix bugs for a customer who isn't using that particular feature, because the fix may cause errors elsewhere in his operating system.

Now so far as producing error-free code, I think I would agree with what Dr. Dertouzos said about theoreticians. I'll paraphrase: basically we're dealing with large programs, with 10 and 20 millions of lines of code. And we have no theory yet that enables us to prove correctness, nor do we have testing procedures that enable us to completely test all the software. Unfortunately it's a fact of life. We test in a brute-force manner, and the combinatorial cases to be checked exceed the life of the program. If we didn't release the program before it was completely tested, the machines would be obsolete—and so would the program—before they were delivered. That I think is an unacceptable difficulty. In the airplane analogy, it was pointed out that crashes do occur, unfortunately. And if you know your statistics, you avoid new planes for the first year after they've been introduced. That's when they're taking all the bugs out of them. New cars have similar problems. But if you have a car that's been on the road for two or three years, you're statistically in much better shape. The diesel engine I bought within the last year-and-a-half is in good shape in comparison to the problems that were reported when the engine was introduced three years ago. And I'm afraid software is very similar to these other products in that sense. We don't have a theory that allows us to write error-free programs.

QUESTION: If a company starts by selling a program that is rather high quality, let's say higher than the quality of other companies selling programs of that kind, and they're selling at a price comparable to the other people in the market, you would assume that they would get more business, they would have more usage in their programs, and then their programs would be debugged more because people would find the bugs in them. Do you at IBM see this as a potential problem?

H. SCHORR: Well, we think we do provide high-quality programs that are well debugged. Consequently, we do have high usage of our programs usually.

QUESTION: Do you feel as others do that there's an impending crisis in terms of experimental computer science research since industries seem to be draining off much of the best talents in the academic world, whereas industry doesn't seem to be having an equal commitment to research endeavors?

H. SCHORR: Well I'm not sure that industry is draining off the best talent. There are plenty of talented people in many of the universities. I'd love to hire an awful lot of people I know in academia—including numbers of faculty members. The quality is high—as high as it is elsewhere. I think, however, the shortage is real because it's a growing field and there's a limited training production of people. But I don't think the problems are any worse than they've ever been, because of the monetary rewards in industry.

QUESTION: Well I'm not sure it's just income. It's a matter of where there are excellent facilities for doing research at this time. That is, with many of the universities struggling for funds at this time, it seems that if you're a graduate student right now in computer science, then many of the better positions in terms of continuing work are now with industry rather than the university environment.

H. SCHORR: Well, I was part of a National Academy of Sciences study, and we looked at the computing resources available at IBM/Yorktown and Bell Labs, versus those available at the leading universities. And they turned out to be very comparable. One could not make that case. You could argue that some of the industry facilities are unique. But I'm not sure that's true if you compare them to those of Carnegie-Mellon or MIT and other places that were well endowed. I think you'll find that they have comparable resources for their students and faculty doing research. Now, the resources may not be the same all over the country for every university. But, on the other hand, there are not that many Yorktowns or Bell Labs in the country either.

QUESTION: I think it's possible to consider a computer as merely a machine for controlling the motion of electrons in the solid state. Do you know of any current research attempting to use computers to force internal electronic currents into patterns representing electronic motions in atoms and molecules?

H. SCHORR: No. Now, let me take the last question.

QUESTION: My question is similar. Could you say what is the possible future of so-called biochips. Is it pure science fiction or is there development going on that may have some future?

H. SCHORR: I think I'll have to pass on that one, too, because I worry more about the systems than about the technology.

Computer Image Synthesis

Shapes

FRANKLIN C. CROW

Xerox Palo Alto Research Center
Palo Alto, California 94304

INTRODUCTION

Considerable effort goes into producing a computer-generated image. An image such as shown in FIGURE 1 can require anywhere from 30 seconds to an hour or more of the time of a "super mini" computer. Typically, the color of around ⅓ million spots or "pixels" (picture elements) must be calculated. The image shown in FIGURE 1 consists of 480 rows each containing 640 pixels, and requires about 15 minutes to compute. This number of pixels is appropriate for use with videotape or other media of limited resolution. However, 35 mm, 70 mm, and even larger formats of photographic film have been used to record images with several thousand rows of several thousand pixels each. Images with more than 20 million pixels are not considered the least unreasonable.

Since a complex, high-resolution image can easily take hours to compute on any but the fastest of today's computers and hundreds or thousands of images are required for an animated sequence, the cost of computer animation is rather high. However, the incredible pace of technological growth in computer hardware is making computer imagery increasingly fast and much less expensive.

While the day is fast arriving when computational costs for computer imagery will be quite reasonable, there remain other problems in the creation of computer imagery that will not automatically disappear. While FIGURE 1 takes only 15 minutes or so of computer time, the arrangement of the shapes and the selection of colors for the image took a couple of man-days. Furthermore, the total investment in designing the shapes depicted in the image amounts to several man-months.

A scene is composed of a collection of objects arranged in space. The objects themselves are often composed of aggregated simpler shapes. Defining a scene is most often a matter of typing in coordinate numbers that indicate the positions of the objects, and rotational values that specify their orientations. An image of the scene must then be generated to verify that the desired arrangement has been achieved. Much of the time investment in modeling and arrangement is directly affected by man-computer interaction factors.

Human interaction with computers occurs at four importantly different rates: (1) At the fastest rate, the computer completes each operation faster than the user can request another. This is known as "real-time"

FIGURE 1

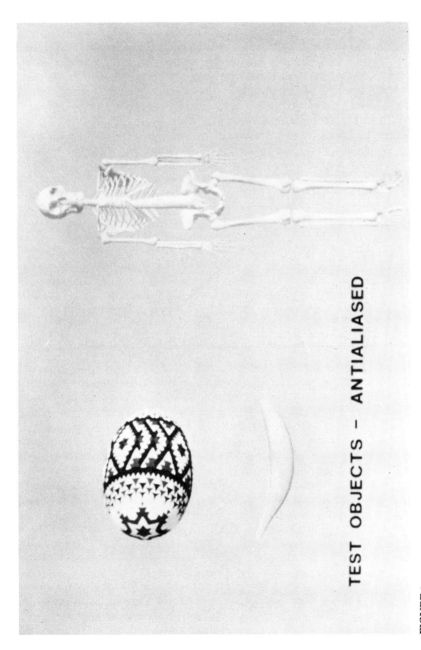

TEST OBJECTS - ANTIALIASED

FIGURE 2

interaction. (2) Somewhat slower rates can be characterized by completion of each operation before the user's mind wanders off onto some other topic. This time has been placed by human-factors researchers at a few seconds. Let us call this "human-time" interaction. (3) Even slower rates may require users to sit in front of the display and daydream or otherwise occupy themselves. This is sometimes known as "quick turnaround." Operations may take up to a few minutes. (4) The slowest rates are those that engender frustration unless the operations are done in a "batch" mode, where the user expects to go off and do something else, returning for the results at some later time.

In general, operations on line drawings at graphics work stations occur at or near real-time rates. Thus a modification of a shape on the screen should take no more than a small fraction of a second. On the other hand realistic images with shaded solid representations take at least "quick turnaround" time. Therefore, shape designing and arranging operations are most often done with line drawings, so that modifications can be made on the fly. We all hope that, in the future, faster processors will allow shapes to be designed using shaded solids. At present, shapes must be verified by making an occasional shaded image, and waiting.

Faster image generation is one way to speed the specification of a scene such as FIGURE 1. In particular, real-time interaction can make many such jobs trivial. However, a complicated scene can be manipulated in real time only by using a highly abstracted line drawing. With no program available for making the abstraction, each adjustment has to be verified by generating an image at "quick turnaround" speed. Only a small number of changes can be made per hour at that rate. For more satisfying performance, an automatic abstraction scheme, which substitutes a rectangular solid for each object in the scene, can be integrated with the display system so that crude drawings can be made at "human-time" rates.

Even with the faster feedback afforded by object abstractions, it is still necessary for the user to type numbers to the display system in order to specify the positions of objects. The next step in making arrangements easier is to use graphical input to point at the place where an object should be, or to "drag" a representation of the object to that position. Recent programs provide that capability and have dramatically increased the speed at which scenes can be arranged.

The shapes of the objects arranged in a scene also have to be described. The shapes in FIGURE 1 came from a variety of sources and were produced by a variety of means, all of which involved computer aids of one sort or another. Building systems for designing shapes is ultimately more interesting than building systems for making pictures of predefined shapes. Image display systems are charged with emulating physical reality, which is reasonably well understood at the required level. Systems for aiding in shape design, on the other hand, must cope with human interaction and avoid stifling creativity or otherwise inhibiting the designer, considerably more difficult objectives.

Systems for computer-aided layout of highly constrained patterns, such as those involved in interconnecting electronic components (circuit boards, integrated circuits), have been highly successful since they act to relieve tedious drudgery and enforce rules that prevent common mistakes. Although similar advantages are conceivable for more free-form three-dimensional design, the less constrained environment makes the problem much more difficult. Commercial systems for three-dimensional shape design, while available, do not come close to meeting the criteria advanced above.

It is fair to say that, in general, people are attracted to computer imagery because it makes production of animation much easier. People thus attracted tend to be impatient with tedious exercises, so there is a strong force to make the definition of shapes easier. In the following, I will explain some of the methods that have been commonly used to generate shapes. The definition of the objects used in FIGURES 1 and 2 will be explained at the appropriate places.

THE CHARACTERISTICS OF COMPUTER-USABLE SHAPE DESCRIPTIONS

In the simplest sense, realistic computer imagery is produced by evaluating the set of surfaces intersected by rays emanating from an observer point. The order in which the surfaces are intersected determines which surface is visible; the angle at which rays from the light sources intersect the surfaces determines brightness. The evaluation of $\frac{1}{3}$ million rays from the observer point, one through each of the spots on the display, produces an image.

Providing shape data as input to such a process means defining surfaces that allow simple evaluation of intersections with arbitrary lines in a three-dimensional space. Therefore surfaces must be described as continuous functions. In practice, a surface of any complexity is extremely difficult to describe as a single function. Nearly all shape data are now described by using a collection of bounded continuous regions. A shape is described as "piecewise analytic," meaning that a surface is assembled from many "surface elements," each a bounded region of a function. These surface elements are fitted together numerically so that a ray piercing the surface passes through only one surface element.

To date, most shape descriptions have used linear surface elements and are therefore polyhedra. However, higher-order surfaces are seeing wider use as display algorithms that can handle them become more widespread. Quadric surfaces (ellipsoids, cones, etc.), cubic surfaces (described by third-order equations), and quartic surfaces (described by fourth-order equations, chiefly doughnuts) are all used. However, since it is far easier to find the intersection of a plane and a line than the intersection of, say, a bicubic surface and a line, polyhedra have dominated shape data for computer display.

The first characteristic of data for shape display is that they unambiguously describe a surface. If I lay down four points on a piece of graph paper, most humans would see the shape thus described as a simple quadrilateral. However, there are other possible interpretations, which yield a pair of triangles. Some image-making systems have restricted surface element descriptions to triangles, to simplify things. However, more or less arbitrary polygons can be handled by many systems as long as they are consistently described.

Polygons are most easily handled if they are planar and convex. However, with some additional complexity in the display algorithm, reasonable images can be made of arbitrary polygons. Unfortunately, existing algorithms will make errors on certain cases of nonconvex polygons. The errors might not be noticeable, in general, but users of such systems must understand them well enough to avoid the pitfalls. This is not always easy.

Automating Hand-Entry Methods

The very first realistic computer-synthesized images were made using shape data entered by hand. A sheet of graph paper was used to draft a simple shape. Then coordinates of a succession of vertices describing the shape could be read from the paper and entered into the computer. An editing program could then be used to format the numbers into a file to be read by the display program. For obvious reasons, most early computer images consisted of shapes such as cubes and other more or less rectilinear solids. However, the graph paper method has no inherent limitations. Only tedium and perceptual ability curb the shapes that may be created in that way.

A large part of the tedium in entering shapes by the graph paper method comes from the need to deal with numbers. Each coordinate pair (or triple) needs to be read from the graph paper and written down, or at least typed to a terminal. The use of a digitizing tablet removes the need to deal with numbers directly, an important step.

A number of techniques have been developed to aid in transferring standard drafted shape descriptions to a form usable by display systems. There is a well-established methodology for representing three-dimensional shapes on paper. In particular, three-view drawings (front, side, and top views) are a widely recognized medium. Three-view drawings have been used very successfully in combination with large digitizing tablets for semiautomated shape definition.

One system for entering three-dimensional data by tablet is described by I. E. Sutherland.[14] Some digitizing tablets allow the use of two simultaneous digitizers. A pair of drawings, say a top view and a side view, allow one of the digitizers to measure the height and width dimensions of the represented object while the other measures the depth dimension.

Surfaces may be developed by mentally breaking the form into polygonal facets and marking the vertices of the polygons on the drawing.

A surface may then be defined by digitizing each of the vertices of each polygon in a prescribed order. As the polygons are recorded, the program being used to take data properly formats a file for the display program.

Since the data are being recorded under program control, various niceties can be added. If a display is handy, the polygons may be displayed as they are digitized, providing visual feedback on the correctness of the measurements. Usually a surface is modeled with adjacent polygons sharing the same vertices. In this case the order of digitization can be used to save redigitizing the same set of vertices for an adjoining polygon. In particular, if a shape can be described by a sequence of cross sections each defined by the same number of points, it is sufficient to digitize the points of each cross section in turn and let the program produce the polygon "skin" using the current and previous cross sections.

A similar technique is in use for reproducing shapes from computer-assisted tomography (CAT) scans used in medical diagnosis. The scan process yields a set of profiles of the shape as though it had been cut into slices. Digitizing each of the profiles in turn, a polygonal mesh can be built up to describe the shape in a manner similar to that described in the preceding paragraph. The skull of the skeleton in FIGURE 2 was produced from a set of skull-section profiles using a program that automatically assembled the polygon mesh as the vertices were digitized.

It is also possible to digitize from photographed shapes using the methods described by Sutherland. In a study done by Parke, several people's faces were digitized.[12] Polygonal outlines were painted on their faces, which were then photographed from two points simultaneously. Fixed markers hung near the faces allowed the measurement of several known positions, which were then used to find the transform that would take measured positions from the two photographs and recover the coordinates of the corresponding point in three-dimensional space.

Using automated entry methods does not change the fact that most data are still ultimately hand generated. Preparing drawings to be digitized still involves excessive amounts of tedious work. Furthermore, if we wish to modify the shape of interest, we are back where we started, unless we are willing to hand edit the data by changing some of the digitized numbers, an odious task at best. Drawings can, of course, be modified and redigitized. Faces can be repainted and rephotographed. However, it would be far preferable to modify the shapes using graphical input to interact with the shapes. Of course if the shapes can be interactively modified, why not design them by computer-aided means in the first place?

MODELING WITH SIMPLE SOLIDS

There are a number of systems for computer-aided shape design that function by providing a small catalog of primitive solids.[13] Most industrial parts can be adequately modeled as collections of connected cylinders, spheres, rectangular solids, and the like. Furthermore, the surfaces of these primitive solids are well understood for purposes of machining.

An object may be built up interactively by pushing representations of the primitive objects around on a display screen. The representations may be relatively simple line drawings, which can be displayed and moved around with little or no lag behind the operator's motions. Thus the primitive shapes can be juxtaposed, viewed from various angles, moved around some more, and then viewed again. When a certain level of satisfaction is reached, a display program can be applied to a file generated from the solids-modeling program to make a high-quality shaded image. Since precise intersections and other object interactions cannot always be deduced from the line drawings, unexpected results from the display program may send the operator back to the solids-modeling program for further adjustments.

Complex shapes are modeled from primitives by combining them using simple rules. Objects combined by a "union" rule enclose the volume occupied by all the primitive objects together. Objects combined by an "intersection" rule enclose only that volume occupied by all primitive objects simultaneously. Variations on these rules allow primitives to act like negative objects. A negative object removes volume from objects it intersects.

Crude chess pieces make good objects for solids modeling. Consider, for example, a rook, which can be made by several easy steps: (1) chop the bottom off of a large sphere to give a base; (2) put a cylinder on top of the base to form the midsection of the piece; (3) add another, larger cylinder to form the top; and (4) use long, thin rectangular solids applied as negative objects to cut grooves across the top of the piece, providing the familiar crenellations at the top.

The class of objects that can be made in this way is very large. However, objects assembled from primitives tend to appear somewhat crude. Furthermore, it is often difficult to see how to create a given shape out of the primitives available. Experienced designers can become very clever at using such systems. However, a more straightforward path to the same results would be preferable. The subtleties of finely blended curved forms cannot easily be achieved from an assemblage of primitives. Therefore, some experimental shape-design systems strive toward a greater flexibility, closer to the possibilities offered by modeling clay.

DEVELOPABLE SURFACES

Many shapes can be produced by sweeping a template along a path in space. The prime example of this method is the solid of revolution. The template is similar to a physical analogue that might be used with a lathe or potter's wheel. The template is swung around a circular path developing a surface as it goes. A program for generating surfaces of revolution is fairly easy to produce. Furthermore, a large class of interesting objects in everyday life can be rendered as surfaces of revolution (e.g., glassware, lamps, and pottery).

To generate a solid of revolution, all one needs is a program that can take a string of vertices describing a template and produce a polygonal surface by stepping around a circular trajectory, producing a row of polygons with each step. On completion of the trajectory, the surface will close on itself. The tipped over champagne glass in FIGURE 1 was produced by a program for surfaces of revolution.

Programs for surfaces of revolution are simple enough that the completed shape can be displayed in human time, or less, in response to a newly entered template. Thus changes in the shape can be quickly appraised. In fact, satisfying real-time interaction with a shape can be achieved by displaying just the profile of the surface, using a mirrored copy of the template to form the other half of the profile.

Templates can be used to develop surfaces in a variety of other ways. Block letters, for example, are easily developed by adding thickness to a two-dimensional representation of the letter. Similarly, a closed string of vertices may be moved along a path in three-dimensional space, sweeping out a shape in the process. The latter process is similar to the extrusion technique used in many industrial forming processes.

The surface of revolution can be significantly generalized to make a much more powerful tool. In addition to defining a template, let us also define that path through which the template is swept. This makes it possible to make fluted shapes, for example. The process can be further generalized to allow several different templates to be used along the sweep path and different sweep paths to be used at different points along the templates. Of course, the different templates and sweep paths should be interpolated one into the next for smoothly changing surfaces.

The broken pieces of column shown in FIGURE 1 were produced, in part, with a generalized surface of revolution system. The column in front of the glass stands on a squarish pedestal. The column itself starts with a rounded base supporting a fluted section, which appears to be broken off at the top. Two sweep paths and four templates were necessary to produce this shape. The two sweep paths consist of a circular path for the base and a wavy circular path to form the fluted section. The four templates are used to produce the broken appearance at the top. All templates are identical except for the top sections. Each top section takes a sharp change in direction at a different height and meets the others at a common point in the middle.

Most of the bones in the skeleton in FIGURE 2 were similarly modeled. The straight bones generally require only enough templates to get the required number of bulges at the ends. In general, two templates per bulge are adequate.

Most any relatively simple shape without holes or long protrusions can be modeled as a generalized surface of revolution. However, in practice, any shape requiring more than a dozen sweep paths or templates has been difficult for any but very experienced users to get predictable results with. The problem is that it is hard to visualize the result from just the collection of paths and templates.

The Easter egg in FIGURE 1 required the greatest effort of all objects in that figure. Although it is basically a surface of revolution, it was carefully designed so that the individual polygons would show an interesting pattern if they were individually colored. Therefore, one section of the egg was designed meticulously by hand and then mirrored and rotated to fill out the entire shape.

A number of programs were written to support the design of the egg.[9] This effort was justified since the shape was made into a 30-foot monument for which the pieces were tooled under computer control. However, many other surfaces can most easily be generated by a program.

ALGORITHMICALLY DEFINED SURFACES

Highly regular surfaces, for example, the checkerboard surface of FIGURE 1, are best defined using a computer program. Given some experience in the style of programming needed to produce files for shape description, a program for generating checkerboards can be produced in from 30 minutes to half a day depending on the ability of the programmer. Programs that can be produced so quickly are often known as "quick hacks" and are sometimes casually discarded after serving the immediate purpose. More often, a collection of such programs grows over time, becoming a useful set of tools that may be easily modified for various purposes. These tools have a distinct drawback, however, in that they are usually designed for a distinct purpose and therefore must be modified for each new use, putting them out of reach to nonprogrammers.

It was realized some time ago that with more careful design, large classes of objects could be generated from a single program by feeding it different parameters as input.[10] An early example of such a program generated 1960s-style high-rise buildings. The parameters controlled such things as number of floors, size and spacing of windows, outside dimensions of the building, etc. Such a program makes it possible to generate whole cities rather quickly. In fact, it becomes quite easy to produce input data for the display program that either overtax its capabilities (if it is badly designed) or require an unacceptable amount of time to generate the image.

Some kinds of stochastic behavior have recently been added to algorithmically defined shapes.[6,8] If the variation in the parameters supplied to produce the buildings making up a city is suitably constrained, then random numbers can be supplied to define each particular building. A similar technique has been applied to simulating landscapes. If the variation in topography over a region can be statistically characterized, then a few points can be set out to pinpoint peaks and valley bottoms, leading the statistical description to supply a likely version of what undulations fall in between. Extremely realistic images of imaginary landscapes have been made in this way.

The mountains in the background of FIGURE 1 were produced by specifying a few parameters for altitude variation and roughness and then applying a variational expansion to a quadrilateral. The quadrilateral was divided into four parts, and the new vertex thus created was assigned a height based on the input parameters and a value picked from a table of random numbers. Succeeding steps subdivided each of the new quadrilaterals, and the process continued for a number of steps specified by yet another input parameter.

Unfortunately, algorithmically defined surfaces cannot easily be modified to suit one's tastes. Since a global process has determined the details, one has no direct control over them. However, when huge amounts of shape data must be created just to use as a background (as in the case of the mountains) or to establish a sense of space (as in the checkerboard), the algorithmic approach shines.

FREE-FORM CURVED SURFACES

None of the above techniques can satisfy a designer with desires for the freedom afforded by modeling clay. One would really like a system that allowed the designer to mold a blob into any shape by pushing and pulling on the surface. Some rather restrictive systems of this sort have been built.[4,5,11] However, any such system suffers from the impoverished access to three-dimensional space afforded by two-dimensional input (digitizing tablet, mouse, joystick) and two-dimensional output (display screen). Some efforts have been made to overcome this limitation by providing three-dimensional input devices,[2,7] but no device has yet achieved much acceptance. Three-dimensional output devices have been even less successful.[15]

Although interaction is awkward using two-dimensional media, modifications to a surface are possible with a few aids. Most of the difficulty arises when trying to isolate the position at which to grab the surface. A line drawing frequently offers little distinction between two or more overlapping surfaces. Typically, the front and back surfaces of an object are both visible, and indistinguishable. If the designer's graphics work station is powerful enough to support real-time rotation, the proper angle can usually be found to clarify the situation. However, additional aids that give better cues are badly needed. Graphics work stations that support perspective views in real time and allow more distant features to be dimmed in proportion to their depth are very helpful.

Once the surface has been grabbed at the desired point, another problem arises. Just what effect should pushing and pulling have upon the surface? Polygon-based systems may be modified by changing the position of a vertex. However, if a smoothly curved surface approximated by polygons is being modified, the smoothness of the original surface should be retained. Moving a single vertex will not, in general, maintain a smooth surface. However, if adjacent vertices are constrained to move similarly but by lesser amounts, then the surface appears to have some elasticity and smooth surfaces are easier to maintain.[5,11] Other techniques using nonlinear surface elements are more successful.

There are some very powerful techniques for using nonlinear surface elements to piece together smooth objects. Coon first proposed a scheme for describing curved shapes by piecing together continuous curved patches of surface and enforcing continuity constraints at the joins.[3] Successors to the "Coons patch" allow very convenient control of a surface without losing desired smoothness. Since smooth continuity at joins between patches is enforced, such a surface behaves a bit like idealized modeling clay.

The difficulty in controlling curved surfaces comes in managing uneven distribution of detail. A more or less evenly curved blob can be modeled very easily. However, a shape like a human face, which has large smooth areas such as the forehead and sharply detailed areas such as the eyes, proves much more difficult. The problem arises because well-understood formulations for curved surfaces require that the density of the patches be about the same over the whole surface so that a regular mesh of quadrilaterals may be used.

The banana shape in FIGURE 2 was produced on a curved surface system,[4] although roughly the same shape could have been produced as a generalized surface of revolution. Eight vertices were arrayed around the banana at six positions along its length. The eight vertices were arranged in four closely spaced pairs to provide high curvature at the creases, where the peel would come apart upon removal, and slowly curving expanses in between. The six positions along the length allowed the definition of the stem (two positions), the main body, with increasing thickness toward the middle (three positions), and the pointed end opposite the stem (one position).

ASSEMBLING A SCENE

The assembly of a scene requires that all the objects be arranged in some intended manner. This can usually be done easily, if the scene is not too complicated, by specifying positions using graphical input. As shown in the introductory section above, a representation of the scene adequate to understanding the spatial relationships among the objects can be manipulated in real time on a reasonably powerful graphics work station. However, a shaded color image of the scene always holds some surprises.

Setting up a scene requires specifying a position from which the viewer sees the scene and a direction in which the viewer looks or, more easily, a point in the scene that represents the center of the viewer's interest. Choosing these positions can be difficult if the image is to be used to illustrate a point in which one object is required to partially obscure another, for example. Here a real-time system is a great advantage.

Building an animated sequence of scenes requires still more effort. The simplest animations merely involve moving the observer position around from frame to frame. Small "quick hack" programs that calculate various eyepoint trajectories have been used for this purpose. However, to make the creation of animation possible for everyone, a means for specifying a sequence of positions and times at which the eyepoint should occupy those positions must be provided. A curved path that passes through all the designated points can then be computed by an animation program. The sequence of positions thereby produced can be written on a file subsequently used to produce the required series of images.

All the objects in a scene can be similarly controlled. A "script" of sorts then consists of initial position and orientation designations for the objects followed by a command to generate the first frame. Thereafter, only those designations that change from one frame to the next need be specified between frame-generation commands. A flexible animation system allows nearly everything to be changed from frame to frame, including the position orientation, color, surface texture, and shape of objects, the color, strength, and location of light sources, and the position and field of view of the observer.

The designation of colors remains a problem. Most systems have not yet managed color in a way allowing the user to exercise subtle control. Most specifications come in the form of percentage designations for the three primary colors. Thus yellow consists of 100% red, 100% green, and 0% blue on a color display. A reddish brown might be made from 70% red, 40% green, and 10% blue. One way of handling color is to keep the equivalent of paint chips around. For example, make a catalog of the all possible colors using five broadly spaced values for each of the primaries. This requires only 125 colors. The user can look up a color close to what is desired, then add a bit of this or that to achieve the desired variation.

Color-naming schemes have been proposed as an alternative to color catalogs.[1] Ideally, a user could specify a color by entering "dark reddish brown." The system would look up its definition of brown (as percentages of the primaries), interpolate $\frac{1}{3}$ the way to its definition of red ($\frac{2}{3}$ of the way would be called "brownish red"), then darken the result by halving the values of all the primaries. Once a system is calibrated so that the users agree on a definition of brown, violet, pink, etc., resulting colors should be quite predictable.

While the computation time to make a scene or animated sequence of computer images may be enormous, the human time required to design it is equally enormous for anything of substantial complexity. The assembly of objects and their arrangement can be made fairly easy using computer aids. However, the problem of creating enough computer aids to give a wide range of expression is substantial. The software required can be expected to be considerably greater than that required to produce the images once the objects are defined and arranged.

SUMMARY

Complicated, realistic computer-generated images are notorious for using tremendous amounts of computer time. However, an interestingly complex realistic image generally requires correspondingly complicated input. Describing and arranging a collection of shapes for display can involve a broad collection of techniques. Using particular images as examples, some of those techniques are explained herein. First, it is explained how shapes must be described for the computer algorithms that must display them. Then, manual, automatic, and computer-aided techniques for numeric realization of the shapes are described. Shape data may be entered by hand from sketches on graph paper or by digitizing equipment from drafted diagrams or pairs of photographs. Data may be generated by programs written specifically for the purpose. Finally, data may be produced by interacting with computer programs that aid in the development of certain classes of shapes. Computer aids are also useful for assembling composite objects and arranging objects in scenes for animation.

ACKNOWLEDGMENTS

The images shown in FIGURES 1 and 2 and many of the systems described were implemented at Ohio State University while the author was with the Computer Graphics Research Group there. The broken columns were created by Rick Balabuck and the skeleton by Don Stredney at Ohio State. The Easter egg was created at the University of Utah by Ron Resch, Robert McDermott, and Jim Blinn. Other objects were created at Utah and Ohio State by the author. Examples of most of the shape-definition and scene-arrangement programs mentioned herein have been implemented by Wayne Carlson and Julian Gomez at Ohio State and by the author at Utah.

REFERENCES

1. BERK, T., L. BROWNSTON & A. KAUFMAN. 1982. A new color-naming system for graphics languages. IEEE Comput. Graphics Appl. **2**(3): 37.
2. BURTON, R. P. & I. E. SUTHERLAND. 1974. Twinkle box: a three-dimensional computer input device. In National Computer Conference: 513–520. American Federation of Information Processing Societies (AFIPS). New York, N.Y.
3. COONS, S. A. 1967. Surfaces for Computer Design of Space Forms. MIT Project MAC Report No. TR-41. Massachusetts Institute of Technology. Cambridge, Mass.
4. CROW, F. C. 1977. A three-dimensional surface design system. In Proceedings, ACM 1977 National Conference. Association for Computing Machinery. New York, N.Y.

5. CARLSON, W. E. 1982. Techniques for the generation of three dimensional data for use in complex image synthesis. Ph.D. Thesis. Ohio State University Department of Information and Computer Science. Columbus, Ohio.

6. FOURNIER, A., D. FUSSELL & L. CARPENTER. 1982. Computer rendering of stochastic models. Commun. ACM 25(6): 371.

7. GEYER, K. E. & K. R. WILSON. 1975. Computing with feeling. *In* Proceedings, IEEE Conference on Computer Graphics, Pattern Recognition, and Data Structures: 343–349. Institute of Electrical and Electronic Engineers. New York, N.Y.

8. MANDELBROT, B. B. 1977. Fractals: Form, Chance, and Dimension. W. H. Freeman and Company. San Francisco, Calif.

9. MCDERMOTT, R. J. 1980. Geometric modelling in computer aided design. Ph.D. Thesis. Computer Science. University of Utah. Salt Lake City, Utah.

10. NEWELL, M. E. 1976. The Utilization of Procedure Models in Digital Image Synthesis. Computer Science Department Report No. UTEC-CSc-76-218. University of Utah. Salt Lake City, Utah.

11. PARENT, R. E. 1977. A system for sculpting 3-D data. Comput. Graphics 11(2): 138.

12. PARKE, F. I. 1972. Computer Generated Animation of Faces. Computer Science Department Report No. UTEC-CSc-72-120. University of Utah. Salt Lake City, Utah.

13. REQUICHA, A. A. G. & H. B. VOELKER. 1982. Solid modeling: a historical summary and contemporary assessment. IEEE Comput. Graphics Appl. 2(2): 27.

14. SUTHERLAND, I. E. 1974. Three dimensional data input by tablet. Proc. IEEE 62(4): 64.

15. VICKERS, D. L. 1974. Sorcerer's Apprentice: Head-Mounted Display and Wand. Computer Science Department Report No. UTEC-CSc-74-078. University of Utah. Salt Lake City, Utah.

Computer Image Synthesis

Rendering Techniques

TURNER WHITTED*

Bell Laboratories
Holmdel, New Jersey 07733

INTRODUCTION

Computer image synthesis is a powerful and flexible tool for producing film and video animation. To use it, one "tells the computer" how to make an image and then goes away for a while. Images produced by the simplest methods have a cartoonlike appearance, while advanced techniques will generate pictures that cannot be immediately distinguished from photographs of real scenes.

Although computer-generated images have long been used for flight training and some scientific and engineering applications, they are increasingly being used for special effects in the advertising and entertainment fields. In spite of this growing application, the complexity of image synthesis techniques continues to intimidate most people. The purpose of this paper is to demystify the image-making process without understating the difficulty that it presents.

DIGITAL IMAGES

Ideally, an image is a continuous function resulting from the projection of three-dimensional objects onto a two-dimensional viewing plane. Representing image functions in a computer, however, requires breaking the image into discrete samples, referred to as pixels (FIGURE 1). A digital image is then an array of sample values stored as numbers in the computer's memory. An image resolution of 512 × 512 refers to a list of 262,144 pixels. This is a commonly used representation because it approximately matches standard television resolution. In addition to being spatially sampled, the image intensity values are quantized into discrete values as well. Since the eye can only distinguish a little over 100 distinct intensity values, 8 bits (256 distinct intensity levels) is a convenient representation for monochrome images. Color images typically have 24 bits per pixel, 8 bits each for the primary colors red, green, and blue.

For interactive applications, a user must see the digital image. This requires that the image memory have two ports—one for the computer

*Present affiliation: Numerical Design Ltd., 133 E. Franklin Street, P.O. Box 1316, Chapel Hill, N.C. 27514.

and one to refresh a video display. Such a special purpose memory is called a "frame buffer." It may be part of the host computer's main memory, or it may more likely be a peripheral device. The low cost of semiconductor memory has made such display systems widely available.

COMPARISON WITH OTHER TECHNIQUES

There are several ways to use computers to make pictures. The simplest is to scan a picture into the computer's memory, manipulate it, combine it with other pictures, and print it back out to film. A second method is to use the computer memory as an artist's canvas. A locator device such as a light pen or graphics tablet becomes the artist's brush.

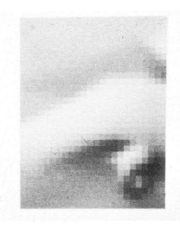

FIGURE 1. The highlighted region of the image on the left is enlarged eight times, showing that it is made from a mosaic of discrete pixels.

The computer "paint" program defines the brush's color, size, shape, and other attributes (all under the artist's careful control, of course). The paint program converts the artist's actions into pixel values, which are stored in the computer memory.

Both of these techniques are inherently two-dimensional. The image is not only the result, but a representation of the image is the primary data structure of the computer programs. Any attempt to represent a three-dimensional world with such programs must come from the artist's skill; the computer program has no knowledge of the three-dimensional world.

A more flexible approach to generating images is to directly model a scene in three dimensions. An image of this scene is created by projecting the three-dimensional model onto an imaginary surface called an "image

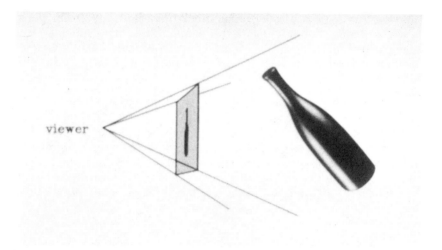

FIGURE 2. Projecting the three-dimensional world onto the image plane is an essential step in image synthesis. The image plane is the computer's geometric representation of the viewing screen.

plane" (FIGURE 2). The image plane is the computer representation of the viewing screen. As an example, if the three-dimensional coordinate system for our model is oriented so that the $+x$ direction is to viewer's right, the $+y$ direction is up, and the $+z$ direction is away from the viewer, then an orthographic projection onto the x-y plane can be achieved by setting the z component of each location to zero. Transformations such as rotation, translation, and scaling are accomplished with simple matrix multiplications.[1] A true perspective view requires that the x and y components be divided by the z component.

Many objects can be represented by straight lines. Since lines are described by the coordinates of their end points, it is a simple matter to apply the geometric transformations to the line segment end points and then connect them to form line drawings. Curved lines are readily approximated by collections of straight line segments. Unlike the painted or scanned-in images, the line drawing is derived from geometric information and conveys mostly geometric information (FIGURE 3, left).

Image synthesis is a process that accepts three-dimensional geometric object descriptions and produces shaded images (FIGURE 3, right). The computer program achieves this transition from object to image by simulating the reflection of light from the objects described by the input data and calculating an intensity value for each corresponding element of the discrete image. In addition the program must decide which elements of the object description are visible to the viewer and discard those that are not.

The computer graphics techniques that work either entirely in the image domain or entirely in the geometric domain are conceptually straightforward. Because image synthesis crosses the boundary between the two domains, it is not simple either conceptually or in its implementation.

IMAGE SYNTHESIS

Computer image synthesis is best described as a pipeline of cooperating processes (FIGURE 4). The front end performs geometric operations on three-dimensional objects to transform them from *world* coordinates to *viewer* coordinates. It also performs a clipping operation, i.e., it discards objects or fragments of objects that fall outside the field of view.

The second stage maps visible parts of each object onto the image plane. Algorithms that perform the mapping are called *visible surface algorithms*. (The term *hidden surface algorithm* is used just as often and means exactly the same thing.)

The final stage of the pipeline is the "shader," a procedure for calculating intensity values for every point on a visible surface.

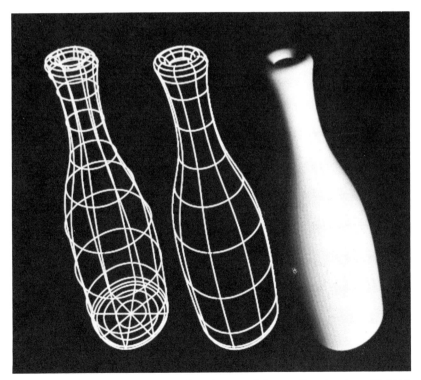

FIGURE 3. An object is displayed as a line drawing (left), as a line drawing with hidden lines removed (center), and as a shaded image (right).

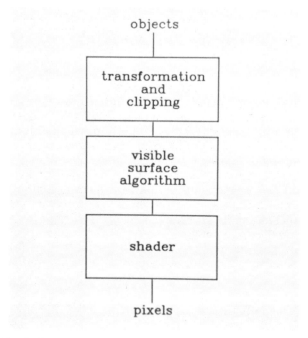

FIGURE 4. The display pipeline.

In this paper, only techniques for rendering polyhedral objects will be discussed. This turns out not to be terribly restrictive since nearly any shape can be accurately approximated by large numbers of small polygons (FIGURE 5). The restriction does simplify the discussion considerably since polygons are easily defined in terms of straight line edges.

VISIBLE SURFACE ALGORITHMS

Image synthesis algorithms evolved from line-drawing methods. In the early days of computer graphics when line drawings were the only possible display, a lot of serious work was devoted to solving the hidden line problem. That is, the goal was to remove lines from a drawing that would normally be obscured by the surfaces that the lines represented (FIGURE 3, center). With the advent of raster displays, it was natural to focus on the "hidden surface problem." Since for a long time image synthesis and hidden surface removal were synonymous, it is instructive to take a look at some simple hidden surface algorithms.

The solution to the hidden surface problem can be stated very simply: *at a given point on the image plane, only the object nearest to the viewer is visible.* This implies that a visible surface algorithm must compare depths while mapping surfaces onto the image plane.

Part of any algorithm for displaying shaded areas is a method of mapping the projected polygon onto the image plane and shading the interior of the polygon. FIGURE 6 shows how this is done for convex polygons. The initial step is to sort polygon vertices by y value to find the top and bottom. Next, vertices are sorted by x to form a list of right and left edges. Finally, the region inside the polygon is filled by assigning intensity values for each pixel that falls between a left and right edge. For the time being, we assume that the intensity value is constant over the interior of the polygon.

The other element of the display algorithm is the visibility calculation. If we have a memory large enough to store the entire image, one solution is to "paint" polygons into the memory starting with the farthest and proceeding to the nearest. When we are done, all nearer objects will have overwritten farther ones at points of overlap. This is the popular *painter's algorithm.*[2]

A similar approach requires that depth information be stored at every pixel. As polygons are written, their depth at each pixel is compared to

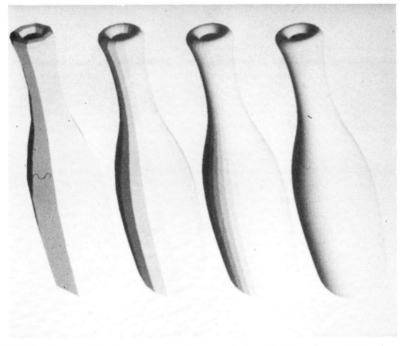

FIGURE 5. A curved bottle approximated successively with 144 polygons, 576 polygons, 2,304 polygons, and 9,216 polygons.

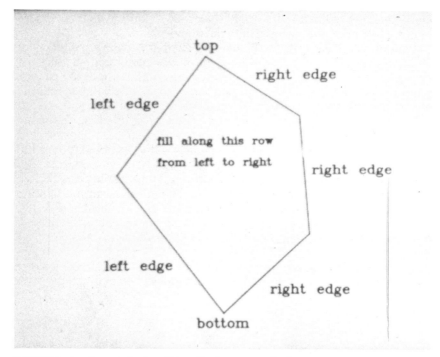

FIGURE 6. A polygon is "painted" into display memory by first sorting its vertices from top to bottom, and then left to right, to form lists of left and right edges. Pixels between the left and right edges are shaded one row at a time starting from the top.

the depth of what is already in the frame buffer. If the current polygon is closer at a given pixel than what has already been written, then an intensity and depth for the current polygon overwrite the frame buffer's previous contents. If, on the other hand, the current polygon is farther away than what was previously written into the frame buffer, the frame buffer's contents are not changed. This is called the z-*buffer algorithm*,[3] and unlike the painter's algorithm it can process polygons in any order.

There are, of course, many opportunities to be clever when designing an efficient display algorithm. One characteristic of both of the polygon display methods described above is the need to sort polygons and edges. In fact, for this class of algorithm, sorting is the principal activity and the efficiency of the sort largely determines the efficiency of the algorithm.[4]

A completely different type of hidden surface algorithm is *ray tracing*, which, as the name implies, simulates a pinhole camera by casting rays from each pixel of the image plane through a focal point and into the three-dimensional scene (FIGURE 7). The algorithm computes the point of intersection of each ray with each object in the scene to determine which object is visible along each ray. It requires no perspective projection, no clipping, and it is probably the simplest display algorithm to implement. It is also the least efficient way to make pictures. The reason for mentioning it here is that it can be easily extended to make highly realistic pictures.

SHADING

When describing the method of filling the interior of a polygon, no mention was made of what intensity value to fill it with. The intensity value should be related to the orientation of the surface with respect to some simulated lighting environment. In the most general terms, reflection from a point on a surface is expressed as the integral over the hemisphere above the surface of an illumination function, $L(x,y,z,\phi,\theta)$, times a reflectance function, $R(\phi,\theta)$:

$$I(x,y,z) = \int_{\phi} \int_{\theta} L(x,y,z,\phi,\theta) R(\phi,\theta) d\phi d\theta \qquad (1)$$

where (x,y,z) is the point of reflection.

The intensity expression is evaluated on a per pixel basis and must therefore be simplified to permit rapid calculation. A grossly simplified reflection model is Lambert's law:

$$I = \mathbf{N} \cdot \mathbf{L} \qquad (2)$$

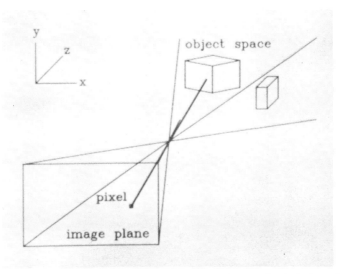

FIGURE 7. A ray-tracing display algorithm "fires" a ray from each pixel, through a focal point, and into object space. The first surface encountered by a ray is the visible one for that pixel.

where I is the reflected intensity, N is the polygon unit surface normal, and L is a unit length vector in the direction of the light source.

The fastest way to apply this model is to fill each polygon with a constant intensity value calculated once per polygon. FIGURE 8, left, shows an example of an image produced in this way. The faceted appearance is due to the use of a polygonal approximation for the torus in the figure. A considerably improved approximation can be obtained by calculating intensity values at the polygon vertices and smoothly interpolating the intensity over the surface of the polygon,[5] as in FIGURE 8, center.

The commonest approach to greater realism is to add better models of light reflection to the existing display algorithms. Lambert's law accounts for only the diffuse reflection of light from a surface. Better models include the effects of specular reflection[6] (FIGURE 8, right) and transparency (FIGURE 9).

These models are only approximations to actual reflection with extreme simplifications. For more realistic images fewer simplifications can be tolerated, and the amount of time required to compute them begins to grow. It is possible to derive very accurate reflectance functions based on the physical properties of the surfaces being simulated.[7,8] It is

FIGURE 8. A polygonal approximation to a torus is rendered using flat shading (left), smooth shading (center), and a shader that simulates highlights (right).

FIGURE 9. Transparency is simulated by painting polygons in back to front order and only partially overwriting background pixels when painting transparent polygons.

more difficult to provide good illumination functions. The point light source in Equation 2 is the simplest illumination function, but it does not account for shadows or reflections from nearby objects. The initial attempts to improve the illumination model added shadows[9] and simulated lighting environments[10] with encouraging results.

The most recent improvement has been to use ray-tracing algorithms to solve the visibility problem recursively.[11,12] That is, when a point on a surface is found to be visible to the viewer, the visible point is taken to be a new viewpoint and the visibility calculation is solved all over again. The objects visible from this new viewpoint are transmitted to the viewer either through reflection or refraction. Since ray tracing determines visibility only along a single viewing direction, many rays are needed to provide a complete view. Typically, for each point visible to a viewer, rays are traced along a single direction of reflection and a single direction of refraction (if the surface is transparent) as if the surface were a perfectly smooth mirror (FIGURE 10). Additional rays are traced to each

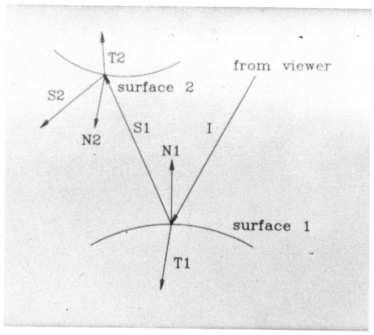

FIGURE 10. Mirror reflection and refraction can be simulated by applying ray tracing in a recursive manner.

light source to determine if the point of reflection is hidden from the light source and thus in shadow. The picture in FIGURE 11 was made in this way, and although it has a realistic appearance, it took several hours of computer time to create.

DIGITAL ARTIFACTS

The finite resolution of digital images introduces an artifact known as aliasing.[13] It is most commonly noticed along edges that appear to be jagged. In animated sequences aliasing artifacts can be terribly distracting as "jaggies" march along polygon edges, as moire patterns dance across the image, and as fine detail periodically disappears from the screen. As FIGURE 12 illustrates, dealing with aliases carefully is absolutely essential for generating realistic images.

Signal-processing theory permits a sampled image to contain only a level of detail that is consistent with the resolution of the sampling points. An expensive approach to reducing the effects of aliases is to increase the resolution of the display system until the artifacts are not noticeable. A more reasonable method is to reduce the level of detail in an image by filtering prior to sampling. However the processing required to do the filtering is difficult to implement and time consuming to execute.

RESEARCH ISSUES IN REALISTIC IMAGE SYNTHESIS

Having looked at techniques for producing synthetic images, we turn our attention to future work in the production of realistic pictures. There are several elements of realism including *geometric fidelity, intensity fidelity, complexity,* and *freedom from digital artifacts.* The visible surface algorithm must insure geometric fidelity; the shader, intensity fidelity; and a procedure for antialiasing removes the digital artifacts. Knowing that the physical world is complex implies that any realistic simulation of the world will also be complex. The efficiency of rendering procedures is therefore of extreme importance.

How does one build a display system that preserves all of these elements while rendering pictures in a reasonable amount of time? One way of answering this question is to take a look at the amount of computing time spent in the different parts of the rendering process. We find that for simple scenes the visibility calculations still dominate the

FIGURE 11. A realistic picture computed using recursive ray tracing.

computing time, but for more realistic images the shader is more time consuming. However, for extremely complex images the shading costs reach an upper limit and visibility costs soar. Furthermore, we know from experience that trying to prevent artifacts by modifying existing algorithm is awkward and tends to at least double the time needed to render a scene. While the task of generating realistic images seems to require both faster computing engines and more efficient algorithms, fast hardware is usually expensive and better algorithms are elusive. For the time being the question remains unanswered.

FIGURE 12. Two images of the same scene rendered with and without antialiasing.

SUMMARY

This paper describes computer image synthesis techniques. Initially, simple algorithms are given. The limitations of the simple algorithms provide a point of reference for discussing the difficulty of producing realistic images. Some approaches are suggested, illustrated, and criticized. In the end, the question of how best to render realistic images remains open.

REFERENCES

1. NEWMAN, W. M. & R. F. SPROULL. 1979. Principles of Interactive Computer Graphics. 2nd edit. McGraw-Hill. New York, N.Y.
2. NEWELL, M. E., R. G. NEWELL & T. L. SANCHA. 1972. A new approach to the shaded picture problem. In Proceedings ACM National Conference.
3. CATMULL, E. E. 1974. A subdivision algorithm for computer display of curved surfaces. Ph.D. Thesis. Computer Science Department. University of Utah. Salt Lake City, Utah.
4. SUTHERLAND, I. E., R. F. SPROULL & R. A. SCHUMACKER. 1974. A characterization of ten hidden-surface algorithms. Comput. Surv. 6: 1.
5. GOURAUD, H. 1971. Computer display of curved surfaces. IEEE Trans. Comput. C-20: 6.
6. PHONG, B. 1975. Illumination for computer generated pictures. Commun. ACM 18: 6.
7. BLINN, J. F. 1977. Models of light reflection for computer synthesized pictures. Comput. Graphics 11: 2.
8. COOK, R. L. & K. E. TORRANCE. 1982. A reflectance model for computer graphics. ACM Trans. Graphics 1: 1.
9. CROW, F. C. 1977. Shadow algorithms for computer graphics. Comput. Graphics 11: 2.
10. BLINN, J. F. & M. E. NEWELL. 1976. Texture and reflection in computer generated images. Commun. ACM 19: 10.
11. WHITTED, T. 1980. An improved illumination model for shaded display. Commun. ACM 23: 6.
12. MAX, N. L. 1981. Vectorized procedural models for natural terrain: waves and islands in the sunset. Comput. Graphics 15: 3.
13. CROW, F. C. 1977. The aliasing problem in computer-generated shaded images. Commun. ACM 20: 11.

Democratic Choice and Technological Change

HARLEY SHAIKEN

Program in Science, Technology, and Society
Massachusetts Institute of Technology
Cambridge, Massachusetts 02139

The context in which I would like to discuss choice and change is the use of computers in manufacturing. But I think the basic issues involved here are much broader than just manufacturing, and span the use of computer technology to reorganize work.

Today we are seeing a very rapid and pervasive application of computers and microelectronics into the workplace. Computer technology makes possible extraordinary changes in the way work is organized and carried out. The word we most often associate with these changes is inevitability, but I think a far more appropriate concept would be choice. In fact the concept of inevitability, the fact that we view these changes as somehow all inevitable, blurs and limits the choices available.

In particular it is too narrow a focus to speak about the impact of technological change. Speaking about the impact implies that microelectronics and computers automatically, as a function of the technology itself, lead to certain consequences either beneficial or negative. Instead I think the way computers and computer systems in manufacturing are designed and used embodies certain values. Whether these values are explicitly stated or merely implied, they govern the way these technologies are designed, developed, and used. And in fact it is technology in the service of these values that leads to many of the consequences you see today, rather than the inherent characteristics of microelectronics and computers.

I would like to focus here on what values technology embodies, the consequences of these choices in the workplace, and the relation between the process of how these choices are made and what the technology actually looks like.

Today, in the real world, technological decision making in manufacturing in particular and the workplace in general is made under extraordinary pressures to raise productivity. And whether the consequences are positive or negative, no matter how negative they might be, they are all justified by saying that unless these steps are taken even more negative consequences will result. So perhaps we should begin by reexamining the definition of productivity.

Defining productivity merely as an output for a given input, let us say the number of cars produced per worker-hour, is far too narrow for the kind of changes that we are seeing taking place today. We have to begin by looking at productivity on the level of the society as a whole, and I think we should define the productive society as one in which each person who wants to contribute to the total output has an opportunity to do so. In other words, even if individual firms can become extremely productive as a result of technological change, as a society we may be totally unproductive if large-scale unemployment is the result.

So this broader social definition of productivity is a key to determining the values and the ways in which new technologies are developed and employed. But it is also necessary to reexamine productivity on the level of the individual firm, because computers tied together in the various parts of a manufacturing operation raise in an unprecedented way new issues for which types of systems are most productive.

I am going to argue that the most effective uses of computers and microelectronics are those in which information and responsibility are broadly shared. This aspect, the effective uses of new computerized systems on the level of the firm, is often masked by the nature of these systems themselves. One reason it is masked is that new technologies that are introduced are generally more capital intensive than those they replace, usually much more capital intensive. So if you merely measure a new system compared to what it replaces, almost by definition the new system would be more productive. But the real measure ought to be the productivity of that system given its potential.

A second aspect that masks the effective use of new technology is the issue of downtime. We speak about the characteristics of new systems as if they always work, but that is like trying to determine how fast a car will cross Manhattan, knowing that we have one Porsche and one Volkswagon and that the Porsche has a higher top speed. In reality that will tell you very little about what Forty-second Street looks like at rush hour and the most effective way to cross it.

What in fact are the choices from which we can select? I would like to examine two broad choices: one is the development of new technologies in the direction of what I would call electronic Taylorism; and the other is the development of human-centered systems.

Electronic Taylorism simply defined is the incorporation of the values of Frederick W. Taylor into the design of a system itself. There are three important characteristics of electronic Taylorism in production: one is centralized command; a second and related issue is the removal of skill; and a third characteristic of electronic Taylorism is increased machine pacing and worker monitoring.

In contrast, I would define human-centered systems as having the following three characteristics: decentralized decision making; the ability to fully utilize worker skill and creativity; and the wide dissemination and distribution of information—in effect, an optimal interaction or the striving toward an optimal interaction of people and computers irrespective of issues of social control. But since decision making is now exclusively in the hands of managers and engineers, managerial and engineering attitudes are very central to determining which set of choices is selected for the design of new equipment.

It would be ludicrous to attempt to characterize the attitude of all managers or all engineers in one sweeping statement, but I think there are pervasive characteristics, often not explicitly stated, that govern the way these choices are made.

A report that was done by the Air Force in its Integrated Computer-Aided Manufacturing Program (ICAM) underlines managerial control as a central goal. "The Air Force learned that managers' interests went beyond increased labor productivity. Industry managers qualified their interest in computer-aided manufacturing concepts on the potentials of extent of return on investment, maintenance of competitive position, greater design flexibility, and greater management control. Of these, industry considered management control as having the greatest payoff potential in computer-aided manufacturing."[1]

If managerial control is the central criterion, that strongly shifts the direction of technological choice, I would argue, toward the direction of electronic Taylorism. But there is also an engineering attitude that moves in the same direction, the attitude that those processes that are most predictable are inherently more desirable. But the way predictability is achieved in an unpredictable environment raises important questions for how human beings are used. In other words, is the most predictable system necessarily the most automatic system? Or could the most predictable system be the one that fully utilizes human skills and creativity?

I would like to put this argument in a more specific context by looking at a hypothetical production process—something so simple that it obviously does not exist in any real manufacturing operation, but nonetheless the points of emphasis are very real and quite appropriate.

Let us look at this model operation from design to production, in this case a computer-aided design terminal at one end, a computerized or numerically controlled machine tool on the other. In this case, utilizing the same basic hardware, work could be organized very differently using the concept of electronic Taylorism versus the concept of human-centered systems.

With electronic Taylorism, an engineer would sit at the computer-aided design terminal, design the part, fully provide the instructions to program that part, and automatically transfer those instructions to the machine tool. The role of the machinist would be merely to monitor the operation, to stop it if something went wrong. On the level of design, control would be centralized. On the level of the shop floor, skill would be minimum. The performance of the machine would be electronically monitored so that every time the machine stopped or did not perform according to program, the engineering office would be notified. This of course would be a very workable system, and probably far more productive than the manual machines and manual draftspeople that are replaced.

In fact, it is characteristic of most uses of this technology in industry today. But is this the only choice? What would a human-centered system look like? Again using the same simple example, an engineer would sit at a computer-aided design terminal and design a part. But in the programming of that part, the provision of the instructions to the machine tool, the machinist would play a central role, which would be analogous to the skilled function a machinist currently performs at a machine tool.

Instead of monitoring the operation of the machine tool electronically, a computer terminal at the machine could provide additional information to the worker about related production processes throughout the plant. Rather than using information as a vehicle of control, the processing of information would be designed to seek to expand the horizons of the person at the machine tool.

What is the difference between going in one direction and going in the other direction? What are the social costs involved in terms of the organization of the workplace using this simple system of electronic Taylorism versus human-centered control? One critical social cost is that with electronic Taylorism, the designer becomes severed from the reality of production. Here something I would term a computer illusion comes into play.

Sitting in front of the computer-aided design terminal without the necessity, technically or organizationally, of having any contact with the shop floor, it is easy to begin believing that the model is the reality. That what exists on the screen is all one needs to know about the actual operation. But in complex manufacturing processes, this illusion could be a dangerous error. Obviously the computer at the point of design offers a wide range of new alternatives. One can look at the characteristics of 600 brackets rather than the 6 brackets a conventional draftsperson might be able to look at in designing a new part. But knowing that there are 600 choices is not all that valuable if one has lost the feel of what a bracket actually does, because computerization does not remove the need for knowledge in production, it merely allows knowledge to be centralized and readily available if that is the choice that is made.

This can lead to some disastrous results. The Council for Science and Society in Britain describes an incident that occurred in a British aircraft factory. The story sounds as if it were made up to make the point, but I have been assured that it actually took place. In this incident, a young engineer designed the igniter for an aircraft turbine engine using the latest in computer-aided design equipment. The design was then reproduced on a numerically controlled machine tool. Somewhere in the process a decimal point was accidentally moved one position to the right—as errors go, relatively small. On the shop floor, the machinist saw the error but decided to produce the part anyway, so the world's largest jet aircraft igniter was manufactured. It required two machinists to carry the igniter up to the engineering office. The engineer who looked at it said that it looked fine, all the design criteria had been met.

This case is kind of humorous, but what about those errors that are not off to this magnitude? What about those errors that are off by a factor of 15%? How does one catch those errors? Where is the check on the shop floor once skill has been removed from that part of the operation?

But even on the level of design, there is also a danger because automation in the service of electronic Taylorism is a dynamic process that does not affect just one part of the production operation. It becomes very easy to think that all the designs can be done with optimized processes, so that for each bracket there is one optimal solution which you can then pull out to design a larger part. For a lot of operations, this works very well. But there are those designs for which this limits choice rather than expands choice. Would it have been possible, for example, for Shakespeare to write *King Lear* with optimized passages? And many engineering designs require at least as much creativity and versatility as writing.

With human-centered systems there is a technological and organizational need for the engineer to have direct contact with the shop floor, because the provision of instructions to the machine is still done by the machinist or at least the machinist has an important role in this. Organizationally it becomes necessary, for production to be carried out at all, for there to be sustained contact between what is taking place on the shop floor and what happens during the design process itself.

But there is a second cost to electronic Taylorism. Removing all human input from production results in processes of extraordinary complexity. The more complex a process becomes, the more prone it is to failure. And here the hidden issue of downtime becomes very central. It is not enough to know the technical capabilities of a system. One must also know how the system performs in practice. How serious a problem is downtime in American industry? Let us look at a previous example of technology, not necessarily a computerized process but transfer lines in the automobile industry—long lines of machine tools from which parts are automatically moved from one machine to another. It was these transfer lines for which the term automation was first coined by a Ford Motor Company executive in the late 1940s.

The Ford Motor Company did a study of 154 transfer systems throughout its operation between 1974 and 1980, and their conclusion was that the systems were functioning between 46% and 64% of the time.[2] Now obviously a variety of factors contributed to this, but downtime is a very central problem and the design of systems to remove human input as a criterion of design in order to establish increased control or greater predictability could in fact have the opposite result.

This process is exacerbated by the role of the military in the design and development of machine tools in the United States. One problem with military production is that the product is complex, so that the production process is also complex and requires the most complicated of machine operations which are then diffused to commercial industry. Whereas in other nations, who have done quite well competitively, principally Japan, the design of machine tools is centered on the commercial applications, which often produces as a start a less complex variety of machine system. But there is another issue as well, one that Dr. Melman has developed, a question of cost maximization and the design of those complex systems in an environment where cost is not an issue. It has led to the reported motto of military involvement in these production systems, "never use a simple system where a complex one will do."

Ultimately many technologies will be developed in the future that are able to reliably replace certain human functions. But the issue of choice is still relevant—Is that desirable? Is that necessarily more productive? But in any case, rushing to deploy the most automatic system as a criterion of design has disastrous results in the short term.

There is a third cost, which may be the most important of all, the impact of new designs and new computerized systems on the work environment itself. In the case of numerical control, the technology I used in the example earlier, many production managers have come to think that the actual operation of numerical control works better with a more highly skilled worker as part of the production process. But if jobs are designed to be idiot proof, then skilled workers are the last people in the world who would want to do those jobs. Yet today, those skills that are the result of a previous generation of training and organization remain vital to the efficient operation of new systems.

What happens as those skills disappear? What happens if a production process by its very organization and deployment of new systems makes it difficult to acquire those skills? In fact many designs of systems that deploy electronic Taylorism have a dramatic role in the quality of the work environment—by removing skills, by removing judgment, jobs become more routine, more monotonous. Under these circumstances, the quality of life on the job can become seriously eroded.

Here Dr. Robert Karasek, at Columbia University, developed a model for stress at work which is very applicable to the evaluation of new computerized systems. In this model, those jobs that have high psychological demands and low decision control are most apt to cause high stress and the resultant diseases that stem from this stress. Those jobs with low psychological demand and high decision control among others cause much lower stress.[3,4]

Today skilled machinists are in that upper left quadrant of high decision control, low psychological demand. It seems quite possible that electronic Taylorism could put them in the lower right quandrant of low decision control and high psychological demand—high psychological demand, increased stress stemming from an operation that is totally out of the control of the worker.

But it is not enough merely to analyze the characteristics of the system and the choices that are available in designing new machines and systems. The process of change itself is critical in evaluating the ultimate outcome, the ultimate choices that are made. It is more than a question of developing new approaches that are user friendly. There is also an issue of power involved here. There is a central question of the development of those institutions that allow workers and their representatives to have input into the design process itself. The choice between electronic Taylorism on the one hand and human-centered systems on the other also requires a decision concerning the development of those institutions that can insure that the people affected by change have an input and a control over the direction and development of that change.

That still leaves one central question unanswered, the social cost of the introduction of new machines and systems. Today, in an era of high unemployment for most workers, the social costs of change are pivotal.

Today we are looking at the introduction of a very potent labor-displacing technology against a backdrop of slow economic growth. The very serious result could be unemployment. It is not enough merely to say that unless these decisions are made, firms cannot compete and therefore even more unemployment will result. That argument is true as far as it goes, but it does not tell us what happens to those people who are displaced in either case, as a result of labor-displacing technology or as a result of a failure to compete. The question is not a technical one. It is essentially a political question, but one that is at the core of whether or not these new technologies will be a social benefit or in fact create new and unfortunate problems, particularly for those people who are directly affected by the changes that have taken place.

The social cost of change, I would argue, must be a central criterion in how the changes are made. Ultimately we also have to look at the effect of an authoritarian workplace on democratic values and the democratic society. It is not enough merely to look at the use of computers outside the workplace when the process within the workplace moves in an authoritarian direction. Even though the promise is extraordinary to develop new choices and better ways of work, the promise and the reality could be very different. Ultimately authoritarian systems in the workplace are incompatible with democratic values. If we have to change one let us make the workplace more democratic.

REFERENCES

1. U.S. Air Force Integrated Computer-Aided Manufacturing Program. 1979. ICAM Program Prospectus: 8. Air Force Materials Laboratory, Air Force Wright Aeronautical Laboratories, Air Force Systems Command. Wright-Patterson Air Force Base.
2. BERRY, B. H. 1981. Detroit's auto industry wrestles with machine downtime. Iron Age (September 16): 31.
3. KARASEK, R. A., JR. 1979. Job demands, job decision latitude, and mental strain: implications for job redesign. Admin. Sci. Q. **24.**
4. NELSON, B. 1983. Bosses face less risk than the bossed. The New York Times (April 3).

Alternatives for the Organization of Work in Computer-Assisted Manufacturing

SEYMOUR MELMAN

*Department of Industrial Engineering
and Operations Research
Columbia University
New York, New York 10027*

The general introduction of computers into industrial work has transformed the nature of the work, as well as the ways of organizing work for optimizing the productivity of capital. This development goes characteristically unrecognized because the emphasis still remains on work as the performance of essentially manual manipulative tasks. Indeed, the rules first propounded by Frederick Winslow Taylor in his classic "Shop Management" are to this day built into consensually validated principles for the organization of work.

Taylor wrote in 1911:

> As far as possible the workmen as well as the gang bosses and foremen should be entirely relieved of the work planning and of all work which is more or less clerical in its nature. All possible brain work should be removed from the shop and centered in the planning or laying-out department, leaving for the foremen and gang bosses work strictly executive in its nature. Their duties should be to see that the operations planned and directed from the planning room are promptly carried out in the shop.[1]

In keeping with this larger view, management during this century has organized industrial work on the following subprinciples. First, work is to be progressively simplified, with every task broken down to sequentially simpler components. Second, each work assignment should consist of a stable set of fixed tasks. Third, the integration of work and the planning and scheduling of work are to be carried out by management. Fourth, the maintenance of equipment is to be planned and executed under managerial directives. And fifth, the control of quality is to be arranged from the management center.

These methods of work organization have become so commonplace, so widely appreciated, and so connected to the concept of industry and the use of powered equipment in production that their origin in the work of Taylor is often forgotten. These elementary ideas, or rules, pervade departments of industrial engineering and operations research, schools of business, and schools of management not only in the United States, but almost everywhere in industrialized society—in the Soviet Union as well.

The introduction of computer control, as in numerical control of machine tools, has in fact altered the nature of worker skill required for optimizing the productivity of the equipment itself. Manual manipulative dexterity is now built into the machine, and the selection of tools and the sequence of machine motions are built into the program. For optimizing the productivity of capital, or of labor, or both, what is then required is the (statistically) stable operation of not only single machines, but of the set of equipments that constitute a process. Reliable machine performance is the most important requirement when, to illustrate, the loss of one man-hour of labor in recent industrial practice would cost about $14, while the loss of one hour of the work of a medium-sized numerical control machining center imposes a cost of about $67. Clearly it is the productivity of capital rather than the traditional focus idea of productivity of labor that in fact controls the terms of economic effect.

All this is amplified by flexible manufacturing systems that use numerically controlled machine tools in coordinated sequences. In order to get high productivity of capital from a series of numerically controlled machine tools, downtime must be minimized by superior maintenance and expert operator intervention. Thus the operator's skill can no longer be defined as simple manual manipulative dexterity or muscular work— instead it comes to be defined as operator understanding of the nature of the mechanism with facility to appreciate the moments requiring intervention. Under current conditions, skill takes on an increasingly important intellectual component; and nothing in the writing of Frederick Winslow Taylor prepared us for this.

I would like to give you an illustration of the consequences flowing from the traditional Taylorite organization of work as against the obverse of those principles in operation—a report of operating characteristics as they prevail in two product-engineering shops. We'll call them Plant A and Plant B. These two shops are in the same industry, indeed they are in the same firm, but in two different divisions of the same firm. They have different local managers though they share the same top manager in the parent firm. While the shops are separated spatially, the local managers deal with the same union, and the two shops have the same types of machines; they both use as their basic equipment a set of numerically controlled machine tools, with 50 machinists employed in each case.

Plant A operates by the classic Taylorite managerial principles. The machinists are assigned to particular machines but the programming of these machines is the sole responsibility of a programming department. No operator has access to the program. Maintenance, scheduling, and quality control functions are all the responsibility of management.

In Plant B, however, bargaining to determine whether the hourly workers would have a hand in the programming of the new machine tools began in 1965. After some years agreement in principle was reached, and arrangements were concluded for training the entire machinist work force in computer technology and programming skills. Eligible candidates first had to be fully qualified journeymen machinists, as that is conventionally understood. These journeymen machinists were then trained in computer technology on work time, and that training was completed by 1983. Now all are competent to use the CAD/CAM technology to make a program. They do not necessarily compose all programs for all the work, but they are empowered and competent to intervene with respect to a program and make modifications or corrections.

It is further the case in Plant B that every Monday morning there is a three-hour maintenance program carried out by each operator. Thus with the pattern of work organization in Plant B, the responsibility and authority of the machinist have been substantially enlarged.

Characteristically, computer and numerical control devices include a lock and key among their controls, which makes it possible for the holder of the key to close off all but stop-and-start controls on the control box. In Plant A the locks are closed, so that if the machinist-operator finds a fault at any point in the operation his main option is to press the stop button and call the foreman, who is in turn responsible for summoning a maintenance man, an electrician, a programmer, or whomever. In Plant B where the locks are left open the machinist-operator has full authority to intervene with respect to machine function. If he wishes, he may call upon other persons but he is not required to do so as he is empowered to act.

Wages in Plant A average $12.50 an hour, and the workers are designated "operators." Wages in Plant B average 14% more at $14.22 an hour, and the workers are classified under the same union contract as "journeymen machinists."

In Plant A where the traditional Taylorite management principles have prevailed, management has tried, under those principles, to use numerical control for deskilling. That is to say, once computer-controlled equipment was installed, management approached the union with the argument that the manifest duties of the operator at the machine had been severely delimited, no longer requiring manipulation of machine controls other than the on and the off buttons. Hence the argument has been made that a lower skill is then required of the operator, hence a lower job classification is called for, hence a wage reduction is arguably appropriate.

The associated results, however, have been increased downtime and rather poor productivity of capital and labor. The uptime, that is the proportion of scheduled work time during which the machines are actually functioning, is under 50% in Plant A—while it has been averaging 97% in Plant B. The work force at Plant B has also become very stable, with turnover virtually at zero. The new organization of work at Plant B aims at a high degree of utilization of the computer controlled equipment. Clearly, this requires a work force that is trained in computer technology to bear widened responsibility and authority at the production site.

The contrast depicted here characterizes a wide array of experience reported by engineers and managers in many countries. The era of Taylorite managerialism as a sufficient guide to productivity growth is at an end.* As computerization becomes increasingly characteristic of industrial work there will be a growing contradiction between the conditions of the physical technology itself and the traditional mode of work organization. Optimized productivity of capital and labor will henceforth have to be obtained by new ideas for the organization of work—including wider responsibility and authority by the operators for programming, programming correction, scheduling, maintenance, and quality control.

It is a general principle that productivity can be optimal as the organization of work is congruent with the material means of production; and the obverse is also true. Ways of organization of work that combine direct operations with planning, maintenance, and quality functions are most congruent with the sophisticated new technology. Accordingly, democracy in the workplace is not an extraneous alternative in the design of work. It has become an indispensable requirement for major productivity growth.

REFERENCES

1. TAYLOR, F. W. 1911. Shop Management. (As published in 1947. Scientific Management, comprising Shop Management, The Principles of Scientific Management, and Testimony before the Special House Committee. Harper. New York, N.Y.)
2. MELMAN, S. 1983. Profits without Production. Alfred A. Knopf. New York, N.Y.

DISCUSSION OF THE PAPER

QUESTION: Dr. Melman, you've convinced me and I suppose everybody else in this room that plant B is the preferable plan. Was management convinced? And if not, why?

S. MELMAN: Oh, I'm pleased to report that the management of Plant B was convinced and pleased and was proud to report on these conditions of work, regarding this as a substantial achievement on their part. The top managers of Plant B saw the implementation of these conditions as representing an achievement by them both in relation to their dealings with the work force, and in their relation to the higher levels of management of the same firm. The top management of the firm has not been heard from.

---

*An extensive discussion and bibliography on this point is contained in Reference 2, Chapters 6 and 7.

QUESTION: How would you see the applications of your ideas to the office place?

S. MELMAN: There is a crucial difference between the industrial point of production and the office. On the industrial plant floor, there is a definable material product. In the industrial office, the "product" is a decision on production that doesn't have a clear physical expression as in the case of a product of a factory. That leaves the productivity of office operators to be dealt with on a "micro" basis—operation by operation—rather than on an aggregated basis as is feasible for a factory.

QUESTION: On the basis of your experience, to what extent do you feel we are moving toward an A society and to what extent do you feel we are moving toward a B society?

S. MELMAN: A major part of the productivity debacle in the United States is associated with sustaining the A pattern. For example, as the values of management have conformed to the values of our schools of business, making money has become the main event, and never mind details of making goods. And that is in keeping with the value criterion that distance from production is the criterion of status. Hence, noninvolvement in the making of goods becomes a source of status. From that reasoning you might infer that the termination of production leads to the high-status society. And indeed, that's been given a name: it's called the postindustrial society. Now, that's a packet of nonsense which needs no great elaboration here. It is axiomatic that a community must produce in order to live. And the elemental requirement of an economy, ordinarily understood, is to organize people to work.

QUESTION: I suggest that management fire their cost accountants in Plant A and hire the cost accountants from Plant B because if Taylorite production was justified on the basis of cost accounting, it should be equally obvious that Plant B is a cost-accounting plus. So that if the function is to make money, they are not fulfilling their function by cost accounting A instead of B.

S. MELMAN: Alas, things aren't always as they seem, as Alice said in Wonderland, and sometimes skimmed milk masquerades as cream. Harley Shaiken noted to us that managerial control, decision power in and of itself, is often treated as a prime goal by managers. In that case, some managers so oriented are prepared to put aside and disregard the productivity gains demonstrated in Plant B in favor of what they see as the established managerial control that is operative in Plant A. In the United States, the introduction of numerical control machine tools has lagged. Thus, by 1978, after 20 years of very intensive discussion, advertising, promotion in the trade and other press of numerically controlled machine tools, only 2.7% of the machine tools in use in the United States were of that sort. One of the very important factors that restrained the introduction of machine tools was the discovery of high cost associated with their operation. The high cost was incidental to major downtime and poor uptime performance. And the difficulties encountered in getting high rates of utilization from the machines were associated with the mode of organization and division of labor according to the Taylorite principles.

Given continuance of rates of wage increase of the 1970s, average industrial wages in Japan will exceed those of the United States by 1986. So that helps us to appreciate the significance of the fact that in the largest machine tool firm of Japan, that of Yamazaki in Nagoya, the stable production system and modes of operation that I have called here Plant B are in use. They yield productivity of labor and capital, making possible the production of a given class of machining center within a three-week production cycle time. That compares to an ordinary standard of five months for the same work in the United States and western Europe.

So my judgment is that these factors of the organization of work have fundamental importance for productivity and for industrial growth in the United States.

COMMENT: I think you just answered my question, but it sounded to me that Plant B was being managed much as I understand most of Japanese industry is managed. And that in fact we in the United States are attempting to emulate that in terms of quality.

S. MELMAN: I don't know how most Japanese industry is managed. We hear more and more about certain leading firms, and I have direct knowledge about the Yamazaki firm. It operates in the manner that I just summarized.

QUESTION: I think you cogently and dramatically illustrated the benefits of Plant B organization over Plant A. However, I think that it was based on a certain presupposition, namely, that the "journeymen" in Plant B had the mental acumen and the ability to rise to the level of complexity in mastering the programming. And the question that I would like to ask, therefore, is will there always be a pool or is it likely that, in our ever-increasingly technological society, there will be enough journeymen who have the capability of assuming that type of responsibility in the Plant Bs of our future society?

S. MELMAN: We'll only know as we try to do it. However, if we are informed by the wisdom of Frederick Taylor, we'll never even try. In another one of his fundamental works, Taylor, who did many of his early studies on work performance in the Midvale Steel Works, Pennsylvania, characterized the iron worker. I paraphrase. He said the iron worker is like an ox, both physically and mentally. If you start with the assumption that the production worker is an ox, you'll never think of training such persons into computer technology. But that is not a valid assumption. It comes out of a Taylorite hierarchical, class-dominated, status-seeking orientation. If that is persistently applied, it will yield further lethal results in American industry.

QUESTION: I have a question, which I think in a way applies both to you and to Mr. Shaiken, but I just want to make a comment about a possible comparison between the automated office and the automated manufacturing plant. Under numerical control of work, it would seem to me that you could make the analogy that at the shop floor and the automated factory, the worker is a machine tender but that with numerical control in the office, the worker becomes the machine since the worker is being numerically controlled by the computer.

Now the question that I wanted to ask was in terms of worker participation. That could mean many different things, and the model that both of you I think were implying is a fairly tame model, and does not seem to deal with real fundamental redistribution of power—issues of ownership, issues of social responsibility, and whether a socially responsible organization can exist in an economically competitive climate. And I was wondering if either you or Mr. Shaiken or both of you could comment on a more definitive model of worker participation?

S. MELMAN: In a forthcoming book called *Profits without Production* in September of this year, I'll have a wide-ranging set of things to say about these larger issues of decision power. But I think Harley Shaiken would be a splendid commentator to that point.

H. SHAIKEN: (*Massachusetts Institute of Technology, Cambridge, Mass.*): I don't know how tame the model is in that it doesn't seem to have received very much acceptance. I think it's ironic though that moving in the direction of increased authority in the workplace is done in the name of productivity. I think that's the fundamental area that we have to begin to explore. Right now our overall viewpoint of this is that on the one hand, there are those people who know how to run technology and that technology might have some unfortunate implications. On the other hand, we have those people who have human concerns but yet we live in a real world. I think that's a very faulty way to look at it. I think even within a competitive system, it is possible that moving in a human-centered direction is a preferable route. There are some cases that really didn't come up in either my presentation or Dr. Melman's presentation— cases where in fact a human-centered use of technology would be less productive. But that's only if we define productivity in the narrowest possible way. And here we can learn something from the environmental movement—viewing the problems of pollution in terms of a production process. So even in those cases, I think it's very important to consider the quality of the work environment as a central part of the changes that are taking place and as a central part of the social cost that applies to these technologies.

Ultimately, to implement a use of technology that is fully human and that moves in a human-centered direction will require, I believe, political change as well as technical and economic change. But to acknowledge this is not to say that there aren't areas today where moving in a human-centered direction would be more productive and beneficial to the society as a whole.

QUESTION: I have two particular questions and one more general one. Are there more planners or programmers in Plant A, because the workers themselves can't exercise any such tasks? In Plant B, how long did it take to recoup the education cost invested in the workers to upgrade their skills? My third question: you seem to say that the resistance comes from management and in this case the creative change came from the unions. What brought this about in the one union in Plant B—their initiative of this change? And what kept the union in Plant A—since it's the same union—from initiating it?

S. MELMAN: I don't know the answer to the latter, and I don't know how long it has taken or will take to recoup the education costs. But I can shed a little light on the extent to which machinists are interested in moving in the direction of broadened responsibility and authority.

During the last two years, Dr. Shaiken and I met with groups of machinists assembled by the International Association of Machinists. And we've found among them an emphatic and near-universal interest in broadened responsibility and authority in work: it makes life more interesting; the work is more challenging; it just feels better to go to work. Are there more programmers in Plant A? I'm not certain of that. The overall size of the staffs and the number of production workers in the two plants are closely comparable. There is no dramatic difference there.

It's important that in the Yamazaki and in other major Japanese machine tools firms, the young engineers and graduates of technical institutes all, without exception, come into the plants and go through assignments on the shop floor as a routine part of their career. They change work assignments from design to assembly to quality control to production, and they do this in three-year cycles. So the work of an engineer as participating directly in production or in the hands-on work of assembling computer-controlled machines is an ordinary part and feature of work performance for the continuing part of a person's life career. I think it is personally damaging to engineers in this country, and damaging to the whole community, to sustain the alienation that has been built into us by making the performance of work into a low-status activity.

Knowledge Engineering

The Applied Side of Artificial Intelligence

EDWARD A. FEIGENBAUM

Heuristic Programming Project
Computer Science Department
Stanford University
Stanford, California 94305

INTRODUCTION: SYMBOLIC COMPUTATION AND INFERENCE

This paper will discuss the applied artificial intelligence work that is sometimes called "knowledge engineering." The work is based on computer programs that do symbolic manipulations and symbolic inference, not calculation. The programs I will discuss do essentially no numerical calculation. They discover qualitative lines of reasoning leading to solutions to problems stated symbolically.

Knowledge

Since in this paper I often use the term "knowledge," let me say what I mean by it. The knowledge of an area of expertise—of a field of practice—is generally of two types: (a) *facts* of the domain—the widely shared knowledge that is written in textbooks, and in journals of a field, which constitutes the kind of material that a professor would lecture about in a class; (b) equally as important to the practice of a field is *heuristic* knowledge—knowledge that constitutes the rules of expertise, the rules of good practice, the judgmental rules of the field, the rules of plausible reasoning. These rules collectively constitute what the mathematician George Polya has called the "art of good guessing." In contrast to the facts of the field, its rules of expertise, its rules of good guessing, are rarely written down. This knowledge is transmitted in internships, Ph.D. programs, apprenticeships. The programs I will describe require, for expert performance on problems, heuristic knowledge to be combined with the facts of the discipline.

Expert Systems

The act of obtaining, formalizing, and putting to work these kinds of rules is what we call "expertise modeling." In the modeling of expertise, we construct programs called "expert systems." The goal of an "expert system" project is to write a program that achieves a high level of performance on problems that are difficult enough to require significant human expertise for their solution. The more common strategy of artificial intelligence (AI) research is to choose a highly simplified problem—sometimes called a "toy problem"—and exploit the toy problem in depth. In contrast, the problems we choose require the expertise of an M.D., or a Ph.D., or, at least, a very highly trained specialist in a field, to solve. An expert system of this type consists of only two things: a knowledge base and an inference procedure. The knowledge base contains the facts and heuristics; the inference procedure consists of the processes that work over the knowledge base to infer solutions to problems, to do analyses, to form hypotheses, etc. In principle, the knowledge base is separable from the inference procedure.

The Scientific Issues Underlying Knowledge Engineering

What are the central scientific issues of the artificial intelligence field from which this more applied research draws its inspiration? I would like to categorize these under three headings.

First is the problem of *knowledge representation*. How shall the knowledge of the field be represented as data structures in the memory of the computer, so that they can be conveniently accessed for problem solving?

Second is the problem of *knowledge utilization*. How can this knowledge be used in problem solving? Essentially, this is the question of the inference engine. What designs for the inference engine are available?

Third, and most important, is the question of *knowledge acquisition*. How is it possible to acquire the knowledge so important for problem solving automatically or at least semiautomatically, in a way in which the computer facilitates the transfer of expertise from humans (from practitioners or from their texts or their data) to the symbolic data structures that constitute the knowledge representation in the machine? Knowledge acquisition is a long-standing problem of artificial intelligence. For a long time it was cloaked under the word "learning." Now we are able to be more precise about the problem of machine learning; and with this increased precision has come a new term, "knowledge acquisition research."

This is the most important of the central problems of artificial intelligence research. The reason is simple: to enhance the performance of AI's programs, knowledge is power. The power does not reside in the inference procedure. The power resides in the specific knowledge of the problem domain. The most powerful systems we will be building will be those systems that contain the most knowledge.

The knowledge is currently acquired in a very painstaking way that reminds one of cottage industries, in which individual computer scientists work with individual experts in disciplines painstakingly to explicate heuristics. If applied artificial intelligence is to be important in the decades to come, we must have more automatic means for replacing what is currently a very tedious, time-consuming, and expensive procedure. The problem of knowledge acquisition is the critical bottleneck problem in artificial intelligence.

A Brief Tutorial Using the Mycin Program

As the basis of the exposition of underlying ideas, I will use a well-known program called MYCIN.* The EMYCIN system, described later, was described by William VanMelle as his Ph.D. thesis.[11] MYCIN is a program for medical diagnosis and therapy. It produces diagnoses of infectious diseases, particularly blood infections and meningitis infections, and advises the physician on antibiotic therapies for treating those infectious diseases. MYCIN conducts a consultation with its user, a physician. This physician is to be distinguished from another kind of doctor who works with MYCIN, the expert. The expert is the person who introduces rules into the MYCIN knowledge base. The user exploits these rules in a dialogue, an interactive consultation that finally terminates in a diagnosis and therapy. The consultation is conducted in a stylized form of English; the doctor never knows about the LISP program underneath. In the consultation the doctor is asked only for patient history and laboratory test results (exogenous data the computer could not possibly infer).

A program like MYCIN is using qualitative reasoning to discover a line of reasoning, leading to a result (in this case a diagnosis). We can expect that it should be able to explain that line of reasoning to the user. In fact, I believe it is necessary that expert consultative systems do so; otherwise, the systems will not be credible to their professional users.

Knowledge in MYCIN

Table 1 shows a piece of knowledge in MYCIN. MYCIN contains about 500 rules, about half of them for blood infections, half for meningitis infections. Each such "production rule" consists of an "if" part and a "then" part (sometimes called a "situation part" and "action part"). The "if part" defines a set of conditions of relevancy such that if each of these clauses is true, then the conclusion follows.† The rule is shown in approximately the way the expert would enter it; and exactly the way the doctor would see the rule if it were displayed. This piece of knowledge will be evoked from the knowledge base if the conditions are true, and will be built into the line of reasoning.

---

*Developed originally as the Ph.D. thesis of E. H. Shortliffe, Computer Science Department, Stanford University. Further developed by the Heuristic Programming Project at Stanford.[10]

†Any logical combination of the "if side" clauses can be used.

TABLE 1. A Piece of Knowledge in MYCIN

If:	(1) the infection that requires therapy is meningitis, and
	(2) the type of the infection is fungal, and
	(3) organisms were not seen on the stain of the culture, and
	(4) the patient is not a compromised host, and
	(5) the patient has been to an area that is endemic for coccidiomy-coses, and
	(6) the race of the patient is one of: black asian indian and
	(7) the cryptococcal antigen in the csf was not positive
Then:	there is suggestive evidence that cryptococcus is not one of the organisms that might be causing the infection.

Inexact Inference

In MYCIN, there is a way for the expert to state to what extent, on a scale from 0.1 to 1.0, he believes the preconditions imply the conclusion: 1.0 is definition certainty; 0.9 is "very strong evidence"; 0.6 is "suggestive evidence"; and so on. These indices are combined in MYCIN with a very simple and easily explained function, yielding an index called a "cumulative certainty factor," an index of "strength of belief" in the line of reasoning.

MYCIN Diagnosis and Therapy

TABLE 2 shows a typical MYCIN diagnosis. Then MYCIN proceeds to conduct a shorter consultation with the physician about such things as the patient's known sensitivities to various types of antibiotics and the resistance shown by certain organisms to various kinds of antibiotics. MYCIN then produces a therapy recommendation such as shown in TABLE 3.

MYCIN's Line of Reasoning

MYCIN's line of reasoning is a chain of rules that concludes the (perhaps uncertain) presence of an infecting organism from laboratory test data and patient history. The line of reasoning is discovered by backward chaining. The search starts with the various possible organisms as "goals to be achieved" and terminates with the data.

TABLE 2. An Example of a MYCIN Diagnosis

INFECTION-1 is MENINGITIS
    +⟨ITEM-1⟩E.COLI[from clinical evidence only]
    +⟨ITEM-2⟩PSEUDOMONAS-AERUGINOSA[from clinical evidence only]
    +⟨ITEM-3⟩KLEBSIELLA-PNEUMONIAE[from clinical evidence only]
    +⟨ITEM-4⟩DIPLOCOCCUS-PNEUMONIAE[from clinical evidence only]

The explanation facility can exhibit selected portions of the chain as requested by the user. It can answer a variety of queries during or after the consultation dialogue, such as "Why (are you asking me for this information)?" or "How (was some particular conclusion reached)?" One interesting form of query is shown in TABLE 4. To answer it MYCIN must be able to recreate the unacceptable lines of reasoning.

MYCIN's Inference Procedure

We can remove the knowledge base of MYCIN and substitute a set of rules from another domain. That is equivalent to saying that the knowledge base and the inference procedure are separate things in an expert system. Removing from MYCIN its infectious disease diagnosis rules yields an inference "engine" which we call EMYCIN (for essential mycin or empty mycin or engine mycin).

TABLE 3. An Example of a MYCIN Antibiotic Therapy Recommendation

My preferred therapy recommendation is as follows:
In order to cover for Items ⟨1 2 3 4⟩:
Give the following in combination:
(1) AMPICILLIN
Dose: 3.5 g (28.0 ml) q4h IV [calculated on basis of 50 mg/kg]
(2) GENTAMICIN
Dose: 119 mg (3.0 ml, 80 mg/2 ml ampule) q8h IV [calculated on basis of 1.7 mg/kg] plus consider giving 5 mg q24h Intrathecal
Comments: Monitor serum concentrations
Since high concentrations of penicillins can inactivate aminoglycosides, do not mix these two antibiotics in the same IV bottle.

BUILDING A NEW SYSTEM WITH THE EMYCIN TOOL: PUFF

Combining with EMYCIN a set of rules for pulmonary diagnosis (diagnosis of lung diseases) produced a diagnostic program called PUFF.[9] In this diagnostic situation, a patient is breathing in and out of an instrument called a spirometer, producing measurements of flow of air in expiration and inhalation, versus lung volume. Data reduction is done by a PDP-11, and data interpretation is done by PUFF.‡ The PUFF report is reviewed by an expert physician, is signed if accurate, put into the patient record, and sent to the referring physician. Currently about 80% of the PUFF outputs are signed without modification. PUFF consists of about 250 production rules of the MYCIN-like type. It produces reports like that shown in TABLE 5.

‡PUFF was developed on a PDP-10 computer at Stanford in collaboration with doctors at Pacific Medical Center in San Francisco, and now runs at the hospital on a PDP-11.[11]

TABLE 4. An Example of MYCIN's Explanation Facility

USER:	WHY DIDN'T YOU GIVE TETRACYCLINE FOR E.COLI IN REC-1
MYCIN:	TETRACYCLINE was discounted for ITEM-1 (RECOMMENDA-TION-1)
	because there is evidence that this e.coli is not sensitive to it.

ANOTHER APPLICATION OF THE EMYCIN TOOL

A group designing airplane wings for the United States Air Force uses a software package called the MARC package§ for finite element analysis. The package is excellent but complex. Its use requires considerable expertise. The design group wanted a MYCIN-like expert system to consult with designers on the use of the MARC package. EMYCIN was used to create the expert system SACON (for structural analysis consultant).[1] An engineer brings to SACON his design specifications for the structure. SACON produces for him an analysis plan, which he can then translate into subroutine calls for the MARC software.

TABLE 6 shows a MYCIN-like production rule for SACON. TABLE 7 exhibits a SACON output-analysis plan.

CONCLUDING REMARKS ON MYCIN-LIKE SYSTEMS

Before leaving the topic of MYCIN-like systems, let me just remark on two trends. The first is a trend in knowledge engineering to put in

TABLE 5. An Example of the Output of PUFF

INTERPRETATION: Elevated lung volumes indicate overinflation. In addition, the rv/tlc ratio is increased, suggesting a mild degree of air trapping. Forced vital capacity is normal but the fevl/fvc ratio is reduced, suggesting airway obstruction of a mild degree. Reduced mid-expiratory flow indicates mild airway obstruction. Obstruction is indicated by curvature in the flow-volume loop of a small degree. Following bronchodilation, the expired flow shows slight improvement. This is confirmed by the lack of change in airway resistance. The low diffusing capacity indicates a loss of alveolar capillary surface, which is moderate.

CONCLUSIONS: The low diffusing capacity, in combination with obstruction and a high total lung capacity would be consistent with a diagnosis of emphysema. The patient's airway obstruction may be caused by smoking. Discontinuation of smoking should help relieve the symptoms.

PULMONARY FUNCTION DIAGNOSIS;
　　1. MILD OBSTRUCTIVE AIRWAYS DISEASE
　　　EMPHYSEMATOUS TYPE.

§For MARC Analysis Research Corporation.

TABLE 6. A Piece of Knowledge (Production Rule) in the SACON System

If:	(1) The material composing the substructure is one of metal,
	(2) The analysis error (in percent) that is tolerable is between 5 and 30
	(3) The nondimensional stress of the substructure is greater than .9, and
	(4) The number of cycles the loading is to be applied is between 1000 and 10000,
Then:	It is definite that fatigue is one of the stress behavior phenomena in the substructure.

software packages what we know about building expert systems. EMY-CIN represents one of the first of these packages. There are other packages, built for different types of inference procedures. The AGE system assists in the building of inference procedures of a type called "blackboard models," first developed at Carnegie-Mellon University in the HEARSAY-2 speech-understanding project. Another package assists with knowledge representation. Called the UNIT package, it is similar to the packages KRL and KL-ONE.

Second, let me mention a unique package that facilitates teaching of knowledge in knowledge bases built for expert systems. This package, called GUIDON,¶ is capable of teaching whatever EMYCIN can reason about. Thus, GUIDON can presently teach infectious disease diagnosis and therapy, pulmonary function disease diagnosis, and the use of the MARC structural-analysis package. GUIDON consists of a set of rules for another kind of expertise, the expertise of good teachers. If you blend the rules of good teaching with the rules of good practice in a field, then you can teach well the rules of good practice in the field. This is important

TABLE 7. A SACON Output (Analysis Plan)

The following analysis classes are relevant to the analysis of your structure: General-inelastic

The following are specific analysis recommendations you should follow when performing the structure analysis:

- Activate incremental stress-incremental strain analysis.
- Model nonlinear stress-strain relation of the material.
- Solution will be based on a mix of gradient and Newton methods.
- User programs to scan peak stress at each step and evaluate fatigue integrity should be used.
- User programs to scan stresses, smooth, and compare with allowable stresses (with appropriate safety factors) should be used.
- User programs to scan deflections, calculate relative values, and compare with code limits, should be called upon.
- Cumulative strain damage should be calculated.

¶Developed as the Ph.D. thesis of William J. Clancy at Stanford University.[3]

because the rules of good practice are almost never taught explicitly! They are usually taught informally, by apprenticeship, as I have mentioned earlier.

HYPOTHESIS FORMATION AND THEORY FORMATION: DENDRAL AND META-DENDRAL

One of the most widely used of the expert systems of knowledge engineering is the DENDRAL system.[2] Initially, DENDRAL analyzed mass spectral data, and inferred a complete structural hypothesis (topology only) for the molecule. DENDRAL was subsequently generalized to produce a set of structural candidates from whatever constraints happened to be available in the problem—not only the mass spectral constraints, but constraints from nuclear magnetic resonance, from other spectral data like IR or UV, or any other information that the chemist happens to know about the problem. Given a set of constraints from various kinds of available data DENDRAL will produce a set of candidate structures that are the best explanations of the data.

DENDRAL's Knowledge and Method

DENDRAL's knowledge sources are shown in TABLE 8. DENDRAL uses a three-stage problem-solving process. The first stage is one in which constraints on solution are inferred from spectral data. Given those constraints, plus all other constraints the chemist has noted, the program generates all structures satisfying the problem-specific and the general chemical constraints. Finally it tests the candidates to choose and rank the best. This method is called a plan-generate-and-test strategy.

DENDRAL's Applications

DENDRAL has been used in thousands of chemical structure analyses. It has users in universities and industries throughout the United States, Europe, and Australia. Some operate over the international TYMNET to Stanford; others use DENDRAL on their own machines. DENDRAL has been "exported" to the United States National Institutes

TABLE 8. DENDRAL's Sources of Knowledge

Graph theoretic	connectivity, symmetry
Chemical	atoms, valences, stability
Spectroscopic	mass spectrometric fragmentation rules, nuclear magnetic resonance rules
Contextual	origin of sample, chemical properties, method of isolation
Judgmental	goodness of fit between predicted and observed data

of Health. The British recoded it for a PDP-10 in Edinburgh, Scotland. It is running at Lederle Laboratories in Pearl River, New York, and at other chemical and drug companies.‖ Developed in LISP, it was rewritten in BCPL for efficiency. It has also been used to teach structure elucidation in the first-year graduate course in organic chemistry at Stanford, and also to check the correctness of published structures.

Knowledge Acquisition

The knowledge acquisition bottleneck is a critical problem. How is it that chemists arrive at their rules of mass spectrometry? They derive these rules or theories by induction from laboratory experience. The META-DENDRAL program was an attempt to model the processes of theory formation.

The "meta" level, or knowledge acquisition level, of DENDRAL accepts as input a set of known structure-spectrum pairs. We have stored thousands of these in our computer. The output of META-DENDRAL is a set of general fragmentation rules of the form used by DENDRAL, viz., some particular subgraph of chemical molecule gives rise to some particular fragmentation. (*If* this subgraph occurs, *then* this fragmentation process will occur.)

META-DENDRAL's method is also a plan-generate-and-test method. The planning process is called interpretation and summarization, interpreting each spectral data point as a fragmentation, collecting evidence for similar processes and bond environments. The generation process generates a space of plausible rules (not plausible structures a la DENDRAL, but plausible rules of mass spectrometry) constrained by the evidence and by some user-supplied context. The test phase tests the plausible rules, using all the evidence—positive and negative evidence—and generalizes or specializes the rules to improve support from the evidence, seeking a better fit between rules and evidence.

In a major knowledge acquisition experiment, META-DENDRAL inferred the rules of fragmentation for a family of complex steroidal molecules whose mass spectral theory was of interest to our chemist collaborators. A total of 33 rules (covering three subfamilies) were formed, all chemically plausible and of high quality (measured in terms of the amount of input data accounted for by each).

How good is META-DENDRAL? To what extent have we succeeded in forming by machine a piece of reasonable scientific theory, i.e., a set of fragmentation rules for mass spectrometry? We chose the classical scientific route for answering that question. We wrote out the results of the experiment described above and sent the paper to a respected scientific journal, as a scientific contribution. The contribution was

‖DENDRAL has been licensed by Stanford University to Molecular Designs Inc. for development and sale to industry.

refereed and published in the journal, the standard qualification for a piece of new knowledge entering the science.

KNOWLEDGE ACQUISITION, DISCOVERY, CONJECTURING: AM

Another attempt at modeling knowledge acquisition and discovery was the development of the AM program.** AM's task is the discovery of mathematical concepts (not necessarily new to mankind, but interestingly complex for a program to have discovered).

AM begins with a set of elementary ideas in finite set theory: the idea of a set, a multiset, set equality, etc. The program contains heuristic knowledge relevant to generating new mathematical concepts, the kinds of heuristics that an expert mathematician would have. It also has heuristics for discarding the bad ideas generated to pick out the interesting new mathematical conjectures. These are the so-called heuristics of interestingness. Thus the knowledge base contains heuristics of combination ("generate") and heuristics of interestingness ("test").

The program searches a space of possible conjectures that can be generated from the elementary ideas, chooses the most interesting, and pursues that line of reasoning. As usual, the program is capable of explaining its line of reasoning. The user can interact with the program to give familiar labels to newly generated concepts, such as "call that concept 'add' "; "call that 'prime'." The program uses the label subsequently, so that the explanation trace is understandable to the human.

With its heuristics, the program searched the space-discovering concepts like list equality (a specialization of general set equality); cardinality, therefore number; add, subtract, multiply, divide; factoring and the concept of a prime; and the fundamental theorem of arithmetic (the unique factorization of numbers into primes). AM made some conjectures in number theory that were almost really new (discovered many years ago but basically unexplored).

The program eventually began exploring a bigger space than it could cope with, for reasons that are related to my earlier discussion of power and knowledge. As AM plunged deeper into number theory, its general mathematical heuristics became less powerful at controlling search. It needed more specific heuristics about number theory. But these were not given initially because of the possible claim that could be made that the program was initially biased toward discovering number theory. The program lost power as it needed the specialized knowledge that it did not have. A new project called EURISKO is exploring how a program can discover new heuristics as it invents new kinds of things (e.g., as it discovers ideas in number theory, how can it invent heuristics about number theory?).

**Developed by Douglas B. Lenat as his Ph.D. thesis at Stanford University.[5]

Two Major Principles of Knowledge Engineering

The two major principles of knowledge engineering have already been mentioned earlier and will be summarized here.

The first is that the problem-solving power exhibited by an intelligent agent's performance is primarily the consequence of its knowledge base, and only secondarily a consequence of the inference method employed. Expert systems must be knowledge rich even if they are methods poor. This is an important result and one that has only recently become well understood in AI. For a long time AI focused its attention almost exclusively on the development of clever inference methods. But the power of its systems does not reside in the inference method; almost any inference method will do. The power resides in the knowledge.

Second, experience has shown that this knowledge is largely *heuristic* knowledge—judgmental, experiential, uncertain. This knowledge is generally "private" to an expert, not because the expert is unwilling to share publicly what he knows, but because he is often unable to. ("What the masters really know is not written in the textbooks of the masters.") This knowledge can be extracted by a careful, painstaking analysis by a second party (a knowledge engineer), operating in the context of a large number of highly specific performance problems. The expertise being modeled is multifaceted; an expert brings to bear many and varied sources of knowledge in performance.

The Promise of Knowledge Engineering

There is presently considerable interest in the scientific, engineering, and industrial use of knowledge engineering techniques. The promise, recognized but barely realized to date, is threefold.

Cost Reductions

There is a possible enormous cost savings in computation and instrumentation by using these methods. Here I would like to make the case concretely, not abstractly. In signal-processing applications, involving large amounts of data with poor signal/noise ratios, it is possible to reduce computation costs by several orders of magnitude by the use of knowledge-based reasoning rather than brute force statistical methods.

One of the expert systems whose construction I supervised[7] involved the interpretation of massive amounts of signal data with very poor signal/noise ratios. The object of the program was to produce a continuously updated "situation understanding" of the objects producing the signals, their positions in space, and their velocities. Using standard signal-processing techniques of cross correlation and autocorrelation, the computational requirements far exceeded the bounds of all computation available for the problem. In the statistical technique, no use was made of a wealth of knowledge available to interpret the signal data, for example: "textbook" information of the objects as signal-generating sources; "good guesses" available to the human controllers about the "most likely" moves of the objects over considerable periods of time; previously discerned patterns of movement; the laws of physics dictating what the objects could possibly do; what neighboring observing sites had observed; and so on. This was the true symbolic "semantics" and context of the problem. The ongoing model of the situation could be inferred almost completely from this symbolic knowledge, with only occasional reference to the massive amount of signal data for hypothesis verification and for noticing changes. The expert system we built using AI's methods of symbolic inference was able to accomplish the task using (an estimated) two orders of magnitude less computation than the statistical methods required. There is an important lesson here. It makes little sense to use enormous amounts of expensive computation to tease a little signal out of much noise, when most of the understanding can be readily inferred from the symbolic knowledge surrounding the situation.

There is an additional cost saving possible. Sensor bandwidth and sensitivity are expensive. From a symbolic model it is possible, with precision, to generate a set of signal expectations whose emergence in the data would make a difference to the verification of the ongoing model. Sensor parameters can then be "tuned" to the expected signals and signal directions; not every signal in every direction needs to be searched for.

Consider the DENDRAL program described earlier. Because the DENDRAL program knew so much about chemistry in general and mass spectrometry in particular, it could solve structure problems using low-resolution data that chemists could solve at that time only by using high-resolution instruments. Low-resolution instrumentation plus knowledge-based reasoning equaled the performance of high-resolution instruments. A low-resolution instrument costs only about $5,000, while a high-resolution instrument costs about $100,000. Therefore, $5,000 plus "smarts" equals a $100,000 instrument.

The Inevitability Argument

There is a certain inevitability to knowledge engineering and its applications. The cost of the computers will fall drastically during the coming two decades. As it does, many more of the practitioners of the world's professions will be persuaded to turn to economical automatic information processing for assistance in managing the increasing complexity of their daily tasks. They will find, in most of computer science, help only for those of their daily problems that have a mathematical or statistical core, or are of a routine data-processing nature. But such problems will be rare, except in engineering, and physical science. In medicine, biology, management—indeed in most of the world's work— the daily tasks are those requiring symbolic reasoning with detailed professional knowledge. The computers that will act as "intelligent assistants" for these professionals must be endowed with such reasoning capabilities and knowledge.

The Most Important Gain: New Knowledge

The methodology that I have been describing allows a field to "get its hands on" the real knowledge of the field. The real knowledge of the field is not in the textbooks of the field. The textbooks lack the experiential, judgmental, heuristic knowledge known to the excellent practitioners of the field. When experts argue, the bases on which they argue are largely unspoken. The methodology we use gives a way of bringing heuristic knowledge to the surface and making it concrete—so that it can be discussed, so that consensus can be achieved. If consensus is not achieved, at least the alternatives to the consensus are available for examination.

In the end it may be irrelevant that a computer program is available to be an "intelligent assistant." The gain to human knowledge by making explicit the heuristic rules of a discipline will perhaps be the most important contribution to the knowledge-based systems approach.

PROBLEMS OF KNOWLEDGE ENGINEERING

Though knowledge engineering has made great advances in the last 10 years, and is witnessing the pressure toward industrial application, it faces persistent problems.

The Lack of Adequate and Appropriate Hardware

Artificial intelligence is largely experimental, not theoretical, computer science. It builds and tests systems. Its laboratory is the computer, and it is suffering from lack of adequate laboratory facilities.

Currently applied AI is machine limited. That was not the case for the first 15 years of AI. The capabilities of computers to process symbols exceeded our ability to conceive interesting ways to process them. In the last few years the field definitely has been limited by the size and power of its computers. For example, the DENDRAL program is now solving much larger and more difficult problems than we ever conceived that it would solve. System designers are always gentle to their systems; they know the computational boundaries of what is feasible, but users do not. The users have real problems that can easily exceed the computational capabilities of the systems that we provide them. Problems in the physical sciences can command any number of large computers, while an AI project is worth only a small fraction of a DEC PDP-10. The scale must be changed.

AI researchers are now discovering how to construct specialized symbol manipulation machines. These computers have not yet been built by industry because the industry does not yet perceive a widespread market. In the past we have adapted the classical computing machines for the symbol-manipulation activities that are indeed more general activities of computing. The list processing systems, particularly LISP, in which most AI work has been done, have been pasted on top of the instruction code of conventional computers. That is a mistake. We need specialized symbol-processing devices.

The silver lining on the cloud is the emergence of machines with large memories and LISP machines. A LISP machine (Massachusetts Institute of Technology 1979), is a piece of hardware and microcode that runs a version of the LISP language.[6] This provides highly efficient symbolic processing in a personal computer environment.

Lack of Cumulation of AI Methods and Techniques

The second problem is the lack of cumulation of AI methods and techniques. The AI field tends to reward scientifically irresponsible pseudoinnovation. That is, it tends to reward individuals for reinventing and renaming concepts and methods that are well explored.

How does one cumulate knowledge in a science? One way is to publish papers and hope that other people will read them and use the ideas. A more traditional way in computer science is to cumulate ideas in software packages, e.g., the cumulation of computational methods of statistics in the large statistical packages. The creation of software packages such as EMYCIN, AGE,[8] ROSIE (at the Rand Corporation), and the various knowledge-representation packages is a hopeful sign that we will solve the problem of cumulation.

Shortage of Trained Knowledge Engineers

One of the problems of knowledge engineering is the shortage of trained knowledge engineers. There is a strong and growing demand for such specialists.[4] The universities are producing very few of them, but are themselves consuming almost the entire product.

There is significant industrial demand. The Xerox Palo Alto Research Center has hired a number of artificial intelligence researchers to investigate the office automation systems of the future—electronic offices. One company servicing the oil industry, Schlumberger Ltd., is working on applying knowledge engineering methods to handle the following problem: the number of interpretations that have to be done for signals (coming from physical instrumentation of oil wells) is growing much larger, and it is expensive and difficult to train new interpretation specialists. Schlumberger is interested in replication of expertise. They want to discover what the expertise consists of and then copy it for use at their outlying sites.

Texas Instruments has established an AI group to explore educational uses of AI, and also some aspects of computer-aided design. IBM has a group in Palo Alto, California, studying the use of AI in diagnosis of computer system failures.

Digital Equipment Corporation (DEC), which already uses an expert system to custom configure its VAX-11 line of computers, is also developing a system to diagnose malfunctioning computer systems.

More recently, we have seen the founding of companies specifically for the purpose of providing expert systems to business, industry, and government users. Among these new companies are Applied Expert Systems (Cambridge, Mass.), IntelliGenetics (Palo Alto, Calif.), Kestrel Institute (Palo Alto, Calif.), Smart Systems Technology (Alexandria, Va.), and Teknowledge, Inc. (Palo Alto, Calif.). There are a number of military applications of AI that are being done now. Hence the defense contract firms are also in the market for knowledge engineers.

Are there any silver linings to this cloud of shortage of people? I think there are. One is the recognition that the AI community must create for itself the equivalent of the aerospace industry to apply its skills and methods to real-world problems. Each new application cannot be done, in the future, by the few skilled technologists at the university laboratories. AI must have an industry that is capable of performing the process and producing usable devices.

The Problem of Knowledge Acquisition

Another problem of applied AI is a critical scientific problem—the problem of knowledge acquisition. Since the power of expert systems is in their knowledge bases, successful applied AI requires that knowledge move from the heads of experts into programs. This is now a largely manual process of working together with experts. If we continue in this way we could be well into the twenty-first century before we get generally powerful intelligent agents. The process is just too slow. Therefore we seek more automatic methods for transferring and transforming knowledge into its computer representation.

We now have knowledge acquisition systems that are interactive, involving semiautomatic ways of steering the expert to the right piece of knowledge to introduce into the system. We have also done experiments in automatic knowledge acquisition, extracting knowledge directly from "nature," i.e., from data, from evidence (e.g., the META-DENDRAL program described earlier).

Thus, there are silver linings with regard to knowledge acquisition, but the problem is an extremely difficult and important bottleneck problem in this field.

The Development Gap

Finally, there is the so-called development gap. There is a lack of an orderly bureaucratic process in the research funding agencies for handling programs after they have achieved their first success as a research project.

Promising knowledge engineering projects, on whose success in application the future credibility of the field depends, have fallen, or will certainly fall, into the so-called development gap. Industries, also, should be educated so that they perceive a commercial self-interest in filling the gap.

ACKNOWLEDGMENTS

It is fitting, in conclusion, and perhaps instructive to the reader, to acknowledge the major sources of research funds for the work of my groups, the Heuristic Programming Project and SUMEX Project at Stanford University. The primary research funding has come from two agencies over the years: the Defense Advanced Research Projects Agency (ARPA); and the Biotechnology Resources Program of the U.S. National Institutes of Health (NIH). Project support for particular programs has been granted by the U.S. National Science Foundation (NSF). Relatively recently we have received support from the U.S. National Library of Medicine, from the Office of Naval Research (ONR), from the National Aeronautics and Space Administration (NASA), from Schlumberger-Doll Research, and from the IBM Corporation.

The work described in this article has been programmed on the facilities of the SUMEX-AIM Computer Resource at Stanford. SUMEX-AIM is a national computer resource for research on the application of artificial intelligence to biology and medicine. The national users (the AIM community) access the computer over the national computer networks TYMNET and ARPANET. The facility consists of Digital Equipment Corporation central host computers (a 2060 with 9 megabytes of main memory, a 2020 with 2.2 megabytes of memory, a VAX 11/780 with 4 megabytes of memory, and 2 VAX 11/750's with 2 megabytes of memory each) and a number of personal LISP work stations (5 Xerox 1100's and 1 Symbolics LM-2). This heterogeneous computing environment is linked together and to other facilities on the Stanford campus by a 3 megabytes/second Ethernet. The research language used is LISP (including the Interlisp, MacLisp, FranzLisp, and ZetaLisp dialects).

REFERENCES

1. BENNETT, J. S. & R. S. ENGELMORE. 1979. SACON: a knowledge-based consultant for structural analysis. In Proceedings of the Sixth International Joint Conference on Artificial Intelligence: 47–49. IJCAI. Tokyo, Japan. (Also Wm. Kaufmann. Los Altos, Calif.)

2. BUCHANAN, B. G. & E. A. FEIGENBAUM. 1978. DENDRAL and META-DENDRAL. Their applications dimensions. Artif. Intell. **11**: 5–24.
3. CLANCEY, W. J. 1979. Transfer of rule-based expertise through a tutorial dialog. Ph.D. Thesis. Computer Science Department. Stanford, Calif. (Also Stanford University Computer Science Report 79-769.)
4. FEIGENBAUM, E. A. & P. MCCORDUCK. 1983. The Fifth Generation: Artificial Intelligence and Japan's Computer Challenge to the World. Addison-Wesley. Reading, Mass.
5. LENAT, D. 1976. AM: an artificial intelligence approach to discovery in mathematics as heuristics search. Ph.D. Thesis. Computer Science Department. Stanford University. Stanford, Calif.
6. Artificial Intelligence Laboratory. 1979. LISP Machine Manual. Massachusetts Institute of Technology. Cambridge, Mass.
7. NII, H. P. & E. A. FEIGENBAUM. 1978. Rule based understanding of signals. In Pattern-Directed Inference Systems. Waterman & Hayes-Roth, Eds.: 483–502. Academic Press, Inc. New York, N.Y.
8. NII, H. P. & N. AIELLO. 1979. AGE: a knowledge-based program for building knowledge-based programs. In Proceedings of the Sixth International Joint Conference on Artificial Intelligence: 645–655. IJCAI. Tokyo, Japan. (Also Wm. Kaufmann. Los Altos, Calif.)
9. OSBORN, J., L. FAGAN, R. FALLAT, D. MCCLUNG & R. MITCHELL. 1979. Managing the data from respiratory measurements. Med. Instrum. **13**(6): 330–336.
10. SHORTLIFFE, E. 1976. Computer-based Medical Consultations: MYCIN. American Elsevier. New York, N.Y.
11. VANMELLE, W. A. 1979. A domain-independent production rule system for consultation programs. In Proceedings of the Sixth International Joint Conference on Artificial Intelligence: 923–925. IJCAI. Tokyo, Japan. (Also Wm. Kaufmann. Los Altos, Calif.)

Knowledge Technology

The Promise

PAMELA McCORDUCK

450 Riverside Drive
New York, New York 10027

The new knowledge technology, especially its form known as artificial intelligence, is sometimes confusing, for as Henry Steele Commager says of America, it had been invented before it was discovered. The invention of America, Commager notes, "embraced the Blessed Isles, the Fortunate Isles, Avalon, El Dorado and Atlantis; even the sensible Edmund Spenser thought that his countrymen might find Faery Land in the new world."[1]

Just so: in science fiction, artificial intelligences in the form of malevolent robots (or benevolent ones, for that matter), in the form of self-aggrandizing computer networks, and anything else the human mind can imagine, have been presented to us in all-talking, full-color, and lurid detail.

The reality, then, is disappointing, and I sometimes wonder if the petulance exhibited by outsiders is less their outrage at the grand dreams than their disappointment that reality is, just now, so far from those dreams. William Bradford first thought Cape Cod "a hideous and desolate wilderness, full of wild beasts and wild men" but later changed his mind. He, at least, lived there: the most vicious—and amusing—attacks on the New World came from Europeans who had not been there, but knew how awful it was and did their very best to expose it for the noxious and backward place it really was.[1]

You have just heard about the reality of knowledge technology. I am going to undertake to talk about the promise, but if your sense of that promise is what you have read in science fiction—in other words, the gadgets—then I must tell you that I am less interested in gadgets than in how they change our lives: our notions of our own possibilities. So then, the questions arise: Are we embarking on a journey to the Atlantis, the El Dorado of the human mind? Or does something more mundane, even more sinister, wait at the end of our journey?

Frankly, nobody knows. Prophets must humbly remind themselves that a nonhuman mechanism with the capacity to reason is a singularity in human history. Since it is a singularity, we can say nothing for certain. We know from looking backward that mechanical amplifications of human memory, in the form of the written word, made profound, unforeseeable changes in our fortunes. We assume that equally or even more profound and unforeseeable changes will come about as the consequence of our invention of a mechanical amplification of human reasoning power.

We can say nothing for certain but we can make some guesses. We can guess that no matter how wonderful thinking machines will be, there are some things they will never be able to do. For example, they will not be able to guarantee the constancy of your lover; they will not instill filial piety into your children; they will not categorically eliminate wickedness from the planet, nor even give you blessed relief from the heartbreak of psoriasis, though they have a better chance of doing that than anything else I have mentioned. They will not give you deeper self-knowledge, I think, if you already resist self-knowledge. In other words, many aspects of human life will remain the same. But some things *are* going to change, in fact will never be the same again, and those are the promises I would like to explore.

There are themes that will recur throughout this discussion, and I want to bring your attention to them right now. The first is the difference that a slight but crucial superiority in knowledge technology can make in resolving shades of gray to unequivocal black and white. The second theme is the order of magnitude effect, the fact that large changes in quantity bring about dramatic changes in quality. A third theme, which I mention because it is implicit in my talk, is the relatively swift rate of dissemination superior knowledge technology has historically enjoyed. Build a better intellectual mousetrap, and the human race beats down your door to get it.

You have heard about expert systems, which in their way are the rudimentary equivalent of the written word. The fifth generation of computers, which Mr. Fuchi will talk about, is the equivalent of the printing press, in that it aims to bring the power of expert systems knowledge technology not only to experts in given fields who might want intelligent assistance, but that same expertise to anybody and everybody who might want it. Or, if I can change the metaphor a little bit, expert systems are the equivalent of custom-built horseless carriages, each one specially designed. Mr. Fuchi and his colleagues intend to bring this horseless carriage of the intellect into mass production.[2]

Let us look at some specific promises, then.

THE ECONOMIC PROMISE

Knowledge is economic power. We sense that knowing more helps us gain more; we also sense that incomplete and vague information, misinformation, or late information is costly to us in the marketplace (and all the more so in the clinic or on the battlefield). We want knowledge, of course, not mere information; we want help with the information glut, help that will automatically pare and shape all that information so that we can, with our limited human brains, comprehend and make use of it. One major promise of the new knowledge technology is that it will give us knowledge we can use, when we need it and in the shape we want it. The raw bulk will be refined, digested, and interpreted in ways that we can put to effective use.

We have good evidence that knowledge has profound economic value. In the manufacture of automobiles, for example, the Japanese have shown us that "working smarter" means a significant difference in productivity, something that Adam Smith was the first to point out in his *Wealth of Nations*. The Japanese have translated that "working smarter" into products so attractive that if a genuinely free market were to operate, most of us would be driving Japanese cars, even as we now all use Japanese consumer electronics.

The new knowledge technology will improve processes of every kind. I mean here manufacturing, management decision making, design, catching fish from the sea, or growing wheat in the heartland. I can illustrate this by telling you about a conversation Professor Feigenbaum here and I once had. He said: "You know, there's no such thing as a machine as smart as a person." You can imagine my surprise. Were all these machines that outperformed the human experts in the oil field or the laboratory or the sickroom nothing more than frauds? I thought I hadn't heard him right, so I made him repeat himself. He did. I still did not get it, but I did begin to see something of the Zen master's smile on his face.

Since I have been a combination of student and straight man of Feigenbaum's for a long time, I gave in and asked him to explain. "It's easy," he said. "You start out with a task you want a machine to do. You specify it precisely, drawing on human expertise. You use all the expertise your team of experts has, but the machine still isn't as smart as they are. But of course the moment you have the program and the knowledge all laid out in detail in front of you, you can immediately see how to make improvements. And suddenly the program has surpassed human performance. But there was no moment you could put your finger on when the machine was just *as* smart *as* the human. For a while it isn't as smart, and then suddenly it's smarter."

Thus even if no *new* knowledge is brought to bear on any process, whether it is design or decision making, manufacturing or harvesting, the very fact of bringing to bear on that process a mechanism that embodies not only the expertise of the very best human experts at it (one expert or, for that matter, many geographically scattered experts) will change the quality of the process significantly for the better. Better processes allow better productivity, superior products, economic leverage. We have seen the first instance of this in the industrial revolution and we know what economic revolution was embedded in those machines. In knowledge machines, I believe the degree of the economic revolution will be orders of magnitude greater.

And then if knowledge technology begins to give us *new* knowledge, knowledge that human beings would not have stumbled on because they do not have the time or energy to do the kinds of searches that might uncover that new knowledge, or because a clever combining of pieces of old knowledge is beyond the wit of our flesh-and-blood brains, the changes will be much more startling.

If we can sum up the economic promise of knowledge technology, it is that it will resolve shades of gray—small advantages of various kinds, whether they are advantages of time, or capital, or slightly better design—into black and white, and that transformation turns only a slight competitive advantage into an overwhelming superiority.

THE INTELLECTUAL PROMISE

Psychologists tells us that our evolutionary legacy is this: the human brain can deal with about four concepts simultaneously, and no more. One part of human history—surely the most humane and honorable part—has been the systematic compensation for that rather pitiful legacy by providing ourselves with a collection of arrangements and tools that amplify our intellects. Written language is one such amplification; and printing, which created a revolution over several centuries by doing no more than mechanizing written language and improving its distribution by orders of magnitude, is another.

But there is a big difference between these instances of knowledge technology, and the instance of knowledge technology the new fifth generation represents. Writing and printing are merely amplifications of, or substitutions for, the human memory. The computer, and particularly its form in new, intelligent machines, amplifies or substitutes for human reasoning power. This piece of technology has been with us for less than 40 years, and we are barely on the threshold of knowing what such technology will do for us. However, we have some indications.

As revolutionary as written language and, later, book publishing were (and I hold that it was the urge toward universal literacy that is directly responsible for the social revolutions of the eighteenth century) these technologies had their drawbacks. For one important thing, books do not lend themselves very well to expressing experiential knowledge. (This is shown in our slightly pejorative term, "book knowledge." No matter how much they have read, we demand of our apprentices that they work in the shop or the clinic or the courtroom before we certify them, because we understand that experience is different from book knowledge, and we understand also that certain kinds of knowledge are transferred more effectively by example than by the abstractions of books.) This is what I meant by arrangements, that we trust the heads of experts to hold knowledge that books cannot. Technology that can indeed hold and even disseminate that experiential knowledge, the nonbook knowledge, is here in a rudimentary form called "expert systems," which you have just heard about. The fifth generation of computers proposes to transform that rudimentary technology into a universal device, one that anybody can use. This means, very simply, that expertise, which is now badly distributed, will be more evenly distributed. In principle, and we hope in practice, the quality of diagnosis and therapy available to a sick person in a prosperous industrial country will be equally available to the peasants of Henan province, the poorest province of China.

Another drawback of the written word is (to repeat) that it is merely memory, not processing. In the computer, however, we have in our hands an instrument that will amplify and substitute for human memory, and more important, human reasoning power. In other words, for the first time in human history, the production of knowledge is taking place outside the human head. There will be—in a modest way, there already is—automatic creation of knowledge. When a machine can use up all the knowledge we have given it and use it systematically in ways that we cannot, and can make inferences more deeply than we can (since it is not limited, as we are, by our evolutionary legacy of about four items we can attend to simultaneously), then what will happen? We do not know. We may forget how to do things. Though it was drilled mercilessly into us in secondary schools, very few adults today remember how to take square roots. Hand-held calculators do the job beautifully; why burden ourselves and our minds?

More interestingly, we shall perhaps begin to use our new powers to think confidently about matters that have up to now eluded us. Problems that are simply too complex for one bright person, or even a group of bright people to cope with will become tractable because the new knowledge technology will be able to help us think faster and deeper than human brains alone (or even with their memory aids) can. For example, one area that has failed to yield very satisfactorily to our present-day knowledge technologies is human behavior: we simply cannot predict how individuals alone or in the aggregate will behave under changing circumstances. My guess is that the new knowledge technologies will be a tool for that kind of understanding.

But aside from certainty about things we already believe we want to know about, what of the human store of knowledge itself? Will it be different? We do not know.

We do not know whether, even given the same heuristics, or rules of thumb, that humans use, a system that can think faster and deeper will necessarily think down the same avenues that humans do. If it should go elsewhere, we do not know what lies at the end of such different avenues.

We do not know whether new knowledge can be discovered by a machine (though we suspect it can and have early intimations of it). If so, we do not know what the implications of such new knowledge might be.

We do not know how to imbue humans with the critical intelligence to evaluate the knowledge they are exposed to. The problem is already a difficult one for readers of the written word. We do not know whether the ability to interrogate a reasoning machine, to make it explain itself, will help with this problem or exacerbate it.

But let us make some guesses. We humans are mythmakers. Throughout human history, every important phenomenon has collected its share of myths, particularly when there was no other way to explain matters. Thus most of our earliest myths are agricultural (including the reproduction of human beings): our ancestors stood in wonder before the mystery of germination, growth, sustenance, and death, and made up stories, often with human actors but sometimes with animals and other fantastic creatures, to explain these mysteries. (The same kinds of myths explain natural phenomena, national histories, and even the technology of the written word.) What generates all these myths is the lack of rational understanding of the phenomena the myths intend to explain.

At the moment, artificial intelligence is in a premythic phase. I alluded earlier to the tales of science fiction—and they go back to Homer, believe it or not—that anticipated artificial intelligence and told us how it was going to be.[3] Those tales were not exactly right, and I suggested earlier that they stand in relation to the reality of artificial intelligence as myths about El Dorado and Atlantis once stood in relation to the reality of the New World. It turned out the New World was far more complicated, and much better than people could have imagined, in its abundance and variety and opportunities for human achievement, but it did not look that way at first, so the folks who had expected to find the El Dorado of their dreams went away mad (or did not go there at all).

Artificial intelligence at the moment contains no mysteries. You can sit down with the code of a program and figure out line by line what is going on, not unlike the score of a piece of music. Moreover, artificial-intelligence researchers are at great pains to make sure that expert systems, while they are in the process of doing a task, must be able to explain their lines of reasoning to users, so that the user can evaluate the correctness of the program's decisions. I think this is highly important.

But what happens when expert systems, or other forms of artificial intelligence, are so far beyond our human capabilities that they really cannot explain in any fashion we humans can comprehend? One young artificial-intelligence researcher suggests that humans will become "hobbyists" of thinking—that is, some of us will do it, but only as gifted amateurs. Many people worry right now that we humans are beginning to lose some essential skills by using calculators and word processors; no need to learn to add or subtract, or spell. True enough, but no great loss to the human race, I believe; but that is another story.

Myself, I would not be surprised to see the return of mystery, magic, and the transcendental to a central place in human life. I suspect that we will eventually stand before our intelligent machines the way our ancestors stood before the cereal crop: in awe, in pleasure, in reverence, and in a certain amount of fear. And then, if we have not begun it already, we shall begin the great cycle of myths of intelligence, and our creativity will flourish apace.

Those of you who are confirmed rationalists may find this return to the irrational to be a giant step backward for the human race. Those of you who are poets may be thinking, at last, and the sooner the better. I hold both views simultaneously and do not quite know how I feel about it. On the other hand, yesterday Bob Lucky suggested that our intelligent machines would push us, willy-nilly, up the evolutionary ladder, and so what has the potential for mystery at the moment may not be the least mysterious to our children. Their patterns of thinking may have changed in ways we simply cannot anticipate, just as writing, and then printing, made humans think in ways that could not have been anticipated but were nevertheless very different from prewriting and prepublishing patterns of thinking.

THE SOCIAL PROMISE

Implicitly, we have been talking all this time about the social promise of knowledge technology, and now we can make it explicit. It is the democratization of knowledge. In the same way that the written word once democratized knowledge (but surely different by orders of magnitude), knowledge is to be made accessible to everyone. There is the sure change in the professions, though not, I think, their dissolution. We ourselves are human beings, and we usually enjoy dealing with other human beings, so it seems unlikely to me that the relationship between professional and nonprofessional will disappear completely.

Since the professions are largely repositories of specialized knowledge, is it possible that with the widespread distribution of knowledge, the professions will somehow become less exclusive? It is not only possible, it seems inevitable. Specialties that were once locked in individual human heads will be accessible to anybody—though not everybody will want such access. The distinction between specialist and layman will become more blurred than it has been, though I doubt it will disappear altogether.

For example, in medicine there has been a change over the last century away from the healing arts and toward science—universal, explicitly science-based techniques. That change has brought immense power to physicians to cure, and it has also brought power to those outside the profession to measure performance. It has equalized the balance between professional and client in a way that has not been seen for many decades. When a performance is found wanting, the patient can complain, or even sue. Thus the malpractice suit is a manifestation of the lay community's new access to knowledge.[4]

When a further diffusion of knowledge takes place—when the knowledge and techniques of the world's finest specialists are easily and clearly accessible not only to other practitioners in the field but to anyone—that transfer will have comparable ramifications. Medicine is the first profession touching ordinary people directly that has undergone a transformation of its certitudes; other professions that touch people directly are likely to undergo similar transformations, and raise similar expectations and standards of performance, such as engineering, design, the management of politics, and so forth.

Surely the dynamics of that relationship between professional and client will change. For one thing, professionals will know more than they know now: they will, of course, enjoy the intellectual leverage that anyone has with access to much more knowledge in much easier ways. But since that knowledge *is* more accessible, they will, as the physicians have discovered, be held accountable in more precise ways. The exclusionary ways of the professions could disappear with the democratization of knowledge the way the divine right of kings disappeared with universal literacy.

We can expect changes in education. The process of education will change because, first, we shall know more about human cognition and, second, we shall be thinking in different ways about different things and, third, the very tools we hold in our hands will be different.

Thus there is promise—as yet largely unfulfilled, I think—that the design of artificial intelligences can illuminate and make explicit some principles of human cognition that have only been implicit, their exercise and cultivation no more than a matter of chance until now.

As for the tools themselves being different, video games, to take one example, which are in their embryonic stage right now, will in their maturity play the central role that books have played in education. These matured forms will bear the same resemblance to what is currently found in arcades as books bear to hieroglyphics on the face of a cliff. What chiseler in stone could have anticipated where runes would end up? Who then could have predicted the great advantages of books and other printed matter: portability, cheapness, ease of distribution; or the profound changes literacy made not only in human thinking patterns, but in what we felt confident now to put our minds to, and all the enormous social changes that examination of the status quo brought about.

We are today as the makers of hieroglyphics. We can observe one form of knowledge technology in video games and guess that portability, cheapness, and ease of distribution are givens. Interaction—the active engagement of human with machine—is very different from the participation print requires, and we guess that difference will be central. But the shape of that importance and its implications are impossible to predict.

We can expect changes in government. If knowledge is power, and most of us would agree it is, and if we are talking about the democratization of knowledge, then we are also talking about the further democratization of power, continuing a trend that began in Europe in explicit ways in the eighteenth century. It was then that we came to have confidence that we could govern ourselves. However, as our polity grew, we could not all gather physically under one roof, and so we devised something called representative government to compensate for the impossibility of hearing from everybody. Knowledge technology will allow us the possibility of at last hearing from everybody, or at least everybody who is interested in any issue of government. It is possible to foresee a collapse of many of the contraptions of government as citizens take over more direct management of their governance.

THE THREAT OF KNOWLEDGE TECHNOLOGY

Knowledge is power. That is embedded in our earliest texts, whether scripture or instructions on how to fight a battle. With more knowledge comes not only more power, but also more responsibility, both individual and collective, and that we shall have to shoulder without excessive or unseemly grumbling. It will not be easy, but it will surely be exhilarating.

For humans who do not value knowledge, we do not know what a world deeply steeped in knowledge will seem like. There have been suggestions that the enormously rich recreational possibilities of computers—barely touched so far—will either sedate or stimulate that disenfranchised group that now scorns knowledge. Knowledge as narcotic is not especially attractive to me, but the other possibility, the computer as a stimulant, is a hopeful one. Since the specific machines you will hear about from Mr. Fuchi, the Japanese fifth generation, are planned to be as easy to use as a telephone or television, it might be heartening to remember that in the United States, the number of television sets grew from 6,000 to 15.5 million in a matter of five years. We might wish the fifth generation such success.

Among our responsibilities—to name but a few—will be the protection of individual privacy (or even its redefinition), the responsibility for educating all young human beings to take their place in a knowledge-saturated world, the equitable assignment of credit for intellectual property (and perhaps its redefinition), which at the moment is there for the picking.

These are perhaps threats. But I personally am optimistic. I want to tell you why. I spoke a little earlier about the concept of knowledge technology resolving shades of gray into black and white; transforming a small advantage into a decisive one. Here is an example of such a transformation.

Many peoples were milling around the Mediterranean basin and the fertile crescent circa 700 B.C. but we really do not talk about the glory that was Mesopotamia, or the grandeur that was the Northern Semitic empires. Instead, we trace our cultural history directly back to the Greek peninsula and its islands. What was it about the Greeks? Why weren't those competing cultures to give us the glory that was indeed Greece?

There is an answer to that question and it illustrates my thesis perfectly. The answer lies in a simple but potent piece of knowledge technology that turned out to be crucial, that made Greek thought central to the western world for the next 2,500 years. That piece of knowledge technology was a better alphabet. Other civilizations surrounding the Greeks had alphabets of a sort, but they were not as good. What the Greek alphabet did because of its superiority was to turn a shade of gray into clear black and white. Greek thought came to dominate its neighbors, its enemies, and eventually, its intellectual offspring, what we are pleased to call Western culture.

Not only did Greek thought dominate because it was easier to disseminate—for the first time in human history, literacy was democratized—but Greek thought also dominated because through the powers of the superior alphabet it found expression in, it got smarter. Thanks to its slightly superior written alphabet, Greek thought became dramatically more perceptive, richer, more precise, more systematic, more encompassing. It did that by changing, in a stunning release, the way people thought. As a consequence, Greek culture easily beat out its rivals, and shaped a civilization for the next 2,500 years.[5]

I have mentioned another piece of knowledge technology, the printing press. It appeared in western Europe about 1450 (although it had already been invented in Korea and China many centuries before) and took the continent by storm. Its single critical feature was the order of magnitude change it could bring about in the dissemination of knowledge. Thus, in less than 50 years, Gutenberg's invention had been carried all over Europe, and from an estimated scores of thousands of volumes, Europeans now had more than 9 million volumes, roughly a doubling rate every seven years, which is not quite as good as computing, but not bad either. The printing press arrived as the Renaissance was already under way, but it amplified that glorious intellectual ferment to a fare-thee-well. It was directly responsible for transforming a little parochial quarrel in Germany into the Reformation, and probably equally responsible for the Scientific Revolution of the seventeenth century. I have no time to tell you of its effect on national languages, literature, and national consciousness, but it was profound and we feel it to this day. I would even argue that it was the main cause of European domination of so much of the planet for many centuries.

Both the Golden Age of Greece and the Continental Renaissance had two other aspects in common with, indeed as a complement to, their knowledge technology. That was a burst of exploration beyond the boundaries of the known world—inspiration itself for fable, celebration, and prosperity.

Thus history is the source of my optimism. Here in 1983 we stand with a new piece of knowledge technology in our hands. It is not a memory machine, as it has been so often in the past, but a reasoning machine, which will amplify human reasoning by the same orders of magnitude that writing and printing have amplified human memory. This new piece of knowledge technology surely has the potential for just that kind of slight but crucial superiority over the competition that resolves shades of gray into black and white. If nothing else, its powers—and by that I mean not only its large knowledge bases and its ability to reason with that knowledge, I also mean its universal distribution—will surely change the subjects we feel confident to address and, of course, the way we think about them. We also itch to break the boundaries of the known world. We are already beginning to, in ways that would have stunned the Greeks or Prince Hency the Navigator, but in ways I think they would have applauded.

Thus we stand, I think, on the threshold of another renaissance, another golden age, with big changes ahead. Those changes will trouble the Establishment (because they will disestablish the Establishment) but excite the adventuresome, and enrich us all. For that is what new knowledge technology has always promised, and always delivered.

If I have been vague about the shape of the Atlantis, the El Dorado, the Blessed Isles, of the new world to come, it is because I know in my heart that my predictions can only look feeble compared to the opulent complexity of the real when we reach those shores. Our little squabbles, our puny anxieties about our prospects will, if they are remembered at all, be charitably forgiven, the products of our lamentably limited minds that were, through no fault of our own, incapable of imagining something beyond our experience.

REFERENCES

1. COMMAGER, H. S. 1977. The Empire of Reason: How Europe Imagined and America Realized the Enlightenment. Oxford University Press. New York, N.Y.
2. FEIGENBAUM, E. & P. McCORDUCK. 1983. The Fifth Generation. Addison-Wesley. Reading, Mass.
3. McCORDUCK, P. 1979. Machines Who Think. W. H. Freeman & Co. San Francisco, Calif.
4. HOLZNER, B. & J. H. MARX. 1979. Knowledge Applications; The Knowledge System in Society. Allyn and Bacon. Boston, Mass.
5. HAVELOCK, E. A. 1982. The Literate Revolution in Greece and Its Cultural Consequences. Princeton University Press. Princeton, N.J.

DISCUSSION OF THE PAPER

QUESTION: One of the changes that this new technology seems to be bringing—and a particular interest of mine because my company's just starting a major report on it—is telecommuting and the new remote work force. And I wondered if the speakers today would make a comment on what they think is going to happen. I'd also be pleased to chat with anyone here over the week about your thoughts or expertise in the area.

P. McCORDUCK: I think Harley Shaiken gave a talk on that very topic yesterday, didn't he? And I'm sure he has much more insight and things to say about it than I do if I heard you correctly.

QUESTION: This is people working away from headquarters—people beginning to work at home.

P. McCORDUCK: Oh, distributive work. Yes, it will happen. But not the isolated electronic cottage. We just love each other too much. We really need to be with each other.

QUESTION: What you and Dr. Feigenbaum have really described is an exciting complement to the human intellect. But it's not a complement to the human soul or spirit or psyche or morality. And the negative way to ask my question would be to say does that threaten to create an imbalance? Or the most positive approach would be to say, what do we need to do to integrate this technology in a wholesome way into our lives?

P. McCORDUCK: Wow.

M. L. MINSKY (*Massachusetts Institute of Technology, Cambridge, Mass.*): Easy, just get a committee to define wholesome.

P. McCORDUCK: Thank you, Dr. Minsky. In fact we talk about that in our book at some length.

QUESTION: Yes, I have several points. One, I'm a bit distressed by your complete dismissal of the Chinese language in favor of the Greek, considering the long cultural traditions the Chinese have. Especially since you cited the work of Sun Tzu who lived in 400 B.C. Second, I'm curious as to what makes you think that the existence of newer technology will substantially change the way the government works. For example, one of the first proposed uses of electricity was to set up in Congress a system whereby each congressman could push a button to vote yes, no, or abstain. The decision was rejected out of hand as being exactly the kind of thing that they did not want. The question there obviously is do you think that new technology will change things? Another example would be of course the direct popular vote, which we certainly have the technology for now.

P. McCORDUCK: Change takes a long time, but it does happen. Those revolutions I was talking about took hundreds of years. Come back in 100 years, and we'll talk about it. But let me address your first question about the Chinese language. Yes, I could have talked about the Chinese language. As it is, I had to leave out large chunks of Western culture too. But I am deeply respectful of the Chinese language and the simply incredible influence it had on the other half of the world. I was very specifically talking about Western culture.

M. L. MINSKY: I'd just like to make a remark about the second comment. The direct vote is not much of an innovation, and this could have been done by pulling strings. The reason people didn't do it is that even in Congress, it's understood that issues are too complicated for popular democracy within the congress itself. The kind of revolution Ms. McCorduck is talking about is where you write an expert program and load it into the giant expert program that runs us all. That's much different from popular democracy. It's where you send an intellectual representative of your preferences. And that should take a few hundred years, shouldn't it? We're not quite ready to do it.

Fifth Generation Computers

Some Theoretical Issues

KAZUHIRO FUCHI

ICOT Research Center
Institute for New Generation Computer Technology
Tokyo 108, Japan

Recent advances in device technology as well as progress of basic research in the various fields of information processing have inspired us with the feeling that innovative computers will emerge in the near future. In this process of development such research efforts have been consistently interrelated. So new computers are being planned to support innovations in the entire field of information-processing technology.

GUIDELINES FOR THE "FIFTH GENERATION"

"Fifth generation computers" here means the computers for the 1990s. Will these computers be merely an extension of the gradual improvements of current computer technology? Rather, will they be innovative computers that will substantially alleviate the problems of today's information processing? But what will such innovative computers be like?

In the search for the image of the "fifth generation computer," there are several approaches that can be considered. One is to analyze the needs for information processing and to boil the findings down to obtain an image of future computers. Another is to forecast such an image, based on the advancement of device technology. The other approach is to obtain an image of future computers by studying research achievements in various fields of information processing.

Assuming the time for innovation of computer technology has already come, various direct and indirect research projects should already have shown some indications of these innovations.

Over the past 10 years, new developments have been made in the various fields of information processing, notably those of basic research. While these are individually attractive, it is particularly notable that research efforts believed to have originated from different motives have later been found in reality to be mutually and deeply interrelated. These interdependent efforts have not yet reached the stage for practical application to computer technology, but they inspire the feeling that information-processing technology will be integrally reorganized in the near future. We have the impression that the image of computers themselves will also be clarified in this process of reorganization.

When computers were invented, substantial contributions were made by basic and theoretical research. Achievements not only in electronics (in those days called electron tube technology) but also in mathematical logic and neurophysiology were skillfully put to use. Turing's theories of logic contributed to the establishment of an image for universal computers (stored-program computers), and McCulloch-Pitts' neurophysiological model was closely associated with the philosophy of logic elements. These were cleverly synthesized by J. von Neumann and others, to form the basis for today's computers.

Since then, however, the development of computers has mainly been technological and autonomous. Automata theory, theory of formal languages, and other theories emerged, but they have not directly influenced the development of computer technology. Rather, computer technology has created more substance than the then-existing theories have.

Another facet of this progress, however, is that computer technology is about to be crushed by the richness of the contents it has created. One example of this facet is the sense of crisis over the overgrown software. One of its causes seems to be the slow clarifying or theorizing of the contents. It is probably due to this aspect that information processing was labeled as an art but not a science.

Early in the seventies, the contents were properly theorized. This theorization belonged, for instance, in the field of mathematical theories of programming. What is of interest is that the progress appears to be conceiving the image of a new computer architecture by outstepping its own creator computers.

Independently, at least on the surface, of mathematical theories of programming, there have been, since the early seventies, gropings toward a new computer architecture. Noteworthy among these attempts is the research on data-base machines and data-flow machines. Another point of interest is that such machines have started exhibiting progress that synchronizes with the progress in mathematical programming theories. It is felt that under a new concept, many of the proposals made so far can be integrated. Similar phenomena are also developing in relation with other fields. Not only will these lead to the establishment of the image for innovative "fifth generation" computers, but they will also give us confidence that these computers will actually be realized.

TRIALS FOR NEW COMPUTER ARCHITECTURE

Principles of the internal structure of computers themselves have not changed much since von Neumann's invention.

Meanwhile, study of the computer architecture itself has been going on for a long time. Such proposals as associative processing, parallel processing, and variable structures were made some time ago. Proposals of techniques, such as stacking, tagging, and hashing, have also been numerous. Architecture based on high-level languages has already been proposed as well. However, even though some techniques such as stacking have actually been put into practice, most of these proposals have not as yet borne fruit in actual computers.

While each of them is excellent individually, the combination of these proposals in the process of partially remodeling existing systems will not necessarily take full advantage of their merits. For their full utilization, a new unified theory will be required that organically positions and makes use of each of the individual proposals. And this is believed to be possible.

This purpose requires an overall viewpoint that will both focus on hardware structures and include programming. So the future computer architect will need the talent of a master as described by Aristotle.

So far, experimental machines for parallel processing and associative processing have been built to provide higher performance capabilities and more sophisticated functions. Ironically, however, the prototype machines have exhibited nearly catastrophic difficulties of programming, despite certain unique characteristics of the systems in some cases.

This situation is about to change. Data-flow-type architecture has lately attracted much attention, not so much due to its uniqueness as a system, but rather because it conforms with the new trend toward research into programming.

The data-flow philosophy describes the computing processes in terms of the flow of data rather than by the conventional approach that is centered around controls. Parallel operations are described along the flow of data. In moving toward the variable architecture that will be required, J. Dennis developed an architecture based on a message-exchanging philosophy.

On the other hand, software engingeering has proposed new-style programming to sidestep the difficulties in conventional programming. One of these was J. Backus' functional programming, which was to become directly linked with the data-flow-machine philosophy. Given the previous experiences with difficulties of programming for parallel machines, this was an epoch-making change. The desirable form from the programming viewpoint and the idea from the hardware side are unified in Backus' approach, which has not been done for a long time since the original von Neumann system. Furthermore, data-flow machines and functional programming provide possibilities for further development into the "inference machine," which will be described later.

To realize the inference machine, tagging, stacking, and so on will have to be utilized fully everywhere. In this respect, most of the excellent ideas proposed in the past may possibly be organically incorporated. Such an inference machine may indeed be considered to be the new-type computer, or the true form of a computer.

The so-called von Neumann type machine was the realization of the principles of hardware simplification. It has also been the type of machine that has been adjusted to low levels of device technology from the days of its invention through the present day. Outlooks on the progress of device technology permit breakthroughs to the next higher level. Rather, they may be said to be looked forward to by the realizing technology side. And the realizing technology side may anticipate these breakthroughs as well.

NEW PROGRAMMING STYLES

For computer technology, the issues of software (programming) productivity and quality assurance have lately become matters of increasing concern. The cost contribution of software to computer systems has been increasing rapidly. Since Dijkstra's proposal for "structured programming," there has been frequent introspection into programming styles as well as its theorization concerning these styles.

Meanwhile, research for clarification of program specifications and assurance of program correctness has also been actively promoted. Such research is expected not only to assure software quality, but also to enhance productivity. This is because presently program inspection and debugging are sharing a very high percentage of the whole process of making programs. The research is also being integrated into the style (methodology) of building programs up while assuring the validity during the process.

The functional programming of Backus et al. is positioned within this stream. Predicate calculus type programming has also been proposed and is recently drawing attention. The proposals of both programming recommend the use of a certain form of logic itself as the programming language. These proposals correspond to the two streams of formal specification language (the function and predicate calculus types), while they also urge examination of how the specification and programming languages should be interrelated. Formal specifications may be regarded as a type of (highly abstract) program. These abstract programs are converted and made concrete in accordance with system requirements. If this transformation could be achieved in the same language (logic), it would provide many advantages. Such a philosophy will probably link up in the future with the "data abstraction" philosophy, which is also one of the mainstreams of software engineering.

Such a programming language will be an "ultra-high-level" language by the standards of contemporary programming languages. One of the reasons for difficulty verifying program correctness and for the slow acceptance by programmers is the low level of languages currently employed. This aspect will ultimately fall to a problem that the existing computer architecture has. Thus one of the causes for the "software crisis" lies in the very system of the existing computers.

Now, verification of the correctness of programs may be restated as confirmation (demonstration) of identical "meanings" of two statements. Accordingly, the "semantics" of programming languages need to be established.

It may be inferred that with "artificial" languages such as the programming language, the definition of meanings should be simple. In reality, however, considerable difficulties have been encountered, when reviewed historically. The syntax of artificial languages is artificial and may be termed simple, but their meanings do not seem to be necessarily "artificial." The situation has paralleled the difficulties in the semantics of natural languages.

From the sixties to the seventies, a number of attempts in semantics were made. One was operational semantics. An abstract machine was imagined, where the meanings of the language were intended to be determined by the descriptions of an (abstract) interpreter. This was developed in the late sixties as the Vienna definition method. Using it for verification, however, presented great difficulties.

In the seventies, axiomatic semantics was started by Hoare and others. This was a development from Floyd's theory concerning flowcharts in the latter part of the sixties. It provided a programming language with an axiomatic system and a set of inference rules, and was intended to render verification based on these. While it is a type of semantic regulation, theoretically it presents a problem in the area of validity of the inference rules and their axioms. More basic semantic rules are required. These are what corresponds to denotational semantics (model theory) referred to in the field of logic.

Around 1970, Strachey and Scott developed denotational semantics of the programming language. Scott established a mathematically accurate model theory relative to self-applicable languages. This regards "computation" as an approximation process and introduces topology there. Scott's theory may also be considered to support axiomatic and operational semantics. With this as a base, the "mathematical theory of programming" has recently been developed.

One of the conclusions drawn from these efforts is that the normally used programming languages are difficult to handle through semantic approaches. Is it because the semantics has been constructed inadequately? Particularly interesting is the fact that items for introspection concerning programming styles, which were intuitively pointed out independently of such theoretical approaches, happened to coincide with difficulties in semantics. In structured programming, for instance, the use of "GO TO" statments was considered to be harmful. Similarly, the semantic construction of "GO TO" is also complicated to analyze.

These situations reinforce the directions toward new programming styles and new programming languages to support them. Conventional languages are dedicated to the von Neumann type machines. Logic-type languages are regarded to be "ultra–high level" as viewed by the standards of conventional types of languages. If this is the case, will logic machines that directly execute such logic languages be ultracomplicated? The semantics of logic itself, however, are rather simple. This inspires one to infer that logic-type machines will not necessarily be complicated and unreal.

Artificial Intelligence and Knowledge Engineering

In information-processing research, the field of artificial intelligence has been trying to understand phenomena of intelligence and their application. Artificial intelligence research reached a turning point in the early seventies with its awareness of the issue of "languages and knowledge." The philosophy at that time of software engineering, database methodology, and the like was against it. Lately, however, these fields have tended to overlap to a great extent, and to become fused together.

Another notable aspect of artificial intelligence research is that in the latter half of the seventies, applications of artificial intelligence techniques actually started taking place. This applied artificial intelligence is called "knowledge engineering" by E. Feigenbaum.

Included in this area is the issue of the programming languages for artificial intelligence. It was an attempt at converting an inference system into a programming language. Such attempts include concepts for pattern matching, nondeterministic (parallel) computation, and multiple data bases. On the other hand, subsequent progress in research on theorem proving (or inference systems) has shown that it is feasible to directly convert an inference system back into a programming system. This is represented by the predicate logic programming (and its language) described earlier.

Research into knowledge representation is a major theme of artificial intelligence, but here too, links with research on data bases have become increasingly evident. Fundamentally, knowledge representation has come to be associated with an awareness of the problems of making data bases more sophisticated. Higher-level retrievals of data bases are precisely a form of "inference" itself. The image of inference machines also appears feasible from the standpoint of data-base machines.

Knowledge engineering started in the late seventies and is intended for practical applications of artificial intelligence. For instance, MYCIN, a medical diagnostic system, is widely known.

Utilization of natural languages and knowledge will be the prerequisite for the office automation of the nineties and for many other information-processing application fields to be opened up in the future. This is the basic technical requirement needed to realize user demands for computer systems that are truly easy for man to use. We believe that future information processing will incorporate knowledge engineering and grow into "knowledge-information processing."

Then, what kind of a machine will be preferable for the support of knowledge engineering? This, in the present budding stage, is being realized by software on regular computers. The limitations of this approach, however, are very apparent. Knowledge naturally varies by expertise, but the mechanisms that support it are more or less universal. The core mechanisms of knowledge engineering systems are the problem-solving function, i.e., the inference function, the knowledge-base-managing function, and also the accumulation and organization of knowledge itself. So the machines to support knowledge engineering must be inference machines and knowledge-base machines.

CONTRIBUTIONS FROM LINGUISTICS

Future information processing must be able to handle Japanese, English, and other natural languages. This is one of the core themes of artificial intelligence and at the same time, an area of linguistics; deep relations exist between theoretical linguistics and computers.

Historically, Chomsky's early period linguistics deeply influences computer technology. His generative grammar dictates the syntax of most programming languages. Categorization of context-free grammar and other grammars also derives from Chomsky. In the sixties, tremendous developments were made in "generative-transformational grammar," which attempted to explain the syntactic phenomena of languages. In the seventies, more emphasis on the analysis of "meanings" subjected the framework of the generative-transformational theory to major changes. This stage of theoretical linguistics also happened to coincide with the developing period of artificial intelligence linguistics that had taken up the issue of meanings as "language understanding."

Meanwhile, early in the seventies Montague's new linguistic theory emerged. This came from a branch of philosophical linguistics, and is directly concerned with the semantics. It extended formal semantics contained in philosophical linguistics, and applied it to a part of English, producing a model that unified syntax and semantics for the first time in history.

Montague's is a logical theory of linguistics. In it, "intensional logic," whose semantics is clear cut, is introduced as the base logic, and a framework and a procedure are given for transforming sentences in natural language to the intensional logic. In this framework, Montague demonstrated a method of applying formal semantics to natural languages.

Intensional logic is a kind of modal logic that has been transformed into functional forms. The semantics of the modal logic (model theory) were introduced by Kripke. They seek to define the meanings of logical formulas in terms of "possible worlds."

Then what is the significance of such developments in linguistics from the standpoint of computer technology? Functional languages are no strangers to the world of computers. The language LISP, for example, has long been used in the world of artificial intelligence. Functional languages have thus regained prominence because of proposals for functional programming in the field of software engineering as well. Intensional logic is an extension of these functional languages.

The denotational semantics of programming languages referred to earlier originally stemmed from formal semantics. One of the interesting aspects is that timings of the breakthroughs made in both the fields roughly coincided with each other.

Furthermore, the model theory of intensional logic, that is, the possible world semantic, is intuitively easy to grasp if viewed as multiple data bases from a data-base standpoint. This suggests that intensional logic has potential for application to the data-base theory, and actually, such research efforts have already commenced.

There will actually be natural limitations to the utilization of natural languages in programming and queries to data bases. The range of natural language needed for computers will be limited to portions that are logically graspable. Were these limitations unnatural, they would support an argument against the use of natural languages. But the range within the limitations is actually believed to be sufficiently wide for natural languages to be used for practical purposes. From this viewpoint, progress in logical linguistics will be highly welcome to the computer side. In the course of this progress it is conceivable that logical linguistics and computer technology will tend to merge as many overlapping phenomena are observed.

So if the Montague theory were implemented as a machine, what would the result be? It would be a universally applicable machine effective for both knowledge engineering and software engineering. It would further be a machine that the future computer architect will wish to design as his major job.

KNOWLEDGE-INFORMATION PROCESSING AND INFERENCE MACHINES

In the various fields of information-processing research, a number of research efforts are presently regarded to be basic and theoretical, and yet appear to be the buds for blossoming in the future. While these appear on the surface to have grown out of mutually independent motives, they tend to intertwine deeply among themselves. Seen as a totality, they appear to be aiming at a new information-processing system, which may perhaps be called knowledge-information processing. There, the best parts of knowledge engineering, software engineering, data-base research, and architecture research are considered to be organically and harmoniously incorporated.

Even when each individual research group draws an image of a "special and dedicated" machine that will be useful for the group, the images seem to converge into one and the same goal. If this is true, the image of a machine with universal applicability will become the core of future computers. Opinions no doubt will vary on what to call it, but a standardized name of "inference machine" may not be such a poor choice. This, however, is not intended to signify only one type of machine to be tomorrow's computer, of course. Many and various types of inference machines will actually emerge, varying in scale and performance as well as in selection of the internal structure.

Within this image, let us now attempt to grasp that of the "fifth generation" computers of the nineties. Will such an approach be overly optimistic? Various related phenomena appear not only to indicate the adequacy of the approach but also to provide us with the confidence for its realization potential. When seemingly accidental phenomena unanimously point in one specific direction, there really must be an unalterable base current deep down.

However, all this is still a hypothesis that will require much time to verify. Even though the research achievements to date constitute the groundwork, research themes requiring future resolution are still numerous. Difficulty certainly is to be expected. It does not, however, mean the unfeasibility of a new age. No progress is possible without the endeavors of people, and you cannot stop people from endeavors.

Some Expert Systems
Need Common Sense

Department of Computer Science
Stanford University
Stanford, California 94305

An *expert system* is a computer program intended to embody the knowledge and ability of an expert in a certain domain. The ideas behind them and several examples have been described in other lectures in this symposium. Their performance in their specialized domains are often very impressive. Nevertheless, hardly any of them have certain *common-sense* knowledge and ability possessed by any non-feeble-minded human. This lack makes them "brittle." By this is meant that they are difficult to expand beyond the scope originally contemplated by their designers, and they usually do not recognize their own limitations. Many important applications will require commonsense abilities. The object of this lecture is to describe commonsense abilities and the problems that require them.

Commonsense facts and methods are only very partially understood today, and extending this understanding is the key problem facing artificial intelligence.

This is not exactly a new point of view. I have been advocating "Computer Programs with Common Sense" since I wrote a paper with that title in 1958.[1] Studying commonsense capability has sometimes been popular and sometimes unpopular among artificial intelligence (AI) researchers. At present it is popular, perhaps because new AI knowledge offers new hope of progress. Certainly AI researchers today know a lot more about what common sense is than I knew in 1958—or in 1969 when I wrote another paper on the subject.[2] However, expressing commonsense knowledge in formal terms has proved very difficult, and the number of scientists working in the area is still far too small.

One of the best known expert systems is MYCIN,[3,4] a program for advising physicians on treating bacterial infections of the blood and meningitis. It does reasonably well without common sense, provided the user has common sense and understands the program's limitations.

MYCIN conducts a question and answer dialogue. After asking basic facts about the patient such as name, sex, and age, MYCIN asks about suspected bacterial organisms, suspected sites of infection, the presence of specific symptoms (e.g., fever, headache) relevant to diagnosis, the outcome of laboratory tests, and some others. It then recommends a certain course of antibiotics. While the dialogue is in English, MYCIN avoids having to understand freely written English by controlling the dialogue. It outputs sentences, but the user types only single words or standard phrases. Its major innovations over many previous expert systems are that it uses measures of uncertainty (not probabilities) for its diagnoses and the fact that it is prepared to explain its reasoning to the physician, so he can decide whether to accept it.

Our discussion of MYCIN begins with its ontology. The ontology of a program is the set of entities that its variables range over. Essentially this is what it can have information about.

MYCIN's ontology includes bacteria, symptoms, tests, possible sites of infection, antibiotics, and treatments. Doctors, hospitals, illness, and death are absent. Even patients are not really part of the ontology, although MYCIN asks for many facts about the specific patient. This is because patients are not values of variables, and MYCIN never compares the infections of two different patients. It would therefore be difficult to modify MYCIN to learn from its experience.

MYCIN's program, written in a general scheme called EMYCIN, is a so-called production system. A production system is a collection of rules, each of which has two parts—a pattern part and an action part. When a rule is activated, MYCIN tests whether the pattern part matches the data base. If so this results in the variables in the pattern being matched to whatever entities are required for the match of the data base. If not the pattern fails and MYCIN tries another. If the match is successful, then MYCIN performs the action part of the pattern using the values of the variables determined by the pattern part. The whole process of questioning and recommending is built up out of productions.

The production formalism turned out to be suitable for representing a large amount of information about the diagnosis and treatment of bacterial infections. When MYCIN is used in its intended manner it scores better than medical students or interns or practicing physicians and on a par with experts in bacterial diseases when the latter are asked to perform in the same way. However, MYCIN has not been put into production use, and the reasons given by experts in the area varied when I asked whether it would be appropriate to sell MYCIN cassettes to doctors wanting to put it on their microcomputers. Some said it would be okay if there were a means of keeping MYCIN's data base current with new discoveries in the field, i.e., with new tests, new theories, new diagnoses, and new antibiotics. For example, MYCIN would have to be told about Legionnaire's disease and the associated *Legionnella* bacteria which became understood only after MYCIN was finished. (MYCIN is very stubborn about new bacteria, and simply replies "unrecognized response.")

Others say that MYCIN is not even close to usable except experimentally, because it does not know its own limitations. I suppose this is partly a question of whether the doctor using MYCIN is trusted to understand the documentation about its limitations. Programmers always develop the idea that the users of their programs are idiots, so the opinion that doctors are not smart enough not to be misled by MYCIN's limitations may be at least partly a consequence of this ideology.

An example of MYCIN not knowing its limitations can be excited by telling MYCIN that the patient has *Cholerae vibrio* in his intestines. MYCIN will cheerfully recommend two weeks of tetracycline and nothing else. Presumably this would indeed kill the bacteria, but most likely the patient will be dead of cholera long before that. However, the physician will presumably know that the diarrhea has to be treated and look elsewhere for how to do it.

On the other hand it may be really true that some measure of common sense is required for usefulness even in this narrow domain. We will list some areas of commonsense knowledge and reasoning ability and also apply the criteria to MYCIN and other hypothetical programs operating in MYCIN's domain.

WHAT IS COMMON SENSE?

Understanding commonsense capability is now a hot area of research in artificial intelligence, but there is not yet any consensus. We will try to divide commonsense capability into commonsense knowledge and commonsense reasoning, but even this cannot be made firm. Namely, what one man builds as a reasoning method into his program, another can express as a fact using a richer ontology. However, the latter can have problems in handling in a good way the generality he has introduced.

COMMONSENSE KNOWLEDGE

We shall discuss various areas of commonsense knowledge.

1. The most salient commonsense knowledge concerns situations that change in time as a result of events. The most important events are actions, and for a program to plan intelligently, it must be able to determine the effects of its own actions.

Consider the MYCIN domain as an example. The situation with which Mycin deals includes the doctor, the patient, and the illness. Since MYCIN's actions are advice to the doctor, full planning would have to include information about the effects of MYCIN's output on what the doctor will do. Since MYCIN does not know about the doctor, it might plan the effects of the course of treatment on the patient. However, it does not do this either. Its rules give the recommended treatment as a function of the information elicited about the patient, but MYCIN makes no prognosis of the effects of the treatment. Of course, the doctors who provided the information built into MYCIN considered the effects of the treatments.

Ignoring prognosis is possible because of the specific narrow domain in which MYCIN operates. Suppose, for example, a certain antibiotic had the precondition for its usefulness that the patient not have a fever. Then MYCIN might have to make a plan for getting rid of the patient's fever and verifying that it was gone as a part of the plan for using the antibiotic. In other domains, expert systems and other AI programs have to make plans, but MYCIN does not. Perhaps if I knew more about bacterial diseases, I would conclude that their treatment sometimes really does require planning and that lack of planning ability limits MYCIN's utility.

The fact that MYCIN does not give a prognosis is certainly a limitation. For example, MYCIN cannot be asked on behalf of the patient or the administration of the hospital when the patient is likely to be ready to go home. The doctor who uses MYCIN must do that part of the work himself. Moreover, MYCIN cannot answer a question about a hypothetical treatment, e.g., What will happen if I give this patient penicillin? or even What bad things might happen if I give this patient penicillin?

2. Various formalisms are used in artificial intelligence for representing facts about the effects of actions and other events. However, all systems that I know about give the effects of an event in a situation by describing a new situation that results from the event. This is often enough, but it does not cover the important case of concurrent events and actions. For example, if a patient has cholera, while the antibiotic is killing the cholera bacteria, the damage to the patient's intestines is causing a loss of fluids that is likely to be fatal. Inventing a formalism that will conveniently express people's commonsense knowledge about concurrent events is a major unsolved problem of AI.

3. The world is extended in space and is occupied by objects that change their positions and are sometimes created and destroyed. The commonsense facts about this are difficult to express but are probably not important in the MYCIN example. A major difficulty is in handling the kind of partial knowledge people ordinarily have. I can see part of the front of a person in the audience, and my idea of his shape uses this information to approximate his total shape. Thus I do not expect him to stick out two feet in back even though I cannot see that he does not. However, my idea of the shape of his back is less definite than that of the parts I can see.

4. The ability to represent and use knowledge about knowledge is often required for intelligent behavior. What airline flights there are to Singapore are recorded in the issue of the International Airline Guide current for the proposed flight day. Travel agents know how to book airline flights and can compute what they cost. An advanced MYCIN might need to reason that Dr. Smith knows about cholera, because he is a specialist in tropical medicine.

5. A program that must cooperate or compete with people or other programs must be able to represent information about their knowledge, beliefs, goals, likes and dislikes, intentions, and abilities. An advanced MYCIN might need to know that a patient will not take a bad-tasting medicine unless he is convinced of its necessity.

6. Common sense includes much knowledge whose domain overlaps that of the exact sciences but differs from it epistemologically. For example, if I knock over the glass of water on the podium, everyone knows that the glass will break and the water will spill. Everyone knows that this will take a fraction of a second and that the water will not splash even 10 feet. However, this information is not obtained by using the formula for a falling body or the Navier-Stokes equations governing fluid flow. We do not have the input data for the equations, most of us do not know them, and we could not integrate them fast enough to decide whether to jump out of the way. This commonsense physics is contiguous with scientific physics. In fact scientific physics is imbedded in commonsense physics, because it is commonsense physics that tells us what the equation $s = \frac{1}{2} g t^2$ means. If MYCIN were extended to be a robot physician it would have to know commonsense physics and maybe also some scientific physics.

It is doubtful that the facts of the commonsense world can be represented adequately by production rules. Consider the fact that when two objects collide they often make a noise. This fact can be used to make a noise, to avoid making a noise, to explain a noise, or to explain the absence of a noise. It can also be used in specific situations involving a noise but also to understand general phenomena, e.g., should an intruder step on the gravel, the dog will hear it and bark. A production rule embodies a fact only as part of a specific procedure. Typically they match facts about specific objects, e.g., a specific bacterium, against a general rule and get a new fact about those objects.

Much present AI research concerns how to represent facts in ways that permit them to be used for a wide variety of purposes.

Commonsense Reasoning

Our ability to use commonsense knowledge depends on being able to do commonsense reasoning.

Much artificial intelligence inference is not designed to use directly the rules of inference of any of the well-known systems of mathematical logic. There is often no clear separation in the program between determining what inferences are correct and the strategy for finding the inferences required to solve the problem at hand. Nevertheless, the logical system usually corresponds to a subset of first-order logic. Systems provide for inferring a fact about one or two particular objects from other facts about these objects and a general rule containing variables. Most expert systems, including MYCIN, never infer general statements, i.e., quantified formulas.

Human reasoning also involves obtaining facts by observation of the world, and computer programs also do this. Robert Filman did an interesting thesis on observation in a chess world where many facts that could be obtained by deduction are in fact obtained by observation. MYCIN does not require this, but our hypothetical robot physician would have to draw conclusions from a patient's appearance, and computer vision is not ready for it.

An important new development in AI (since the middle 1970s) is the formalization of nonmonotonic reasoning.

Deductive reasoning in mathematical logic has the following property, called monotonicity by analogy with similar mathematical concepts. Suppose we have a set of assumptions from which follow certain conclusions. Now suppose we add additional assumptions. There may be some new conclusions, but every sentence that was a deductive consequence of the original hypotheses is still a consequence of the enlarged set.

Ordinary human reasoning does not share this monotonicity property. If you know that I have a car, you may conclude that it is a good idea to ask me for a ride. If you then learn that my car is being fixed (which does not contradict what you knew before), you no longer conclude that you can get a ride. If you now learn that the car will be out in half an hour you reverse yourself again.

Several AI researchers, for example Marvin Minsky, have pointed out that intelligent computer programs will have to reason nonmonotonically.[5] Some concluded that therefore logic is not an appropriate formalism.

However, it has turned out that deduction in mathematical logic can be supplemented by additional modes of nonmonotonic reasoning, which are just as formal as deduction and just as susceptible to mathematical study and computer implementation. Formalized nonmonotonic reasoning turns out to give certain rules of conjecture rather than rules of inference—their conclusions are appropriate, but may be disconfirmed when more facts are obtained. One such method is *circumscription*, described in Reference 6.

A mathematical description of circumscription is beyond the scope of this lecture, but the general idea is straightforward. We have a property applicable to objects or a relation applicable to pairs or triplets, etc., of objects. This property or relation is constrained by some sentences taken as assumptions, but there is still some freedom left. Circumscription further constrains the property or relation by requiring it to be true of a minimal set of objects.

As an example, consider representing the facts about whether an object can fly in a data base of commonsense knowledge. We could try to provide axioms that will determine whether each kind of object can fly, but this would make the data base very large. Circumscription allows us to express the assumption that only those objects can fly for which there is a positive statement about it. Thus there will be positive statements that birds and airplanes can fly and no statement that camels can fly. Since we do not include negative statements in the data base, we could provide for flying camels, if there were any, by adding statements without removing existing statements. This much is often done by a simpler method—the *closed world assumption* discussed by Raymond Reiter. However, we also have exceptions to the general statement that birds can fly. For example, penguins, ostriches, and birds with certain feathers removed cannot fly. Moreover, more exceptions may be found and even exceptions to the exceptions. Circumscription allows us to make the known exceptions and to provide for additional exceptions to be added later—again without changing existing statements.

Nonmonotonic reasoning also seems to be involved in human communication. Suppose I hire you to build me a bird cage, and you build it without a top, and I refuse to pay on the grounds that my bird might fly away. A judge will side with me. On the other hand suppose you build it with a top, and I refuse to pay full price on the grounds that my bird is a penguin, and the top is a waste. Unless I told you that my bird could not fly, the judge will side with you. We can therefore regard it as a communication convention that if a bird can fly the fact need not be mentioned, but if the bird cannot fly and it is relevant, then the fact must be mentioned.

REFERENCES

1. McCARTHY, J. 1960. Programs with common sense. *In* Proceedings of the Teddington Conference on the Mechanization of Thought Processes. Her Majesty's Stationery Office. London, England.
2. McCARTHY, J. & P. J. HAYES. 1969. Some philosophical problems from the standpoint of artificial intelligence. *In* Machine Intelligence 4. D. Michie, Ed.: 463–502. American Elsevier. New York, N.Y.
3. SHORTLIFFE, E. H. 1976. Computer-Based Medical Consultations: MYCIN. American Elsevier. New York, N.Y.
4. DAVIS, R., B. BUCHANAN & E. SHORTLIFFE. 1977. Production rules as a representation for a knowledge-based consultation program. Artif. Intell. **8**(1): 15–45.
5. MINSKY, M. 1974. A Framework for Representing Knowledge. MIT Artif. Intell. Memo 252.
6. McCARTHY, J. 1980. Circumscription—a form of non-monotonic reasoning. Artif. Intell. **13**(1,2): 27–39.

DISCUSSION OF THE PAPER

QUESTION: You said the programs need common sense, but that's like saying, If I could fly I wouldn't have to pay Eastern Airlines $44 to haul me up here from Washington. So if the programs indeed need common sense, how do we go about it? Isn't that the point of the argument?

J. McCARTHY: I could have made this a defensive talk about artificial intelligence, but I chose to emphasize the problems that have been identified rather than the progress that has been made in solving them. Let me remind you that I have argued that the need for common sense is not a truism. Many useful things can be done without it, e.g., MYCIN and also chess programs.

QUESTION: There seemed to be a strong element in your talk about common sense, and even humans developing it, emphasizing an experiential component—particularly when you were giving your example of dropping a glass of water. I'm wondering whether the development of these programs is going to take similar amounts of time. Are you going to have to have them go through the sets of experiences and be evaluated? Is there work going on in terms of speeding up the process or is it going to take 20 years for a program from the time you've put in its initial state to work up to where it has a decent amount of common sense?

J. MCCARTHY: Consider your 20 years. If anyone had known in 1963 how to make a program learn from its experience to do what a human does after 20 years, they might have done it, and it might be pretty smart by now. Already in 1958 there had been work on programs that learn from experience. However, all they could learn was to set optimal values of numerical parameters in the program, and they were quite limited in their ability to do that. Arthur Samuel's checker program learned optimal values for its parameter, but the problem was that certain kinds of desired behavior did not correspond to any setting of the parameters, because they depended on the recognition of a certain kind of strategic situation. Thus the first prerequisite for a program to be able to learn something is that it be able to represent internally the desired modification of behavior. Simple changes in behavior must have simple representations. Turing's universality theory convinces us that arbitrary behaviors can be represented, but they don't tell us how to represent them in such a way that a small change in behavior is a small change in representation. Present methods of changing programs amount to education by brain surgery.

QUESTION: I would ask you a question about programs needing common sense in a slightly different way, and I want to use the MYCIN program as an example.

There are three actors there—the program, the physician, and the patient. Taking as a criterion the safety of the patient, I submit that you really need at least two of these three actors to have common sense.

For example, if (and sometimes this is the case) one only were sufficient, it would have to be the patient because if the program didn't use common sense and the physician didn't use common sense, the patient would have to have common sense and just leave. But usually, if the program had common sense built in and the physician had common sense but the patient didn't, it really might not matter because the patient would do what he or she wants to do anyway.

Let me take another possibility. If only the program has common sense and neither the physician nor the patient has common sense, then in the long run the program also will not use the common sense. What I want to say is that these issues of common sense must be looked at in this kind of frame of reference.

J. McCARTHY: In the use of MYCIN, the physician is supposed to supply the common sense. The question is whether the program must also have common sense, and I would say that the answer is not clear in the MYCIN case. Purely computational programs don't require common sense, and none of the present chess programs have any. On the other hand, it seems clear that many other kinds of programs require common sense to be useful at all.

Panel Discussion

Has Artificial Intelligence Research Illuminated Human Thinking?

Moderator: HEINZ R. PAGELS

Panel Members: HUBERT L. DREYFUS, JOHN McCARTHY,
MARVIN L. MINSKY, SEYMOUR PAPERT, AND JOHN SEARLE

H. R. PAGELS (*The New York Academy of Sciences, New York, N.Y.*):
A few years ago, I asked a colleague of mine at Harvard what was the
future of artificial intelligence. He simply said: "Heinz, if you took the
smartest two dozen people of the eleventh century and put them in a
room together and instructed them to put together a model of the physical
universe, there's no question that they would come out with something
that would be absolutely brilliant. But it would be all wrong, because the
concepts were not to be invented until several centuries in the future.
That's similar to the case for the AI proponents—they are very smart
people, but the right concepts are not yet available."

People who work in artificial intelligence research have to contend
with critics of that kind, and I'm sure we'll hear a good deal about that. I
once asked Marvin Minsky why this field of study was ever called
artificial intelligence. I said, "Why didn't you call it something more
general, like cognitive science?" And Marvin responded: "If we ever
called it anything other than artificial intelligence, we wouldn't have
gotten into the universities. Now that we're in, and the philosophers and
the psychologists know that we're the enemy, it's too late."

Some of the topics we're going to discuss here revolve around the
issue of consciousness. There is a problem with regard to consciousness
which can be stated very simply. I know that I'm conscious. I'm a
thinking, experiencing being. I can close my eyes and think; I can dream;
I know that I'm conscious. But as philosophers have shown in debate over
the centuries, there's absolutely no way that I can prove to you that I am a
conscious being. You wouldn't know, for example, that I wasn't a
mindless machine put together molecule by molecule by an extraterres-
trial civilization and sent here to confound you. Even if you knew what
was going on in every single neuron in my brain, you could not prove that
I was a conscious being.

Some people on this panel may contest that, but the real question is,
Can we determine whether or not machines are conscious? Many
decades ago Alan Turing addressed that question and came up with the
famous Turing test, a purely behavioral model, and I'm sure some of the
panelists here will allude to that test.

I want to emphasize that artificial intelligence does not have to do
with the technology—with the microchips and the miracles being per-

formed by electronics engineers. Artificial intelligence as viewed by its proponents is really a philosophy, almost "the world view." And in many ways, it's competing with other, older world views and confronting philosophical problems that have been with us for a long time.

I want to point out that the speakers are not divided into two classes—those in favor of AI and those in opposition. The individuals who are here all differ among themselves. At this point each of our panelists will very briefly describe his position and outlook on artificial intelligence and the question before us: "Has AI research illuminated human thinking?" And then we will engage in an open discussion. Professor Minsky will begin.

M. MINSKY (*Artificial Intelligence Laboratory, Massachusetts Institute of Technology, Cambridge, Mass.*): I believe the question that we're trying to discuss is, If you made a machine that looks as if it thinks, would it really think? And there are two parts to that. There's the "if"—Can you make a machine that appears to be intelligent? We don't know the answer to that of course, but I think it will be yes, and that after a long time, when we solve such problems as commonsense reasoning and representation of knowledge, the computer programs and machines that are built according to those principles will get smarter and smarter and more lifelike in some ways.

Then there are other issues about how similar the machines will be to humans and how much they'll resemble us. There's another question yet, which is, What does it feel like inside them? These issues are complicated. For example, one of the things that I've worked on recently is the theory of jokes and humor. Many people will say they can see how you could make a machine intelligent, but not how you could make it understand humor or fear. Well, those people are wrong. They can't see how to make a machine intelligent, yet they think somehow that it's easy and that it's the emotional aspects that are difficult. This just isn't true; it's a major superstition of our culture that feeling an emotion is very deep and hard and difficult to understand, whereas intellect—how we get ideas, how we think—is easy to understand. In that perspective, many of the issues that we're about to discuss here will seem silly to me because they're missing the point of what's hard.

Say, somebody tells you he just got an idea. He could build a car with eight wheels and it would go over bumps easier. Instead of criticizing the idea, suppose you ask him how he got that idea. What will he say? He might say it just popped into his head or he just thought of it, or it came to him. Isn't that shocking? Yet if he says he feels bad and you ask him why, then he'll tell you something pretty interesting and simple—"Well this room I went into reminded me of the one that my sick friend was in." He'll tell you why he felt. I believe that's why Freud worked on emotions, not because he thought they were deeper, but because he thought they were shallower.

So everybody's got it wrong. It seems to me that we understand emotions rather well. But when it comes to ideas, my image is that people see themselves living in a world of thoughts with a brain that has an almost impermeable shield around it, but that every now and then some idea leaks through and gets in—and that's about it. The problem with these people who say that you could make a machine think but it wouldn't really feel like us is that they don't seem to have thought about the real problem. I'll end with that.

S. PAPERT (*Artificial Intelligence Laboratory, Massachusetts Institute of Technology, Cambridge, Mass.*): The question that I would like to talk about is, Has what's been done in artificial intelligence led to deeper understanding of better ways to think about human intelligence? And by human intelligence I mean everything that happens in the human mind, in the broad sense to include jokes and feelings as much as reasoning.

First, I want to make the distinction that the question of whether artificial intelligence has illuminated human intelligence is very different from the question of how intelligent machines really are or ever will be, or whether they work the same as people do, and so on. It's quite clear, for example, that one way to illuminate human intelligence is by contrast. In a sense it could well be that the more machines think in different ways from people, the more valuable they will be as means of illuminating our understanding of ourselves. To understand something, you want to know what else it's like, but you also want to know what else it's different from.

Clearly, until very recently, attempts to understand the human mind in terms of what it's different from have been of two types: one is by comparison with animals, and the other by comparison with various mythical, invented beings such as gods and other mythical creatures.

We now have a third point of comparison, namely, computers. And I do think that, at the very least, we have been led to be much more precise in a lot of the thinking about our own minds by having this new point of comparison, by being able to discuss whether we are like or unlike these machines, irrespective of whether the answer is yes or no.

I would push that a little further and say that one of the effects of artificial intelligence has been to introduce more structure into our thinking about human thinking. Because if you think of thinking only as one kind of thing, you can't get your teeth into very much. To be specific, what I think is probably the best-developed, detailed attempt to make a theory of human thinking that actually matches the way people think is Newell and Simon's attempts to simulate the solving of certain puzzles and the playing of chess. Well is this a good model of how people think?

There's a terrible pun in that. I believe it's pretty obvious what the answer is, that sometimes people think like Newell and Simon describe and sometimes, most often, not. I don't believe I'm thinking like that now, for example. But the fact that they have described this particular model of one particular way of thinking in a lot of detail means I can talk in a much more dense and technical way about other ways of thinking and so put more structure into comparative ways of thinking. This is the most fruitful way in which AI has illuminated human intelligence, by enabling us to be more specific about different ways in which the mind might work. Before AI, there was very little structured classification of ways of thinking.

I would like to push that in another direction. I take it that the question Has artificial intelligence illuminated the human intelligence? means Has AI acted as a searchlight for psychologists or other people to understand better how human intelligence works? But you could twist those same words around and ask whether it has made human intelligence work any better than it did before. I believe that this might be as much of a contribution of artificial intelligence to the world as the making of robots. I've seen some examples of this working with children. Giving children very simple AI models—extremely simple models of how the thought process works in certain situations—enables them to think more clearly about their own thinking and so be more critical about themselves and so be more constructive in taking the next step further. I choose and emphasize this example of children because I think it pushes to an extreme a remark I made at the beginning. These models of thinking that we give to these children have no pretention to be universal and complete models of how the mind works. They are only a little theoretical model that captures enough of what's happening there for you to think about it.

Now ultimately all theoretical models are of that sort. By simplifying reality and pulling out some aspect of it that you really want to think about now, they enable you to think better about reality. And I do think that artificial intelligence has done this quite irrespective of whether we think that present machines are suitable models for the whole human intelligence (which they certainly aren't), or even of whether we think they ever will be. That's the main point I wanted to make to take some sort of position for discussion.

I would now like to make a brief comment on a point raised by Marvin Minsky about whether feelings are harder to understand than thinking. I'd like to make two remarks about that. The first is that, when he expressed such an unpopular position, it reminded me that we are all very inhibited and often embarrassed about expressing what we really think about our own minds and what goes on in them. I believe this very much colors discussion on these issues and that, very likely, the attempt to make explicit models breaks down these inhibitions. This is another way in which AI is helping, by provoking us to let people see more into how we think and lay it out more than we used to.

The second is that I don't think emotions are harder to understand than ideas are, but consider the following. If you made a machine that simulated intelligence, I think it's obvious that we could argue about whether it is intelligent. And I think that most people would go along with the assumption that simulated intelligence is at least some kind of intelligence. I'm going to contrast this with the question that simulated feelings are in a very different state, that is, whereas most people would go along with the statement that simulated thinking is thinking, simulated reason is reason, most people would have serious doubts about whether to go along with the statement that simulated feelings are feelings. And yet I think this difference, which is a matter of house psychology, has very little to do with the substance of what machines can do and what they can't do.

J. McCarthy (*Department of Computer Science, Stanford University, Stanford Calif.*): The question is whether AI has illuminated human intelligence, and I think the answer is obviously yes. AI and psychology influenced by AI are responsible for destroying behaviorism as a serious approach to psychology and turning psychologists toward information processing models. Presumably a psychologist would be more competent than an AI person to speak about that influence.

Now I want to deal with the issue about whether a machine really thinks or believes. This is an elaboration of a point I made in my paper. Namely, we will find it necessary to use mentalistic terminology in describing what we know about machines. Of course, if we understand how a thermostat works, we don't have to adopt the mentalistic stance of saying that the thermostat thinks the room is too warm.

Indeed I picked the thermostat example precisely because we can understand it both ways—mechanistically and mentalistically. Just because we can understand its mechanism is not a reason to bar the use of mentalistic terms. There's an illuminating analogy with the number system and its historical development. Suppose someone said that he didn't think that one is a number, arguing that if you have only one thing you don't have to count. Indeed most languages treat one differently from the other numbers. Some treat two differently also, and in Russian numbers up to four take the genitive case. The introduction of zero to the number system is even more recent, and I believe it was controversial. The justification is that the number system as a system makes more sense if both zero and one are included. Likewise, a systematic treatment of belief by machines will have to start with the easy cases.

A more complex case arises when we say that a dog wants to go out. We cannot practically reduce this to a propensity to behave in a certain way, because we may not know what the dog will do to further this desire. It may scratch the door or yelp or whatever. Secondly, we may not know the evidence that the dog wants to go out. Therefore, the fact that the dog wants to go out is best treated as primary.

Another useful idea comes from Dan Dennett—the notion of the "design stance." Suppose we are designing a dog as an artificial intelligence. It will be convenient to design in the desire to go out as a possible state. We have a variety of choices as to what will cause this state and what our dog will do to realize the desire. In designing computer systems, we will also find this notion of *wanting* a useful intermediate point.

As far as I can see, the purely intellectual terms are easier to handle for machines than are some of the emotional terms. "It believes" is easier than "it hopes," which is easier than "it likes me" or "it doesn't like me." And as to whether the machine is suffering, all I can say is that it complains a lot.

When we ask whether it is conscious, there are a lot of criteria for saying no. No, because it doesn't know about its physical body. No, it doesn't even refer to itself. On the other hand it might claim to be alienated, but it has just read Marcuse. Well that's how most people who claim to be alienated come to claim it. It's something they read about.

H. L. DREYFUS (*Department of Philosophy, University of California, Berkeley, Calif.*): I want to respond to both these questions: Where are we in artificial intelligence? and What has the work in artificial intelligence taught us about thinking? I agree with Seymour Papert that it has taught us a lot, if in no other way than by contrast.

But first, I want to catch up on what was happening this morning, because I want to take off from what we heard about expert systems. As Marvin Minsky said, expert systems only work in microworlds. Microworlds have bracketed off all of commonsense knowledge. I think that's a very important remark to enable us to see where the interesting and essential problems arise for an attempt to understand the mind on an information processing or computer model.

Now the successful expert systems are in a way like games. They operate in a circumscribed domain where what's relevant or not relevant has been settled before the game starts. The easiest way to see that is to think about a game like chess, which is a microworld. It's always relevant where each piece is placed, what kind of piece it is (whether it's a rook or a bishop), and whether it's white or black. It's never relevant how heavy the piece is, what temperature it is, whether it's fancy, carved, or plain, whether it's in the middle of the square or on the side, whether it's clean or dirty, etc. In the same way, DENDRAL, the program that is an expert in spectrograph analysis, deals only with spectral lines—a problem that relates to human beings can never arise. That is a completely circumscribed microworld or domain. Even a program like MYCIN, which looks like it deals with human beings, deals specifically only with objective scores on blood tests. It doesn't connect up with everyday human activity.

When you do connect up with everyday human activity, when you try to make an expert system that captures the expertise of ordinary people, then you get out of microworlds and into the problem of what's called commonsense knowledge. Commonsense knowledge deals not only with facts about the everyday world such as the physics of the everyday world, but also with exceptions—the *ceteris paribus* rules of the everyday world. That's a fancy way of saying rules that say, "everything else being equal, then such and such." Marvin Minsky gave a good example of that—as a rule, birds are animals that can fly; and when people talk about birds, you can assume that they're talking about birds that fly. But if their wings are broken, as Minsky said, or if they are toys, or even if they're penguins, then birds can't fly.

A way to connect this with the talk this morning about expert systems is to use as an example the problems that arise when you try to automate a travel agent. The travel agent is an interesting area in which the microworld, or isolated domain, where expert systems have worked and will do important things shades over into the everyday world. You can give your automated travel agent lots of facts. You can tell it about airports, rates, and distances. You can also give it the kind of facts that expert travel agents know. Facts like, Don't try to go to another airline terminal when changing planes at an airport if you only have half an hour, etc.

But there's something else which is harder and so will give you an idea of what I mean by commonsense knowledge. If for instance you say to this automated travel agent, "I'd like a flight to San Francisco leaving at around 6:00." And it tells you that there's a flight leaving Kennedy at 6:30. Then you say, "No, I'd like something a little bit earlier." And it looks up its schedules and says, "There is a flight leaving at 6:29." Something has gone wrong: 6:29 is a little bit earlier than 6:30 alright, but it's not something any human being would want to know. The automated travel agent doesn't contain any knowledge of human temporality—what spans of time are important to human beings.

Now you might think that you could just fix that. But it's not so easy. You can't just give it a rule like "a little bit earlier means at least 15 minutes earlier," because that is a *ceteris paribus* rule, the kind of rule human beings could use if they were travel agents. But everything else often isn't equal. Sometimes you really do need a flight ten minutes earlier if it's a tight connection. And sometimes even an hour earlier might be okay, if you're flying to Australia for example. So what you need is some sense of the background of everyday needs and experience that human beings bring to the question, Do you have something a little bit earlier? And that means you not only have to put into your expert system all the facts about airports and airplanes, but something like the facts about what it is to be a human being. Because a computer hasn't the slightest idea of what it is to be a human being. You have to tell it everything that there is to know about human beings if it's going to have the kind of commonsense background knowledge that human beings have.

Now of course, it won't need to know *everything* before it gets pretty good. Indeed, if you really tried to tell it everything, it would be an infinite task. There's a general agreement between John McCarthy and Marvin Minsky that it might take, say, 300 years before you get common-sense knowledge into a machine. What they mean is that in 300 years we might get enough of the facts about human beings into the machine so it will begin to be able to behave intelligently, and we could then get expert systems out of microworlds into the real world and start capturing the kind of expertise that travel agents and bankers and literary agents have, which is always an expertise that opens out into the rest of human common sense.

That's the first half of what I have to say. Now I want to talk about how human thinking differs from computer thinking, because the question before this panel comes down to, How do humans deal with common sense and is their way different from the way computers would deal with common sense?

My view is that if commonsense understanding were just knowledge, then programming it would only be an infinite task and we could get on with it and maybe we'd be somewhere with it in 300 years. But I think commonsense understanding isn't a kind of knowledge at all. And that's where I want to agree with Seymour Papert that we can learn a lot by contrasting computer "thinking" and human thinking. What we will learn by contrast is that people don't have a lot of facts and rules in their minds for understanding the everyday world. They've got a kind of skill for coping with things. Therefore, as Minsky says, the right action usually just pops into their head. They're able to see what the issues are and to see what's relevant in a situation.

This ability that people have, to see what's relevant and to have the right thing pop into their head, presupposes something like knowing what matters. But I don't think computers as we now understand them have anything like mattering or concern. It also requires having images and having memories since it involves seeing the current situation as resembling earlier situations, where resembling is a tricky notion because resembling doesn't mean identical with respect to any particular features, which is the way machines always have to analyze resemblance, but simply overall similarity.

Since human intelligence is not a matter of knowledge but a matter of understanding, AI is not even moving in the right dimension. To work at the commonsense knowledge problem is like trying to get to the moon by climbing higher and higher in a tree. You're just not going to get there that way although you are getting a little bit closer.

Now we don't need commonsense *knowledge* to be intelligent and know what matters to our kind of being because we *are* it. We don't need to *know* about bodies because we *are* bodies, and the same for emotions and situations. That is, we *are* our bodies, we *have* emotions, and we're in situations whereas computers are outside and have to be given knowledge of all that. That, I think, poses an insurmountable problem for AI as it's now practiced and lets us see how our kind of thinking is totally different from the computer's kind of thinking.

J. SEARLE (*Department of Philosophy, University of California, Berkeley, Calif.*): Well I'm distressed to find that I agree with a lot that everybody said. However, I'm going to try to state some positions where I disagree with what I take to be certain common tendencies in artificial intelligence.

I want to remark that the question we're supposed to be talking about got subtly rewritten. It says, Does AI illuminate human thinking? At some level, that means the kind of stuff that's going on in us now. Not all of our thinking is conscious, of course, but some is and some of it's unconscious. I want to focus a little bit on the question of what sorts of significance we should attach to artificial intelligence research into thought processes, conscious and unconscious.

In doing that, it seems to me we ought to make some distinctions. The computer is a terrific tool and there's no question but that it's going to be a useful tool in studying human beings and human thought processes just as it's a terrific tool in studying fires or patterns of crime or the marginal propensity to consume or all sorts of other things. But when you read the AI literature, you discover something amazing. There are a lot of people who don't think we can just use the computer to study understanding the way we can use the computer to study five-alarm fires and big rain storms in California. Rather, it turns out that they think the appropriately programmed computer literally does think in exactly the same sense that you and I think—that it literally has the kind of mental processes that you and I are having. So I want to distinguish what I call "weak AI," which is the view that says, "Sure, use the computer; it's a terrific tool," from a much stronger view that says: "It isn't just that we're simulating thinking or studying thinking. Our appropriately programmed computers with the right inputs and outputs will literally have thought processes, conscious and otherwise, in the same sense that you and I do." I call this view "strong AI."

Now I like that thesis because it's clear that we know exactly what somebody's saying when he says, "Look, my machine or the machine we're going to eventually build has thought processes in exactly the same sense that you and I have thought processes." It's clear, and it is false, and it is demonstrably false. I'm going to take a couple of minutes to demonstrate its falsity, so there won't be any illusion that we're all one big community of agreement.

The way I like to demonstrate the falsity of strong AI is to get you to imagine yourself instantiating a computer program for a certain kind of thought process. It's very important in these discussions to take the first-person point of view, to ask, What would it be like for me? Because that's what we know of being conscious and having thought processes. So imagine that there's a computer program for understanding Chinese, so that if you punch a question in Chinese into the computer, the computer can give out the right sort of answer. It has the right sort of data base and the right kind of program so that it can process questions in Chinese and give the right answers.

Now imagine that you are the computer. You're locked in a room and a lot of Chinese symbols are in the room together with a whole lot of rule books for shuffling these Chinese symbols around. This will only work if you don't know Chinese. Like me; I don't know a word of Chinese. I don't know what any of these symbols mean. So there I am in the room shuffling these symbols around. The questions come in. I look up what I'm supposed to do when I get a squiggle squiggle sign and I go and match it with a squaggle squaggle sign. That is called a computational process over a purely formally specified element. These are what Simon and Newell called physical symbols; and I am now acting as a physical symbol system.

Let's suppose these guys get good at writing the programs. I get good at shuffling the symbols. The questions come in, and I give out the right answers. One guy in responding to me said, "Suppose one of the questions is 'Do you understand Chinese?' " And I shuffle around—now I don't know what any of these symbols mean—and put out the symbol that says: "You bet I understand Chinese. And how! What could be more obvious? Why do you keep asking me these dumb questions?" What I want to say is that it's quite obvious, once you look at it from the first-person point of view, that I don't understand a word of Chinese and I wouldn't learn Chinese from instantiating the Chinese understanding program.

Why not? What is it that I have in English that the computer doesn't have in Chinese? Notice that if I don't understand Chinese in that story, then neither does any other computer program understand Chinese, because the program hasn't got anything that I haven't got in the story. What is it that I've got for English that the computer program doesn't have? Well I like commonsense answers. The difference is that in English, I know the meanings of the words, and in Chinese, I don't know the meanings of the words—all I've got is a set of formal symbols with a set of computational rules for manipulating the formal symbols.

The point of the parable about the Chinese room is to reveal a deep point about the character of artificial intelligence research and human thinking. This is the point I want to leave you with, that is, from syntax alone you can't get semantics. From purely formal, symbolic operations, you can't get the mental content. So what I'm trying to remind you of with this story about the Chinese room is something we know independently anyway, namely, what the computer has as a computer is a purely formal level of operation. That's its great appeal. The same program can be put in a complete variety of different kinds of substances, in different kinds of hardware. But as far as we know anything about how the real world works, the world in which we live, our mental states have to be something much more than just a set of syntactical processes because we actually do have thoughts and feelings. We actually have mental contents.

Why is it that the computer doesn't have those in the sense that we do? Let's take the case of thirst, because I'm now thirsty. As far as we know anything about it, thirst is produced in the hypothalamus by the action of angiotensin, which is synthesized by the secretions of renin from the kidneys. The point is that there's a quite specific story about how it works, and the result is that I now feel thirsty. Now think about what an AI program would do. An AI program would say, "Well look, there's just a set of formal syntactical processes; that's all there is to feeling thirsty." The way to see that this can't be right from what we know about how the world works is to imagine that we put the thirst feeling program in some completely different sort of system. Make your computer out of old beer cans, take millions of old cans and let them bang together to simulate the neuron firings of the synapses. Now notice what strong AI has to claim. It can't be just claiming: "Well who knows, maybe the system of beer cans is thirsty. I mean do we know so much about what it's like to be a beer can that we're sure that the beer can isn't thirsty?" That's not the claim. The claim has to be that the system *must* be thirsty because all there is to being thirsty is instantiating the formal computer program for being thirsty. I want to say that if we know anything to be false, we know that to be false. We know it quite independently of these discussions because we know that from a formal level of symbol manipulation by itself, you don't get semantic content.

Well why do people get in this bind? I mean why would anybody want to maintain these views? There are a couple of reasons. One is the constant adoption of a third-person point of view. We're always asked how would we know that some other system was thirsty or understood Chinese. That's the whole point of the Turing test—take the third-person point of view. But I want to tell you something about the mind. At some point, you'll only understand what a mind is and what it's like to have a mind by having one, by being one, by adopting the first-person point of view.

So there is this objectivizing tendency. It's part of modern life that we think all of knowledge must be described from a third-person point of view. But it's obviously false, if you think about the character of our mental states.

The second feature—and this is a kind of linguistic problem that gets into these discussions—is that we find it completely natural to use mental terms in a metaphorical extended sense. It seems to me we do that all the time. I mean I apply all kinds of mental vocabulary to my car, and sometimes not very sympathetic when the thing won't start. But we don't take it seriously in supposing that the car has mental states in the same way that we do. I want to say the same thing about my computer. I ascribe all kinds of mental properties to it. It's completely natural. The mistake is if we suppose that those are to be taken at face value.

But a third and really important reason, and I think the deepest reason, that leads to this mistake is oddly enough that in all of these discussions with all of their technical vocabulary, there is an old-style philosophical mistake that goes back to the seventeenth century—it goes back to Descartes, and frankly it goes back to Plato. This is the mistake—it is the refusal to think that the mind is just a biological phenomenon like any other. That is, in all of these discussions you get the idea that intelligence is something very abstract, that it can't be just a fact of biology like digestion, or the secretion of bile, or mitosis or meiosis.

I want to say that it is a kind of contempt for biology or a willingness to ignore the obvious facts of biology that leads to what is essentially the dualist view that mental states and minds are just programs.

M. L. MINSKY: I'd like to say a couple of words about the things Dr. Searle said. This consciousness thing is a very complicated business. And Searle is imagining a machine that looks up rules and executes them, and he's saying, "Well how would it feel?" But I think he's confusing what's going on in the process with what somebody else might feel when he's looking at it. Of course, if you look at somebody's brain cells with the right instrument, you'll see the nervous impulses going around, and you can say it's just adding and subtracting or whatever it's doing with those electric currents. To think that you know what it feels like to be a typewriter and that if you were a typewriter, you wouldn't feel anything, and to assume from that that if you were a machine a billion times as complex as a typewriter, you wouldn't feel anything is an extraordinary extrapolation. It seems to me this is very similar to his remarks at the end about consciousness and digestion being biological. Everybody knows that there's no vital mystery to digestion if you just know how the enzymes work. There isn't, in a certain reductionist sense, any such thing as digestion.

Now you might say that I'm missing the point because that would mean there isn't any such thing as consciousness. But my complaint is that the people who think there is such a thing as consciousness are trying to simplify it so much. Suppose I ask myself if I was aware four seconds ago of saying the word consciousness. What is consciousness to me? What does it mean to be self-aware? Now think of that Chinese machine that interpreted and answered questions in Chinese without knowing it. Suppose I asked it the question in Chinese, "Were you aware that four seconds ago you translated the word kumquat into mandarin orange or some erroneous such thing?" The machine, if it said yes—and Searle has to grant it says yes because he's assuming that it did all of the things it needed to do to translate correctly—it certainly would have said, "Yes, I was conscious." What does it mean to say that? If I say that I was conscious of doing something a few minutes ago, that means that somewhere in my data processing, I must have made a pale copy of the state of the machine. So you see it's true that if the machine had no trace of its past state, like the old typewriters, then it can't answer questions about how it felt and it wouldn't mean anything to ask it such a question because you know that it's amnesic—every second is disconnected from the next, there's no trace. But if I translate a word and if I can say later, "Yes, I knew I did that," I could only answer that if I made little fuzzy copies. What I'm saying is that the mind is very complicated. When I say I and when Searle says first person, there's no such thing as first person. There are a lot of processes going on. If I ask how did I feel when I met so and so and an hour ago, I go back and I run these processes, but it's not that there was a way I felt. If you've read anything about the mind, you know that there are many parts of my mind, some of which I don't know about for years, some of which I know right away. And what do I mean by I? You see, I'm falling into the trap. There are five parts of the mind. This one has some copy of the state of that one a while ago, this of that, this of that. When you say first person, when you say I felt, a little piece of machinery inside of all this that's connected to the mouth and won't stop, is pretending that it knows what happened there. That it was conscious. That it could be responsible for the things that went on in all the other parts. Well this is all so absurd. A thing like saying a machine can't feel pain really gets you into very complicated issues. It's no use to say a syntactic process can't feel because syntax is in fact the technical word for describing what doesn't happen in a process.

S. PAPERT: One might have said that watches are definitionally made up of wheels turning, and something that doesn't have wheels turning isn't a watch. If one had a commitment to this point of view, obviously these digital things that many people are wearing would not be watches. They'd be simulations of watches. And they wouldn't keep time. They'd do something like seeming to keep time.

Obviously, machines think not in the same way exactly as people think. And obviously people are biological. And when we say Is it true that machines think? we're asking whether we would like to extend the notion of thinking to include what machines might do. That's the only meaningful sense of the question, Do machines think? Newton said the sun exerts a force on the earth. And one might have said, "No, forces are what you do with your muscles, it's biological," but we'd be missing the point. Newton was introducing a new technical concept of force. And AI, if it's going to be taken seriously, is introducing a new technical concept of thinking, one that is not the same as the concept of thinking that's existed since Aristotle and before.

So I've got to agree, of course, that surely machines don't think in exactly the same way as I do. I'm not sure Searle thinks in exactly the same way I do either, or whether any two people think in exactly the same way. But what is obvious to me is that machines don't think in exactly the same way as me or in exactly the same way as one another. And one would deliberately—in working with artificial intelligence—try to make machines think in very different ways so as to have a comparative study of the different ways that this sort of function that we're all interested in can operate.

So I think that Searle's conclusion is true, but I don't know what it's relevant to. Of course it might be that if you poke around in the artificial intelligence literature as he says, there really are some people who have said machines think in exactly the same way as people do. Maybe they meant it, maybe they didn't mean it. Maybe this was a slip of the tongue. Maybe they were philosophically naive. All this is rather irrelevant I think to any fundamental considerations about the nature of thinking and whether something that is shared by us and potential machines is a more coherent, more useful, more powerful notion than this pretechnical sense of thinking that's rooted in the biological.

H. R. PAGELS: Dr. Papert, I'm a little confused. Your remarks make a strong distinction between the kind of "thinking" that a computer might do and the kind of thinking that a human being does. You seem to suggest that these two kinds of thinking have nothing to do with one another. In other words, AI-type thinking has nothing to do with human thinking. But that was not the impression that I got from your earlier remarks.

S. PAPERT: Well let's take the example of Newton expanding the concept of force from someone pushing to something that the sun might do to the earth. He has extended the notion of force, he has changed it. To go from that to saying that his notion of force has nothing to do with what might happen when I push the table is absurd. I think that this is what the theory of intelligence is about, that we are constantly extending the theory or thinking, whether it's in the psychology lab or in the philosophy seminar or in making machines. We are constantly extending and defining our notion of thinking and making new notions of thinking—technical ones. It's not true to say they have nothing to do with the previous ones. So I don't think that there's anything in Searle's argument that could be construed as trying to prove that what happens in the machine has nothing to do with what happens in the person. What he has argued for—and I'm accepting this for the sake of argument—is that it's not exactly the same thing. And I think his argument depends essentially on the attempt to want it to be exactly the same thing.

H. R. PAGELS: So if I understand you, there is a more general idea of thinking which includes both machine thinking and human thinking.

S. PAPERT: And the theoretical enterprise is trying constantly to extend.

J. McCARTHY: I'd like to go back to the Chinese room. There is a confusion between the system consisting of the person and the person himself. I agree with Robert Wilensky who made the same point earlier. The system knows Chinese, but the person who is executing the system may not. This is analogous to an interpreter running in a computer, the interpreted program often has capabilities the interpreter does not. It's just that we don't have experience with systems in which a person carries out a mental process that has properties different from those of the person himself. We get the same confusion with computers. Someone asks me whether LISP can do calculus problems. No, LISP cannot do calculus, but some LISP programs can.

The example of thirst is different. A program that simulates thirst is not going to be thirsty. For example, there is no way to relieve it with real water.

Searle has said that the people in AI take the third-person view of mental qualities. That's correct. We do, and we'll claim that it's a virtue. He says we consider the problem of intelligence as distinct from biology. Yes, we hold that intelligence is something that can be dealt with abstractly just as computation can be discussed and dealt with abstractly. One can ask whether a computer calculates the sum of 3 and 5 to be 8 in the same sense as a human does. I suppose Searle would agree that "calculate" is being used in the same sense for both human and machine in this case.

Now there's the point Dreyfus made about it taking 300 years. I have been saying that human-level AI will take between 5 and 500 years. The problem isn't that it will take a long time to enter data into a computer. It is rather that conceptual advances are required before we can implement human-level artificial intelligence—just as conceptual advances were required beyond the situation in 1900 before we could have nuclear energy.

Pursuing the nuclear energy analogy, the question is whether the present AI situation corresponds to 1900 or to 1938 when Rutherford, the leading nuclear physicist, declared nuclear energy impossible. The situation of 1938 is interesting in that experiments exhibiting nuclear fission had already been done but had been misinterpreted. Perhaps someone has already done experimental research that, when properly interpreted, will make possible human-level AI. I would be very surprised. When we talk about future conceptual advances, we don't know where we stand at present.

Dreyfus made a point about a reservation machine not knowing whether 6:25 will do as a little earlier than 6:30. The program would have the same problem if it were making a reservation for a robot. Whether even a 6:29 reservation will do depends on circumstances. So the fact that the reservation is for humans isn't the problem.

Finally, let me defend Searle on one point. He was discussing whether a computer can think in the same sense as a human—not does it think in the same way. In my opinion the thermostat thinks the room is too warm in the same sense as a human might, and he would disagree. Likewise about whether the dog simulation wants to go out.

H. L. DREYFUS: I want to be very brief because I think there are two separate issues and the bulk of the questions have been directed at John Searle's issue. Let's distinguish the issues. That will help people be clear what's going on. There's the question of whether programmed computers of the sort that we now have with the sorts of programs that we now have could ever behave like human beings. And I want to say they can't. And then there's the question, Even if computers behaved exactly like human beings, would they be thinking? Would they be intelligent? Would they have meaningful mental states? Searle wants to grant the first point hypothetically, i.e., that programmed as at present, computers could be intelligent, and then to say even if they behave exactly like human beings, that still wouldn't tell us anything about thinking because such machines wouldn't be thinking.

To return to issue one, McCarthy brought up the conceptual advances required before we reach the level of commonsense artificial intelligence. I agree we need some breakthroughs, but it all hinges on what you mean by conceptual advances. I think we're not in the same position as we were with respect to atomic energy in 1900 or in 1938, but more like the alchemists were with respect to atomic energy. That is, it's not just a question of the right conceptual advances. We're not even in the right dimension. We're trying to use computers that have programs. And the programs operate using facts and rules stored in complicated data structures. I just think that that's not going to get us common sense because that's not the kind of knowledge that gives us common sense. It seems to me highly unlikely that we could ever cash what gives us common sense into enough knowledge to make a computer seem to have common sense.

The travel agent might have the same sort of problem I mentioned with Martians as with robots. Of course, if Martians were enough like us, the travel agent would not have the same problem, but if they lived 100 times faster, or died in a day like mayflies, then their concerns about a little earlier and a little later would be very different from ours. And so you have to understand how human beings live in time or how any other kind of creature lives in time to see what kind of problems it has and the best way to know how it experiences time is to be of the same species.

J. SEARLE: Can a machine think? Well I want to tell you that's a fairly tricky question. So let's slow down and go through it. There is a sense in which each of us is a machine. We're each a material system. We just have an awful lot of neurons up there. And in that sense, it seems to me the answer to the question is obvious—of course machines can think; we are thinking machines.

So maybe we're trying to ask another question. We're trying to ask the question, Could an artifact think? Could you make a thinking machine? But there again, I don't see any difficulty in principle. Suppose we got the billions of neurons with their axons and their dendrites and synaptic clefts, and neurotransmitters and all the rest of it. If you can duplicate the causes, then you can duplicate the effects. So that wasn't the question we're trying to ask.

Here's another version of the question—Could a digital computer think? We're getting closer now. Even that's a little bit tricky because we want to say just about any system has a level of description where you can describe it as a digital computer. You can describe it as instantiating a formal program. So in that sense, I suppose, all of our brains are digital computers, and in that sense a digital computer can think.

The question we're driving at is this—and that is really the heart of the matter—Could a system think solely by virtue of being a digital computer? That is to say, solely by virtue of instantiating the right program with the right inputs and the right outputs? And there the answer is no. And it has to be no for the reasons that I said earlier. Namely, the purely formal processes can't by themselves give you the content. The same formal processes can be instantiated in any number of different kinds of substances which have quite different biochemical features, most of which will simply be incapable of duplicating the powers of the brain.

There are two very simple axioms on which my whole argument rests. One, the brain causes mental states. And just as a slogan, "brains cause minds." If we know anything about the world, we know that much about how it works.

Two, formal processes by themselves are not sufficient for semantic or mental content. I put that in the slogan by saying "From syntax, you can't get semantics." I don't mean to confine it to linguistics. That's just a mnemonic for reminding us of the difference between the formal, the purely formal, and the content.

So the question we were trying to ask was, Could a system think solely by virtue of being a digital computer? And the answer to that question has to be no. But now we can make a derivation from these two axioms— number one, brains cause minds, and number two, from syntax alone, you don't get semantics. What follows is that the way the brain does it can't be by instantiating a computational program alone. It can't. When we explain how the brain produces mental states, we will not be able to do it entirely by the fact that the brain instantiates formal programs. And indeed, where we actually know something about the operations of the brain, we don't have to appeal to a formal or abstract level. What we do appeal to is quite specific biochemical facts about the operation of the brain as we appeal to quite specific biochemical facts about the operation of the digestion or the operation of the liver or the pancreas or anything else.

Now there are two other little points I want to take up. Throughout these discussions, we tend to think there must be some technical solution to this problem. If you watch the discussion, people will often say that we get so far with computers, but there's always that extra little bit we can't go. So they will say, "Can you program a computer that will fall in love, have a sense of humor, or whatever?" But I want to say that that really misses the point. The point is not that the digital computer doesn't get quite all the way to having a mind, it doesn't get started. It's not in that line of business.

You can always say, of course, "Well it's just an extended notion of thinking. Why not have a larger notion of thinking?" I have no objection to using words in an extended sense provided you make clear the extension. Now I want to say computers think and have thoughts and feelings and consciousness in the same extended sense of feelings, consciousness, and thought that computer simulations of rainstorms leave us all drenched, or computer simulations of five-alarm fires burn all the buildings down. It's only an extended sense of leaving us all wet or burning the building down. I have no objections to that kind of talk, provided you realize that there is a sense in which it just abandons the claim of strong AI.

Indeed, I want to conclude by saying, why does anybody feel tempted to adopt strong AI? That is, McCarthy has written, and I quote this verbatim because it made a big impression on me, "Even a machine as simple as a thermostat can be said to have beliefs." And he means that quite literally—beliefs in the same sense that you and I have. I've discussed this with McCarthy enough to know that he thinks the thermostat literally has beliefs. I once asked him what beliefs the thermostat had? And he told me the thermostat has three beliefs. It believes it's too cold in here, it's too hot in here, and it's just right in here.

What I want to conclude with is this—it seems to me unnecessary, in order to pursue what I think is the really fruitful part of artificial intelligence, for people to adopt strong AI. I mean the computer is a wonderfully exciting tool. And computer science is a very exciting field of human investigation. It isn't necessary either for the success of artificial intelligence or even for the getting of substantial research grants that we should make exaggerated claims.

H. R. PAGELS: I want to move the discussion in a different direction. I'd like to know the panelists' viewpoints on where this discussion might be in 5 or 10 years. Is it possible that an advance in neurobiology, computer design, or the conceptual foundations of artificial intelligence research might resolve this issue one way or the other?

Another area we might discuss is potential collaboration between philosophers and people working in artificial intelligence research.

M. L. MINSKY: I don't have much to say about that. I think as things are discovered and demonstrated, then—barring paradigm shifts of very large magnitude—attitudes will drift a little bit when machines seem more intelligent, people will tend to think that they're more intelligent or that they'll think.

But there are things that never change until there's a paradigm change. For example, very often someone will ask me, "What is intelligence?" And I'll say, "Well I don't know—I'm trying to find out." And they'll say: "Well I didn't mean that. I mean how do you define it? How do you define intelligence?" And I go back and say, "Well how do you define life?" The word "life" doesn't have much place anymore in science, as many of you know. There's a sort of continuum. We know that crystals can copy certain patterns and that a million billion years ago, events started to happen where these very complicated systems started appearing. And if you ask a biologist what he's studying, he'll say he's strying to study some facet of the digestion microworld. To develop a theory to understand a complicated system, we have to cover very small areas until it's all covered up and then sew it all together with exceptions or other theories. I think what will happen in artificial intelligence is that to a large extent, these side issues will decay. Obviously the machines that we have now, whether they think or not in the weakest sense that John McCarthy suggested, are nothing at all like us. They can't remember why they did things. People put in programs to help them. And so it makes very little sense to talk about them having much in the way of consciousness or sensitivity or whatever.

As for 10 years or 200 from now, we don't know. I want to point out that we don't have to spend all the time of the future figuring out what common sense is. We may be able to make learning machines that will cleverly watch their own behavior and decide that certain principles they're using don't work and edit them.

Gradually, the attitude and the respect for intelligent machines will change as they become more intelligent. But in our culture, until there's a revolution, the idea will persist that they're just simulations. people will say, "It's crying terribly out there, that robot. Don't you think you should let it in?" And other people will say, "No it's just simulating. It doesn't really feel bad." I wonder if Searle thinks that the brain gets wet when it thinks about rain. Whatever the process is, why should it matter what the substance is as long as the impulses are there. When we look at a picture of a pretty girl, let's face the fact that we're not seeing a pretty girl, we're only seeing a lot of little colored dots on the retina. And then let's face the next fact, when we see a real pretty girl, we're still just seeing little dots on the retina, if you confine the system to that. I think that's what one means by you can't just look at the interpretation process, you have to look at the system of the person carrying out the rules. We never see anything. Does that mean that we do never see anything? It just depends on the size of the system to which you make this attribution.

So unless there's a revolution that says words like "life" should be removed, everybody will still feel there's a difference. That these robots are maybe intelligent but not alive, or that they have pseudointelligence but not real. And the attributions that you use there will depend on your purposes. Are you worrying about them getting legal rights and inheriting your property? Are you worried about having to share? Are you worried about feeling guilty that they might have the same feelings as you although maybe John Searle is right and one could never prove such a thing? Because it's just a style of thought itself. These questions will depend on too much to answer.

S. PAPERT: I'd like to say something about the question of where we are going, and maybe this is relevant to what kind of cooperation there might be between AI and the different kind of philosopher—a philosopher concerned with reality, with social reality and with people's concerns.

I'd like to put this into a different context. Can machines be intelligent? Can they think? There's a certain form of this question that is of very vital concern to all of us, because there will be machines that will be better than people at doing whatever their jobs are. If your job is being a doctor, there will be a machine that can make a better diagnosis and decide on a better treatment of your patient than you can. Or if you want to invest in the stock exchange, rather than go and ask a human advisor, you should get a machine. The machine will know much better than you—probably will have made millions of dollars already. I think that most people are more concerned about this they than are willing to admit. Because it really is frightening.

Now given that people think this is even slightly likely, they might want to be reassured. And I believe that a lot of people have found reassurance in the writings of Dreyfus and Searle. They read what these philosophers say as somehow reassuring that this isn't going to happen, That people are always going to keep their unique special position in the universe, that maybe the diggers of ditches and the drivers of horses have had their jobs taken away from them, but we intellectuals will always have our jobs and prestige and all the things that come with our particular kind of work.

Can machines ever make us intellectuals obsolete? Dreyfus has said no, they can't because there are certain things that machines will never be. And Searle takes a slightly different position, saying that whatever machines do, we won't call it thinking but we can't define what they'll do or won't do from the outside.

I think it's a little bit chancy to make predictions about what machines can't do, because some clever engineer will come along and make the machine do that thing. So I think a lot of people would rather have something like the Chinese room argument which doesn't depend on competing with the technicians about what is technically possible. Undoubtedly this kind of argument has acquired a certain social popularity for that reason.

But I would like to say, concerning the consequences, that I feel that this is a very dangerous situation. I think it's socially dangerous for people to be lulled into a sense of security that there won't be machines to threaten their positions. I think that these are important issues of what it really means to our sense of ourselves to allow ourselves to face the social issue of what machines will be doing out there—what life will be like—after 300 years or 3 years or whatever.

To go back to a point I made at the beginning—that machines are changing the way people think because machine thinking is often useful as a model for human thinking. It's also sometimes dangerous as a model. For example if you think that Newell and Simon machine that solves puzzles in a certain way is a good model for us to follow, you might be concerned about whether this is a good model for our children to follow. Finding the appropriate context for discussing that is a matter of vital social concern, and it's not dealt with—it's only covered over—by saying, "Well that machine is not thinking because it's not biological, or because it's just following rules, or because it's not semantic." The point is, you give it a problem, it gives you an answer. You ask it why it did this and it gives you reasons. And then you're going to tend to follow that kind of reason or not follow that kind of reason. Or pass them on to your children or not pass them on to your children. I'm just suggesting this as somewhere that AI is going. And the kinds of consideration that have come up here can be dangerously misleading if we don't keep them rigorously separated from all issues of this kind.

J. McCARTHY: The question is, What will be the situation 5 to 10 years from now? Let me make it 10 or 15. I think there'll be a paradigm shift among the public that will give John Searle the following problem. He will want to come to the symposium to correct our use of mental terms, but he won't even get here, because he'll have to correct his secretary who will tell him, "It promised to process your travel advance, but I don't think it will, because it's puzzled about whether the expenditure for flowers was intended and necessary for the business's goals."

Thus in 10 or 15 years, quite mundane systems used for business and personal purposes will require the use of a certain amount of mental terminology in order to be used effectively.

Also let me repeat my warning to philosophers that if they insist on discussing commonsense reasoning only at the general level of today's discussion, they will lose the jurisdiction. We need to consider the conditions for the ascription of particular mental qualities, and this may require collaboration among philosophers and artificial intelligence researchers.

We attempted such a collaboration several years ago, but I think the particular attempt was unsuccessful largely because it considered overly general questions. This was partly because the AI people succumbed to the temptation to become amateur philosophers rather than raising the AI issues to which philosophy is relevant.

H. L. DREYFUS: I think that I'm the one, not John Searle, who's lulling people into a sense of security. I just think it's not a *false* sense of security. I think that you should be confident and trust your natural intuitions and your grandmother's natural intuitions that you are not a machine. Not that you are not a material thing, you certainly are. But you are not the sort of machine that, by using a program manipulating facts by way of rules, produces the kind of behavior we call intelligent.

Now I want to make clear that that's not to say—as people have rightly said—that computers won't fall in love, etc. A recent *Time Magazine* essay, claiming to be giving my views, said that I think that computers won't be able to pray, won't be able to look you in the eye while shaking hands, and so forth. Of course I think that. But that's not important. What I want to say is that even though computers can do really complicated things like analyze spectrograms and play chess, computers as we now understand them and program them can't even understand the sort of stories that four-year-old children understand. Moreover, I think they will never be able to understand the sort of stories that four-year-old children understand because such stories involve emotions like jealousy, everyday practices, seeing one situation as similar to another situation, and the sort of rules that include a clause saying "everything else being equal," without spelling out what everything else is, or what counts as being equal. It's that sort of thing, it seems to me, that the current way of trying to produce artificial intelligence will never achieve. And so I don't think computers will ever behave like human beings if the current direction of research continues. And you can be secure that there won't be the sort of robots around doing the sort of things we do and thinking like we do in your lifetime or even in the foreseeable future.

Let me take the rest of my time to try to answer Dr. Pagel's question, Where will we be in 10 years? When I wrote *What Computers Can't Do* 10 years ago, nobody seemed to think that the problem of making computers intelligent required programming commonsense knowledge. People were trying to use shortcuts to get computers that seemed to be intelligent. Now, 10 years later, everyone thinks there is a big problem concerning commonsense knowledge. Where will we be 10 years from now? I think 10 years from now people might realize that it's not a question of commonsense knowledge at all. That common sense includes feelings, having a body, having images, responding to similarities, etc. Then maybe the field will switch to something that I feel would be more promising, simulating the brain by neural nets with changing thresholds rather than storing facts and rules. And in that new dimension, in x number of years, maybe we'd get somewhere. But I don't think we'll get somewhere by trying to treat our commonsense understanding as if it were knowledge.

J. SEARLE: I always have the disconcerting sense in these discussions that I'm busy saying over and over, "Look, 2 plus 2 is really just 4," while other people are saying, "Yes, but if 2 plus 2 were 5 or 7, think of the terrific derivations that we could make."

Now what will this discussion look like in 10 or in x number of years? I have very great confidence in human rationality. People are going to say, "Yes, 2 plus 2 is just plain 4." And the specific form I think that's going to take is this. Mentality is a biological phenomenon. We don't know an awful lot about how it works in the brain, but suppose we really did know how it worked. Suppose we had a perfect science of the brain or even a pretty good science of the brain. Suppose we were able to explain how the behavior at the neuronal level caused consciousness and thought processes at the same degree that we can now explain how the behavior of H_2O molecules causes the liquidity of the water in this glass.

Once we get to that point, then nobody will make these confusions. Ignorance is one of the reasons that lead to strong AI. Notice what the strong AI partisans are saying. They're saying the brain doesn't matter. And that is literally incredible. It is incredible to suppose that the brain doesn't matter to the mind, that any system whatever, whether it's beer cans or, as Weizenbaum said, rolls of toilet paper with stones laid on the squares, any system at all will have to have mental states in exactly the same sense that you and I do because all there is to having mental states is instantiating the right program.

I believe this discussion will peter out when people realize that that's a preposterous view.

Another reason that it's still possible to propound strong AI is that there's still a certain mystique surrounding the computer. We're not as at home with the computer as we are with cars and telephones and so on. It still seems for most of us a kind of mysterious object, and that leads to a kind of mystification. And that will peter out as the computer becomes more common.

So my answer to the question of what is likely to happen over the years is that people will see that strong AI, the idea that the computer program is sufficient for having mental states, is in a way a last gasp of a Cartesian metaphysics. The last gasp for the idea that the mind is something special. That it isn't part of the biological universe like the rest of the biological facts about our life.

I'd like to end on a more constructive note. I do see enormous possibilities for collaboration between AI and the sort of philosopher that I am. In fact, I've engaged in some of this. And this seems to me the real world of AI. Suppose you have a language and certain rules for speech acts and you also have rules for understanding indirect speech acts, that is, rules for understanding how it is that when a guy says "You're standing on my toe," you know perfectly well that's not just a remark about your geographical location. He's actually trying to get you to do something about it. I think those are rational processes. Now the beauty of AI, and this I really do admire, is that it forces you to pose those questions precisely and forces you to state your theory precisely. In fact the things I've written about—metaphors and indirect speech acts and so on—a great deal of it has been programmed by people working in various AI labs. So I think, in fact, that AI is an immensely useful tool in the study of language and the study of the mind, just as it's a useful tool in the study of rainstorms or the economy or anything else. I feel fairly confident that in the end, the exaggerated and I think implausible and preposterous kinds of strong AI will be abandoned.

What McCarthy says is surely right, we will come to make all these attributions of intentional states to computers as we now make attributions of mental states to cars and adding machines and photoelectric cells and so on. It's quite harmless. Nobody supposes that his car literally has thoughts and feelings. And in the same way, we will come to the point where we realize that our PDP-10 or even our beloved Apple II doesn't actually have thoughts and feelings. And when that happens, then we'll be able to see what is really useful in AI, namely, it is itself a tremendous intellectual advance in the development of computer science and, even more important, it enables us to make further intellectual advances in other fields.

Fundamental Physical Limitations of the Computational Process

ROLF LANDAUER

International Business Machines Corporation
Thomas J. Watson Research Center
Yorktown Heights, New York 10598

The tremendous progress of computer technology, over three decades, leads to the question: How far can that continue? Our precedent for this question comes from thermodynamics, which arose in the nineteenth century out of the attempt to understand the limitations on the efficiency of steam engines. The efficiency question was answered through the second law of thermodynamics, in a way that did not require anticipation of every possible steam engine invention. Another precedent comes from Claude Shannon's channel capacity theory, which sets limits on the information transmitted through a noisy channel, without having to anticipate every clever way of coding messages. Therefore, we distinguish our concern with *fundamental* computer limits from the more prevalent attempts to assess the potential of specific existing or proposed technologies. While we are willing to be very broad-minded and optimistic in the storehouse of parts that we allow, we do want the components of our computing system to obey the laws of physics and do want to understand the interactions of the parts in a total system.

This study of ultimate computer limits is in its infancy; it is easier to ask questions than answer them. To the extent that we have answers, the limits are terribly far away from reality. Therefore, we cannot claim to be guiding the technologist. Then why are the limits interesting? It is a matter of basic science; we are starting a physical theory of mathematics. Most mathematicians have little sympathy for the assertion that their subject requires a basis in physics. Information, however, whether it is in biological systems, in a digital computer, or handled by pencil and paper, inevitably has a physical form. Information is represented by a mark on a piece of paper, a hole in a punched card, a magnetic material magnetized one way or the other, a charge that is present or absent, a Josephson junction that is superconducting or not, etc. Information can come on a much smaller scale, e.g., in the molecular configuration of DNA or, conceivably, even through the spin of a single electron which can be pointed up or down. It is impossible to get away from this sort of physical embodiment. As a result, manipulation of information is inevitably subject to the laws of physics.[1,2]

Mathematics taught us that we know what π is because we have rules that permit us to calculate as many decimal (or binary) places of π as we wish. Now we come back with questions of the following sort: Can we really tie enough of the universe together into a single computing system so that we can go on writing down the digits of π without limit? Even if we have enough storage available for that, if we keep computing successive digits, won't the early ones be disturbed by noise while we are still continuing to do a terribly long calculation? Undoubtedly, we have methods that enable us to calculate each digit of π with very high reliability. But if we cannot have one-hundred percent confidence in each step, can we really go on indefinitely in our calculation of π? Another question: Do the inevitable deterioration mechanisms present in all hardware set a limit to the maximum number of steps that are available? Or can we always transfer a calculation, after it has run long enough, to a heftier and more rugged computer, and thus assure a high probability of freedom from machine failure? We have not made any progress towards answering questions that are quite as basic as the ones just listed. Instead, we have answered some related, more narrow questions. As a result of studying the more easily formulated questions, limits that were initially presumed to be apparent have receded. The reader must be warned: Don't take this too seriously. The real limits, implicit in the sample questions we have cited, will be there. We just do not yet know how to talk about them.

We aim to give a brief road map of this field and a somewhat personal evaluation of its current status. This will be a little more than an annotated bibliography, but less than a structured review of the subject matter. For the latter the reader is advised to turn to some of the papers from a 1981 conference, Physics of Computation.[3] We particularly draw attention to a selected subset of these conference papers,[4-9] closest to our discussion. Our discussion will, initially, follow the historical development.

The notion that there may be ultimate physical computer limits is almost as old as modern computer technology, but throughout the fifties this was primarily a subject for informal and casual discussion, with limited ability to phrase precise questions. Thus, for example, Brillouin's book, despite its chapter "The Problem of Computing,"[10] contains no references to the actual logic processes involved in a computer, e.g., to a logical "and" or a logical "or," and contains no references to a total working computer system, such as a Turing machine or a cellular automaton.

Arthur Burks, in a volume published nine years after von Neumann's death, attributed to von Neumann the notion that a computer operating at temperature T must dissipate at least $kT \log_e 2$ (about 3×10^{21} J at room temperature) "per elementary act of information, that is per elementary decision of a two-way alternative and per elementary transmittal of one unit of information."[11] This statement comes much closer to a sensible discussion of digital computation than does Reference 10, but still involves the unfortunately vague phrase "per elementary decision of a two-way alternative." Indeed, as stressed in Reference 7, the phrase "elementary transmittal of one unit of information" is also ambiguous, and the mere transmission of information, by itself, does not really require energy dissipation.

A failure to distinguish clearly between computation, communication, and measurement is apparent in Reference 10, which states: "The machine may be compared with a transmission channel, including coding and decoding. Under ideal conditions, the message is correctly transmitted, and the information content is kept constant. Errors and approximations in the computing result in a loss of information." This lack of distinction between computation and communication has, unfortunately, persisted to this day, and is apparent in several of the papers in Reference 3, as well as in other recent contributions.[12,13]

Certainly communication, measurement, and computation have a close relationship, but hardly a clear identity. Indeed, the computer, acting as a relatively closed and well-defined machine during the progress of a program, is easiest to discuss. The computer does not confront us with the nasty questions: When are we actually doing a measurement? What is the act of information transmission, of information reception? We shall return, briefly again, to the measurement process a little later.

Questions about the ultimate limits of miniaturization and about the ultimate limits of speed have been particularly troublesome. If we are willing to be somewhat model dependent, some answers can be given.[14-16] Unfortunately we have no easy guide to the phenomena that can be utilized in a computer; conceivably the internal degrees of freedom in the nucleus can serve this purpose. Thus we are not restricted to the scales set by solid-state phenomena, or even by atomic physics. The questions in our field that have been attacked with some success include the minimal energy dissipation, where kT, the average thermal energy of an oscillator, sets a natural scale. We can also say something about immunity to noise, and about the limitations (or more exactly the lack of limitations) that come from the quantum mechanical uncertainty principle.

By 1961, it was understood that the processes in a computer that really require energy dissipation are those that throw away information,[17] and they require of the order of kT energy loss per step. Erasing a bit in a memory is an example of information loss. Any logic operation with two inputs and one output inevitably discards information; we cannot deduce the input from the output. In Reference 17 it was already clear that such operations were not essential to computation; we could rely on one-to-one logic operations. That meant, however, that we would generate lots of unnecessary outputs along the way, only needed for the step-by-step preservation of information. It was not clear, at that time, what to do with the extra outputs once the end of the computation was reached, without incurring the energy dissipation penalty connected with a belated erasure. The failure to perceive what could be done with this surplus information history was undoubtedly rooted in a subtle misconception.[1] It was tempting, but incorrect, to equate computers that can perform only one-to-one mappings with table lookup devices. The latter can only do computations done in advance by the designer and thus are not very interesting. Computers, however, that use only invertible logic functions are not limited this way; they can clearly perform all the operations done in ordinary computers, and ordinary computers certainly carry out programs that have not been foreseen by the designer.

The reference to what it is that can be, or has to be, foreseen by the designer deserves a clarifying remark. We, and others, have stressed the need for schemes that can be part of a Turing machine, or else have access to unlimited storage in some other way. This arises because a finite machine has a limited number of programs it can execute, all of which could, in principle, be foreseen by the designer. In other words, a finite machine looks too much like a table lookup mechanism to seem interesting. But our emphasis on machines of unlimited size seems really unreasonable, when we suspect that nature will not allow that. What we need is a mode of analysis that comes closer to the real world, where finite machines do a great many tasks not understood in advance by their designer; finite machines are more than table lookup devices. We need to characterize finite machines by a figure of merit that characterizes the universe of calculations they can do compared to the complexity of the machine's own structure. Unfortunately, such an approach does not yet exist.

Subsequently we will point to the desirability of *some* dissipation, i.e., friction, in the computational process. Friction, however, in a system at a temperature T, above the absolute zero, is inevitably associated with minimal and unavoidable noise sources, often labeled thermal equilibrium noise. Despite the presence of this noise, we can obtain any desired reliability in computation, if we are willing to compute sufficiently slowly. This was explained in 1969.[18]

The central concept in this field is that of reversible computing, introduced by Charles Bennett in 1973.[19] Bennett recognized that the surplus information piled up as a result of the use of invertible logic operations did not have to be erased. We have to be careful and use one-to-one logic devices that not only are logically invertible, but that actually permit us to push back the information through the device and thus to undo the operation. That is very different, of course, from the behavior of a transistor circuit. If we use devices that are not only physically but also logically invertible, then after arriving at the termination of the program and copying the desired results from the output register, we can simply reverse the computation and thus return the computer to its initial state, without the need to erase any undesired information.

An earlier paper[20] listed some of the detailed models of reversible computation that have been proposed subsequent to Reference 19. This list must be supplemented by Reference 8, which is the first electrical example of reversible computation. These models are illustrated schematically in FIGURE 1. Computation consists of motion along paths that do not merge and do not split, with a separate trajectory for each program. In the presence of frictional forces proportional to the velocity of motion the energy losses, per step, can be made arbitrarily small by pushing the system sufficiently slowly. If we are pushing the system very weakly then the computation, under the influence of noise, will jump backwards, against the small applied force, almost as often as it goes forward. On the average, however, just like an electron in a solid under a weak electric field, it will drift forward. For the remaining details the reader is referred to the cited discussions, particularly Reference 9. Noise that only affects the intended motion (rather than noise that causes equipment deterioration) only reduces the speed of computation and not its reliability. Note that this is true, not only if the noise is limited to the inevitable minimal thermal equilibrium amount, but even if there are other additional noise sources present. The noise immunity of reversible computers transcends that originally found in Reference 18 in another important way. In the reversible systems characterized by FIGURE 1, we obtain noise immunity even if we are doing fast computing, under larger forces, and dissipating appreciable energy in the process.

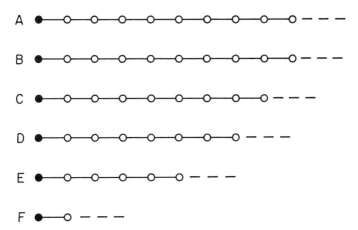

FIGURE 1. The left-hand end of a horizontal chain represents the initial state, and forward computation represents motion to the right, through a sequence of states represented by successive circles. Different letters correspond to different initial states, i.e., different programs.

All of the reversible computation schemes share a problem. They all assume, somewhere, the availability of very large forces, forces that have to be made larger if the computation is to be made more reliable. In Bennett's reversible Turing machine,[9,19] for example, we need "hard" parts that lock different logic variables together in a way that permits us to view the progress of the computation as motion along the single path shown in FIGURE 1, rather than as the independent evolution, in time, of many degrees of freedom, exerting some influence on each other. The real universe may not be all that cooperative in supplying us with an unlimited store of these large forces, or hard parts.

We can go on to ask whether friction and the accompanying minimal noise are essential to the computational process. Two models have been proposed to demonstrate that computational processes can, in principle, be executed in dissipationless systems. One of these is discussed in Reference 7. The other, more well-known, and particularly ingenious version[6] is illustrated in FIGURE 2. In this latter scheme information is represented by the absence or presence of billiard balls, and the interaction of signal streams is obtained by collisions. Reflecting walls, or "mirrors," are also needed to guide balls toward further collisions. These dissipationless computers are, however, somewhat pathological. They have to be flawless; they allow for no manufacturing tolerances. A mirror angled incorrectly, for example, will cause a billiard ball to deviate from its intended direction. This will result in incorrect deflection angles in subsequent collisions, and finally in mirrors or collisions that are missed

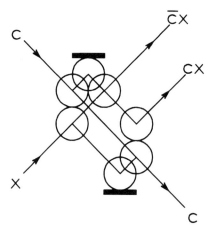

FIGURE 2. Two inputs c and x interact by the direct collision of billiard balls, and their subsequent reflection by mirrors.

totally, or in the occurrence of unintended collisions. Similarly, the billiard balls cannot interact with the internal degrees of freedom present in the billiard balls and present in the mirrors. Such interactions are the source of noise and damping, and would also lead to unintended errors. After all, even small unintended velocity changes will, after a sufficiently long time, cause major mishaps in this system. Thus the continual relaxation towards thermal equilibrium, invoked in the dissipative reversible computers proposed by Bennett[9] and others, has an essential role in computation. If unintended history is not erased by dissipation, it will eventually cause errors.[1]

The requirement for friction is, of course, not a requirement for strong friction. Some reversible computer schemes require almost complete thermal equilibration at every step.[8] But as in the case of an electron moving through a solid, where the mean free path can be large compared to interatomic distances, in some embodiments of FIGURE 1 the thermal relaxation process can be spread over a number of successive computer events.

Let us now return, briefly, to a discussion of the measurement process. The discussions of Maxwell's demon led to a resolution by Szilard, who showed that the measurement process requires energy dissipation.[21] The measurement process, typically, involves coupling the system to be measured to the system that contains the meter, and letting the former influence the latter. Reference 17, however, stated, "The mere fact that two physical systems are coupled does not in itself require dissipation." Then why is the measurement process dissipative? We believe that this question is obscured by many of the existing discussions of the measurement process. As explained in Reference 9, "the essential irreversible act . . . is not the measurement itself but rather the subsequent restoration of the measuring apparatus to a standard state in preparation for the next measurement."

Thus, we can see from the discussion of the communications process in References 7 and 20, and the discussion of the measurement process in Reference 9, that the two processes and the computational process do in fact, despite our earlier protest, have a strong commonality. In each of these cases the dissipation arises from the erasure of information.

The connection between information loss and energy loss that we have emphasized is apparent in many situations. If we drop a ball, in the presence of friction, it will eventually end up lying on the ground. Thus, we have erased the information in the ball's original elevation. Dissipation takes states that are originally distinguishable and maps them on top of each other. The information in the ball's position has, of course, not really disappeared; it has passed into the vibrational modes of the ball and of the ground, and into air currents. As these disturbances spread out, the information may, or may not, continue to be retrievable, in principle. Certainly in a world that permits a limited precision in the handling of information, it must eventually get lost.

The obvious prevalence of friction and information loss leads to the questions: Are there counterbalancing processes? Does information get generated, or does it only disappear? The generation of information must be the opposite of its destruction. Thus, systems that are initially indistinguishable must develop a recognizable difference. There are several possible explanations. The one that is most widely accepted is that the noise that reaches our system from external sources (or from any degrees of freedom not explicitly described in the system's equations of motion) causes system members, which were initially together, to diffuse apart. One can then go on, of course, to argue that the information did not really arise, but reflects information originally in the noise sources, and is transferred to the system of concern. Once again, however, in a universe with limited precision, the noise cannot be followed back in time and distance to any desired accuracy. Thus, the distinctions in behavior produced by noise can be considered to be "generated."

In recent years it has become possible to invoke chaotic processes, instead.[22,23] These are processes in deterministic nonlinear systems, possibly systems with only a few degrees of freedom, which are not periodic or quasi-periodic. Nearby trajectories diverge exponentially in time, instead of the typical $t^{1/2}$ divergence caused by noise. Once again, that exponential divergence, by itself, does not really produce information. We must also claim that two systems that originally were very close, but not identical, are nevertheless in some "in principle" sense indistinguishable. Or, alternatively, we can fall back on the limited precision of information handling and physical laws and claim that we cannot follow all the fine details of this irregular and divergent motion, for a very long time.

Amplifiers can also serve to push signals apart that are close together, initially. Amplifiers need not have the form of transistor circuits with a well-defined input and output, and with limited gain. In parametric amplifiers, to cite one example,[24] we can utilize a departure from the neighborhood of an unstable state and can achieve exponential growth in time for the energy in a resonant circuit. The growing separation of these signals will be accompanied by dissipative effects, i.e., by a compression of phase space for other degrees of freedom.

It is not clear whether one of the mechanisms cited above has to be regarded as the most fundamental. If a choice is necessary, then our preference lies with the direct effects of noise. After all noise clearly exists, and is pervasive, whereas noiseless dynamic systems do not exist.

We add one cautionary note. Quantum mechanics, despite an intimate relationship to probabilities, contains no built in noise sources. It does not provide for a growing spread in nearby systems; entropy is conserved in quantum mechanics just as in the classical case.

We have taken a classical viewpoint, up to this point, and have not invoked quantum mechanics. This takes us to the obvious question, Does quantum mechanics impose additional restrictions on the computational process? Answers to this question have been given repeatedly by invoking the uncertainty principle, $\Delta E \, \Delta t \sim \hbar$, to suggest that very fast switching requires a great deal of energy expenditure. A rebuttal has been provided.[7] A more fundamental quantum mechanical approach, modeled upon the notion of reversible computers, also exists.[5,25,26] This viewpoint has been clarified and expanded in an unpublished discussion by K. Wilson, by several members of the Information Mechanics Group at the Massachusetts Institute of Technology, and most particularly by R. P. Feynman.

The gist of these quantum mechanical approaches is that computation can, in principle, be achieved by a frictionless, energy-conserving system, following its quantum mechanical laws of motion. These quantum mechanical theories of computation proceed very formally, providing a mathematical rule that describes how the bits in the computer change with time. This rule is carefully constructed so that it is consistent with the laws of quantum mechanics, but in contrast to the classical theories, the rule is not accompanied by a description of the apparatus that is characterized by the rule. Furthermore these quantum theories are most clearly satisfactory in describing the internal progress of the computation, and are, perhaps, still incomplete in their description of the interaction of the computer with the outside world. The quantum theories only describe the evolution of the information-bearing degrees of freedom, without reference to any other degrees of freedom providing the physical supporting structure, or providing the linkage between the information-bearing degrees of freedom. Additionally, these quantum mechanical frictionless computers, just like their frictionless classical counterparts, are unlikely to have the immunity to noise, and to "construction" tolerances, exhibited by the classical reversible computer models.

REFERENCES

1. LANDAUER, R. 1967. Wanted: a physically possible theory of physics. IEEE Spectrum **4**: 105–109.
2. BREMERMANN, H. J. 1977. Complexity and transcomputability. *In* The Encyclopedia of Ignorance. R. Duncan & M. Weston-Smith, Eds.: 167–174. Pergamon Press. New York, N.Y.
3. FREDKIN, E., R. LANDAUER & T. TOFFOLI, Eds. 1981. Conference on Physics of Computation. MIT. Int. J. Theor. Phys. **21** [Part 1 (3/4), Part 2 (6/7), Part 3 (12)—1982].
4. TOFFOLI, T. 1982. Physics and computation. Int. J. Theor. Phys. **21**: 165–175.
5. BENIOFF, P. A. 1982. Quantum mechanical Hamiltonian models of discrete processes that erase their own histories: application to Turing machines. Int. J. Theor. Phys. **21**: 177–201.
6. FREDKIN, E. & T. TOFFOLI. 1982. Conservative logic. Int. J. Theor. Phys. **21**: 219–253.
7. LANDAUER, R. 1982. The uncertainty principle and minimal energy dissipation in the computer. Int. J. Theor. Phys. **21**: 283–297.
8. LIKHAREV, K. K. 1982. Classical and quantum limitations on energy consumption in computation. Int. J. Theor. Phys. **21**: 311–326.
9. BENNETT, C. H. 1982. The thermodynamics of computation—a review. Int. J. Theor. Phys. **21**: 905–940.
10. BRILLOUIN, L. 1962. Science and Information Theory. Academic Press, Inc. New York, N.Y.
11. VON NEUMANN, J. 1966. Theory of Self-Reproducing Automata. A. W. Burks, Ed. University of Illinois. Urbana, Ill.
12. BEKENSTEIN, J. D. 1981. Energy cost of information transfer. Phys. Rev. Lett. **46**: 623–626.
13. DEUTSCH, D. 1982. Is there a fundamental bound on the rate at which information can be processed? Phys. Rev. Lett. **48**: 286–288.
14. SWANSON, J. A. 1960. Physical versus logical coupling in memory systems. IBM J. Res. Dev. **4**: 305–310.
15. LANDAUER, R. 1962. Fluctuations in bistable tunnel diode circuits. J. Appl. Phys. **33**: 2209–2216.
16. LANDAUER, R. & J. W. F. WOO. 1971. Minimal energy dissipation and maximal error for the computational process. J. Appl. Phys. **42**: 2301–2308.
17. LANDAUER, R. 1961. Irreversibility and heat generation in the computing process. IBM J. Res. Dev. **5**: 183–191.

18. KEYES, R. W. & R. LANDAUER. 1970. Minimum energy dissipation in logic. IBM J. Res. Dev. **14:** 152–157.
19. BENNETT, C. H. 1973. Logical reversibility of computation. IBM J. Res. Dev. **17:** 525–532.
20. LANDAUER, R. 1981. Fundamental physical limitations of the computational process. *In* Sixth International Conference on Noise in Physical Systems. P. H. E. Mejier, R. D. Mountain & F. J. Soulen, Jr., Eds. Publication No. 614: 12–17. National Bureau of Standards. Washington, D.C.
21. SZILARD, L. 1929. Über die Entropieverminderung in einem thermodynamischen System bei Eingriffen intelligenter Wesen. Z. Phys. **53:** 840–856.
22. SHAW, R. 1981. Strange attractors, chaotic behavior, and information flow. Z. Naturforsch. **36a:** 80–112.
23. FORD, J. 1983. How random is a coin toss? Phys. Today **36**(4): 40–47.
24. WOO, J. & R. LANDAUER. 1971. Fluctuations in a parametrically excited subharmonic oscillator. IEEE J. Quantum Electron. **7:** 435–440.
25. BENIOFF, P. 1982. Quantum mechanical models of Turing machines that dissipate no energy. Phys. Rev. Lett. **48:** 1581–1585.
26. BENIOFF, P. 1982. Quantum mechanical Hamiltonian models of Turing machines. J. Stat. Phys. **29:** 515–546.

The Formation of Three-Dimensional Biological Structures

Computer Uses and Future Needs

CYRUS LEVINTHAL

Department of Biological Sciences
Columbia University
New York, New York 10027

A large part of the science of biology is concerned with three-dimensional structures, their formation, their interactions, and their functions as part of an intact organism. However, when we talk of three-dimensional structures, it must be kept in mind that the reference is to structures of very different levels, size, and complexity. At the molecular level, the dimensions are of the order of nanometers; cells and cell organelles have dimensions of the order of micrometers, and collections of cells have dimensions of the order of millimeters, centimeters, or even meters. In all of these cases, we know that three-dimensional structures and their relationships arise, in part, from the one-dimensional information encoded in the DNA molecules and, in part, from the local environment of the individual structures or even the environment of the organism as a whole.

However, the greater the detail used in examining biological structures, the greater is the degree of complexity that must be dealt with. During the past four decades, the information that has been accumulated concerning molecular structure, details of neuroanatomy, interaction of cells with each other and with small molecules that control their function, and many other features of biological systems has become enormous. There is now virtually no area of biology in which even the simple process of keeping track of the data can be handled without the use of digital computers. The hundreds of thousands of nucleotides in DNA sequences that have been determined in the past five years are routinely handled by computer as are protein sequences and coordinates[1] and a large amount of other data currently being accumulated in molecular biology.

MOLECULAR MODEL BUILDING

However, the use of computers has not simply involved the handling and distribution of experimental data but has also been essential for the interpretation and analysis of experimental results and, most important, for the attempts to simulate biological processes as part of the efforts to understand them. About 30 years ago, when Perutz,[2] Kendrew,[3] and their collaborators initiated the determination of the structure of protein molecules, it became clear that the calculations needed to deduce the structure from the x-ray diffraction patterns were sufficiently complex so that carrying them out by hand was prohibitive. Crystals have to be formed from the native protein and from molecules in the same relative positions but with a heavy atom at a unique position. The crystal structures must be isomorphous; the relative positions of all the protein atoms must be the same in each of the crystals. The diffraction pattern must then be obtained from each of the crystals, Fourier transforms calculated, and extensive further calculations carried out in order to determine the electron density in the unit cell of the crystal. The known subunit amino acids that comprise the protein must then be fit into the electron density distribution in order to arrive at an atomic model of the large molecule.

Other aspects of molecular structures have also been worked out during this period without making use of three-dimensional crystals or x-ray diffraction of isomorphic forms. By knowing the structure of the subunits of which the larger molecule is composed, it has sometimes been possible to deduce the three-dimensional structure of the large entity by selecting those conformations or arrangements that satisfy certain chemical constraints. It was by these methods that the secondary substructures, alpha helices and beta sheets, of which most of the 3D structures are made, were first deduced by Pauling and Corey,[4] and it was also the way in which Watson and Crick deduced the structure of DNA.[5] Initially, these operations were done by hand and involved the construction and manipulation of plastic or metal models.

Starting in 1962, when interactive computer graphics at Massachusetts Institute of Technology's Project MAC was first introduced, we have been using a combination of computer graphics and extensive computation in order to study various aspects of molecular structure and function.[6] I undertook this work at the time because of a set of genetic experiments that we had been carrying on with a bacterial protein. A structural proposal that arose from the experiments required the construction of a set of rather complex molecular models. Our attempts to build such models were continually frustrated by the fact that they fell down and did not maintain the shapes into which we tried to put them. Most of these problems were solved very quickly when we began to use interactive computer graphics combined with the computations necessary to minimize the energy of interaction while molecules and parts of molecules were being packed.

Throughout this period, one of the most challenging problems in molecular biology has been the attempt to deduce the three-dimensional structure of proteins from the sequence of the amino acid subunits of which they are made. There are very good experimental data indicating that the three-dimensional structure does in fact arise entirely from the amino acid sequence, which is in turn encoded in the DNA. Many proteins can be completely denatured by altering the pH, salt concentration, and temperature of their solution so that they lose all of their unique 3D shape, and they can be later restored to their unique natural structure in which they are functionally active by returning their environment to its original state.[7]

Since we believe that we know most of the forces that determine the interaction between atoms in a large molecule, it has seemed reasonable to suggest that, if we were clever enough and had enough computer time, we should be able to simulate the protein-folding process leading to the unique three-dimensional structure that the protein will assume spontaneously. In this way, we could in principle predict the 3D structure of a protein, if we knew its amino acid sequence, even if its crystal structure had not been determined. There are however several important difficulties with this process which have, to date, prevented any such successful simulations or predictions. Probably the most serious of these difficulties are due to the fact that the total energy difference between a folded and an unfolded protein can be small compared to even one of the interactions between a pair of atoms. Furthermore, there is good evidence that the process of folding involves a sequential interaction of different portions of the molecule in such a way that a kinetic pathway is found.[8] The requirement that structures be consistent with such kinetic pathways is one of the major constraints on the process of biological evolution.

Another major problem is the lack of adequate computing power. When a real protein molecule folds either in a cell or in a test tube, each atom is subject to the forces exerted by other atoms and moves accordingly, in a simultaneous manner. Thus the process is inherently parallel. The vibration frequencies of certain modes are very high, and therefore, very small time steps are required if one is carrying out a numerical integration. The net result is that for the total protein-folding process, such molecular dynamics calculations in which each atom responds to the forces according to the laws of classical mechanics require computation times many orders of magnitude beyond those now available. On the other hand, there are many interesting and important biological problems that are within reach when we consider the changes in protein structure brought about by mutation or those that take place during the physiological functioning of the structure.

At one point, there was an optimistic hope that, by using interactive computer graphics to guide the processes of energy minimization and kinetically driven protein folding, one would be able to make use of the chemical insight of the investigator to direct the processes into those pathways that occurred spontaneously within cells. The only trouble with this notion was that it became evident rather quickly that our chemical intuition of these enormously complex problems is so limited as to be virtually useless in guiding the overall folding process. More recently, however, as many more proteins have been solved crystallographically, one has begun to see some of the order and systematics in the way protein structures are assembled. And even more important, the power of recombinant DNA techniques has made it possible to modify genes that encode the sequence of amino acids in proteins. Several groups have started to modify proteins in defined ways as a mean of testing models generated on a computer. This approach can also provide additional information as to the general arrangement of the amino acids within such

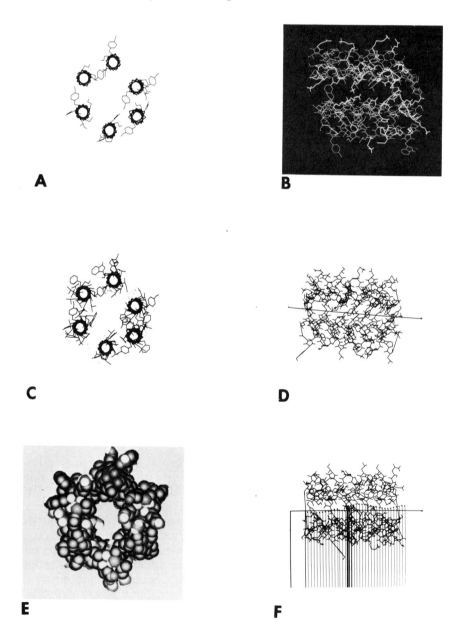

a structure and give a great deal of insight into the way in which protein molecules carry out their complex functions.

In our laboratory, we have been working on several problems with these techniques. With a bacterial toxin called colicin E1, we have shown that a rather small portion is able to insert itself into a planar phospholipid membrane and produce an ion channel which is detectable by conventional electrical measurements. This peptide contains only 152 amino acids, and it must transverse the membrane several times in order to make a channel through which the ions can pass.[9] These general features lead to a large number of chemical constraints which can be fed into the model-building process. Using these constraints, we have generated a small set of molecular models which appear to be consistent with all of the currently available data (see FIGURE 1). In order to distinguish among these models and provide further tests as to the nature of the structure, it is possible to use recombinant DNA techniques to change the amino acid sequence and ask what differences are produced in the behavior of the altered molecule. Each of the molecular models we have generated by means of computation and theoretical physical chemistry makes different predictions with respect to the consequences of certain of the mutations. Therefore we have procedures that are sufficient for evaluating the models experimentally.

So far, six different altered proteins have been made and their properties are consistent with the general features of our models. By making a large number of such mutations, it should be possible to provide rigorous tests for each of the models and deduce the correct one, even without detailed data from diffraction studies. A more ambitious project for the future involves modifying the channel in such a way that it has different electrical conductance properties. In this case, our interest is in producing channels with particular ion selectivity and electrical gating properties, similar to those found in the neurons that conduct electrical signals in the brain.

Another protein in which alterations are being made by chemical modification of the gene is the antibody molecule. In this case, computa-

---

FIGURE 1. The figures in the two plates are all computer generated. FIGURE 1E was produced on a Grinnel image-processing system, and the remainder in both FIGURES 1 and 2 on an Evans and Sutherland picture system 2. FIGURES 1A, 1B, and 1C represent end views of a hypothetical model of the 152 amino acid fragment of the colicin E1 protein which forms an ion channel through a phospholipid membrane. A number of different arrangements of six helical regions were tried and evaluated in order to obtain one that seems to satisfy all of the known constraints. In order to explore all possible arrangements, a great deal more computer time would be needed than has been used to date. FIGURE 1D is a side view of the structure, 1E shows an axis down the center of the channel, and 1F shows the path taken by a sphere whose diameter is the maximum that can pass through the channel. The calculations needed to determine the maximum diameter involve simulating an electric field acting on the sphere and giving the amino acids facing into the channel opening their natural flexibility. We do not, at present, have sufficient computing power to simulate the motion of all of the ions, water molecules, and protein atoms that interact so that we can calculate the electrical conductance predicted by our model.[16]

tion of the effect of changes in the amino acid sequence should be possible because of the enormous amount of information that has been collected with respect to antibodies made in nature.[10] Thus, computational generation of molecular models combined with recombinant DNA techniques will provide us with a set of novel, modified molecules. These should be especially useful in providing new insights into the process of protein folding, as well as providing new molecules of practical importance in medicine and industry.

THE DEVELOPMENT OF NERVE NETS

A very different type of three-dimensional problem in biology is that associated with the formation of the complex nerve net of a vertebrate

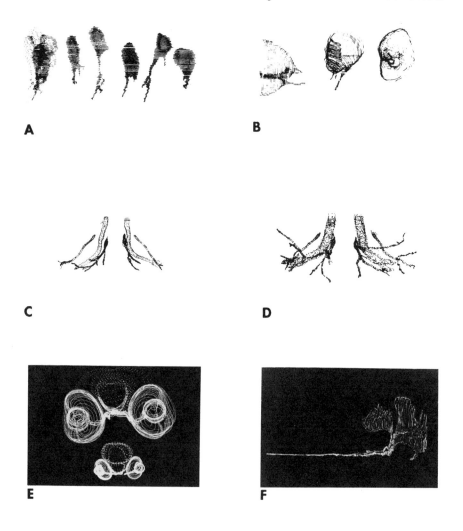

brain. In attempting to deduce the rules governing the formation process, we have made extensive use of computer graphics to reconstruct the three-dimensional structure of parts of a growing nerve net.[11] We are attempting to understand the mechanism by which individual nerve fibers reach their "correct" destination during early development. Our experiments have been possible because we are able to follow the detailed anatomy of growing fibers while the growth is taking place.[12] In order to observe sufficient detail of the growing fibers, one must use electron microscopy and the material must be cut into very thin sections before it can be used in a microscope. Obviously one cannot follow the growth in a living system; however, it is possible to obtain embryos of some organisms at closely spaced times and thus determine the sequential process. We use small animals where it is also possible to obtain an organism with a uniform genetic backround at the ages of interest (see FIGURE 2).

As a result of these studies, we have shown that one of the major factors in the development of a neuronal array is the ability of fibers to follow along the path already established by their older neighbors in the same array.[13] Obviously this "neighbor following" cannot, by itself, be sufficient to determine the pattern of connectivity. There must be "leader" or "pioneer" nerve fibers which, at a very early developmental stage, must follow nonneuronal elements in the growing embryo. At later stages in development, it is clear from studies with simple invertebrates[14] that individual fibers grow in such a way that they follow certain signposts, some of which are other neurons and some of which are not.

The techniques necessary to carry out 3D reconstructions from serial

---

FIGURE 2. FIGURES 2A and 2B are reconstructions of nerves in the visual system of the small water flea, *Daphnia magna*, during early embryonic development. In 2A, five nerves are shown which form a cluster and are "contacted" by the same fiber that grows from one of the cells in the eye. The outlines of the five cells are traced into the computer separately and therefore their anatomy can be examined either separately, to the right, or together, to the left. FIGURE 2B shows one of the cells as it was first being "contacted" by the fiber from the eye. This reconstruction allowed the detailed study of the region of space in which the incoming fiber was being wrapped by the target cell. The interactions and the anatomy of the cells during their subsequent development suggested that the target cell might be "instructed" as to its further development by the incoming fiber.[17] This theory has been further tested by Dr. Eduardo Macagno.[18] FIGURES 2C and 2D show a set of identified nerve cells which mediate the tail flip escape reaction of a small tropical fish. The organisms are from the same brood and have been grown in such a way that the individuals have identical genetic structures, like human identical twins. These two figures show differences in branching complexity in two such genetically identical animals. Further experiments by Dr. Françoise Levinthal have suggested that the differences are due to variations in the environment within the body cavity of the mother. The fish used for FIGURES 2C and 2D are of the natural species *Poecelia formosa*, and the further experiments with genetically identical animals were done with the common zebrafish. FIGURE 2E shows reconstructions of adult (top) and newborn (bottom) visual systems of the zebrafish showing the very short and direct path taken by the optic nerve of the developing system, and FIGURE 2F shows nerve fibers following other, more mature nerve fibers in the developing optic nerve. Several hundred serial electron micrographs were used to make these reconstructions,[13] and it was necessary to be able to follow the same fiber from its cell body to the growing tip in order to establish the overall topology.

sections have required several new devices for producing aligned film-strips from serial section micrographs. In addition, we have used digitizing tablets and 3D graphics as a type of notebook for recording structures that the investigator can recognize when projecting the filmstrip. However the rate-limiting step in all of these experiments is the manual tracing of recognized features into the computer. We are now using a high-speed laser digitizer and automatic pattern recognition programs to aid the investigator in speeding and reducing the tedium of the tracing process.[15] Full automation on these noisy and frequently indistinct images does not seem feasible at present, but sufficient progress has already been made in this direction so that the investigator's task has been made significantly easier. As more use is made of the knowledge we have about the properties of nerve fibers and their 3D continuity, we expect that there will be a continual improvement in our ability to automate contour extraction and fiber following. However, whatever improvements take place, the need for investigator intervention to guide the program will certainly continue into the foreseeable future.

CONCLUSIONS AND PROSPECTS FOR THE FUTURE

In spite of efforts by our group and many others, it has not been possible to carry through a successful simulation of either protein folding or the development of a nervous system except for very simple subsets of the real problem. There are rather clear reasons for this lack of success, even if we assume that all of the rules governing the interactions and the folding and growth processes are known. The most obvious difficulty is that both for nerves in the brain and atoms in a protein, as well as virtually all other processes that take place in living organisms, there is an enormous level of parallelism which we have no way of simulating at present, even for comparatively simple systems. When a protein molecule is folding, several thousand atoms of the molecule and additional thousands of water molecules are all interacting to drive the protein toward its unique stable configuration in which it can carry out its biological function. In experimental systems, it has been possible to show that the folding process takes place in times that are of the order of milliseconds. However, if we try to simulate the motion of each atom with current computers (e.g., a VAX 11/780 plus an array processor), we require about a day to calculate the path that the atoms would follow in a time of the order of picoseconds (10–12 seconds).

Very significant increases in speed can be achieved by building special-purpose, pipe-lined computing engines to carry out the molecular calculations and obtain an increase in speed of several thousand-fold. And within a few years, we will certainly be able to use parallel VLSI architectures with such special-purpose devices to increase the overall speed of the system by a much larger factor. However, in addition to increasing computational speed, we will also require new insights into the physical chemistry and the computational mathematics of these sequential and very highly parallel physical processes.

Very much the same comments can be made about the processes of brain development, except that, in this case, we know a great deal less about the rules governing the elementary interactions than in the case of the atoms in a protein. Experiments directed toward determining these rules represent a significant part of current experimental research in developmental neurobiology.

For all of the problems mentioned in this paper, it is sometimes possible to answer specific questions that are too complex to solve using computer modeling by using physical models either of the brain, or parts of the brain, or space-filling molecule models. In these cases, one uses the ability of humans to recognize patterns and human intelligence to make inferences as to the nature of the structure and how it develops. Carrying out these processes computationally can be referred to as artificial intelligence or simply as designing a complicated program. However they are described, they involve writing programs to simulate extraordinarily complex processes which take place very rapidly and spontaneously in nature. As biologists, we are trying to understand the sequential processes at as mechanistic a level as possible. Fundamentally, this means that we must be able to simulate them by well-defined algorithms, interpretable in terms of ordinary physics and chemistry. The models necessary for such simulations should be sufficiently well defined so that they can be tested experimentally. However, at present, we are frequently limited by the fact that we do not have the computational tools necessary to determine the specific consequences of the general models that seem reasonable. Without detailed simulation, the models do not lead to sufficiently well-defined predictions to yield testable consequences. In the future, we can anticipate more use of special-purpose computing engines, more use of computing in parallel, and much more sophisticated algorithms to handle these problems.

REFERENCES

1. ORCUTT, B. C., D. G. GEORGE & M. O. DAYHOFF. 1983. Annu. Rev. Biophys. Bioeng. **12:** 419.
2. GREEN, D. W., V. M. INGRAM & M. F. PERUTZ. 1954. Proc. R. Soc. London Ser. A **225:** 287.
3. KENDREW, J. C., R. E. DICKERSON, B. E. STRANDBERG, R. G. HART, D. R. DAVIES, D. C. PHILLIPS & V. C. SHORE. 1960. Nature **185:** 422.
4. PAULING, L., R. B. COREY & H. R. BRANSON. 1951. Proc. Nat. Acad. Sci. USA **37:** 205.
5. WATSON, J. D. & F. H. C. CRICK. 1953. Nature **171:** 737, 964.
6. LEVINTHAL, C. 1966. Sci. Am. (November): 213.
7. EPSTEIN, C. J., R. F. GOLDBERGER & C. B. ANFINSEN. 1963. Cold Spring Harbor Symp. Quant. Biol. **28:** 439.
8. LEVINTHAL, C. 1968. J. Chem. Phys. **65:** 44.

9. CLEVELAND, M. vB., S. SLATIN, A. FINKELSTEIN & C. LEVINTHAL. 1983. Proc. Nat. Acad. Sci. USA **80:** 3706.
10. KABAT, E. A., T. T. WU, H. BILOFSKY, M. REID-MILLER & H. PERRY. 1983. Sequences of Proteins of Immunological Interest. U.S. Department of Health and Human Services. Public Health Service. National Institutes of Health. Bethesda, Md.
11. LEVINTHAL, C., E. R. MACAGNO & C. TOUNTAS. 1974. Fed. Proc. Fed. Am. Soc. Exp. Biol. **33:** 2336.
12. LEVINTHAL, F., E. R. MACAGNO & C. LEVINTHAL. 1975. Cold Spring Harbor Symp. Quant. Biol. **40:** 321.
13. BODICK, N. & C. LEVINTHAL. 1980. Proc. Nat. Acad. Sci. USA **77:** 4347.
14. GOODMAN, C. S., T. A. ROPER, R. K. HO & S. CHANG. 1982. *In* 40th Symposium, Society for Developmental Biology. S. Subtelay & P. Green, Eds.: 275–316. Alan R. Liss. New York, N.Y.
15. SOBEL, I., E. R. MACAGNO & C. LEVINTHAL. 1980. Annu. Rev. Biophys. Bioeng. **9:** 347.
16. FINE, R. M., Q. R. LIU, M. B. CLEVELAND & C. LEVINTHAL. (In preparation.)
17. LOPRESTI, V., E. R. MACAGNO & C. LEVINTHAL. 1974. Proc. Nat. Acad. Sci. USA **71:** 1093.
18. MACAGNO, E. R. 1978. Nature **275:** 318.

Selective Networks and Recognition Automata*

GEORGE N. REEKE, JR. AND GERALD M. EDELMAN

Department of Developmental and Molecular Biology
The Rockefeller University
New York, New York 10021

INTRODUCTION

One of man's most ancient and perplexing problems has been to understand the nature of his own mental processes. The invention of the computer has, for many, suggested a promising approach based on the study of information processing and artificial intelligence. However, we would like to suggest that animals, including ourselves, face some problems that computers do not have to face: We are exposed to an unpredictable environment and must respond adaptively in order to survive. We can get information only in real time through the senses, not precoded on a magnetic tape. Above all, we must function without a preestablished program that would specify appropriate responses for all contingencies. In other words, we have to decide for ourselves what the problem is; it is not given to us.

In this paper, we shall consider an essentially biological approach to the problem that draws its inspiration from the Darwinian theory of natural selection and that stands in marked contrast to the information-processing approach. As we shall see, selective systems provide a way to overcome the principal difficulties of the information-processing approach: the needs to provide preestablished external information in the system along with a code for representing that information and algorithms for processing it. These needs arise from the formal separation of hardware and software in information-processing theory, a distinction that has no place in a biological theory of the mind. We believe that category formation and categorization lie at the heart of the matter; that memory and other higher brain functions depend on associations between stimuli that are intimately related to category formation; and that the way we perceive categories involves combinations of functions that are quite unlike those used to date for computer category perception. Accordingly, we will concentrate on problems of pattern recognition and category formation in this paper. We will review a theory for biological pattern recognition that is based on a selective principle, will describe briefly a pattern-recognizing automaton that we have constructed based

*We thank the Henry J. Kaiser Family Foundation and International Business Machines Corporation for their support of this research.

on this principle,[1] and will try to relate the results obtained with this automaton to the broader questions we have raised.

We begin with the seemingly spontaneous perception of pattern or Gestalt that occurs whenever we recognize objects in the visual world. How we are able to do this is a deep problem as suggested by just two simple illustrations.

In FIGURE 1 we reproduce a fragment from M. C. Escher's *Metamorphosis II*. The tower in the center is perceived as a rook in a chess game when viewed in the context to its right, but as part of an Italian town when viewed in the context to its left. The illustration is a kind of visual joke, deliberately ambiguous, but it does illustrate the importance of context in shaping our perceptions.

FIGURE 2 gives another example, again somewhat extreme. It illustrates the concept of a polymorphous set, a set with no singly necessary and jointly sufficient conditions for set membership. Everyday concepts often have polymorphous characteristics—they are not as logical as we would like to think. For example, the reader might attempt to construct a list of necessary and sufficient conditions to define an object as a piece of furniture. Quite likely, no such conditions can be found—only a list of characteristics, some of which are shared by any particular piece of furniture. Or, consider the everyday definition of a bird. Most people will mention that "a bird flies," even while knowing perfectly well that there are birds that do not fly. A large body of psychological literature (for a review, see Smith and Medin)[2] suggests that we identify categories by a mixture of two procedures: comparison with exemplars, and probabilistic feature matching. Not only that, but we slide back and forth between these two methods depending on the situation at hand. One of the main points of this paper is that both methods in combination are necessary for more complex functions such as the formation of associative memories, not because we are careless or illogical, but because the need for them is built into the structure of the underlying system. For this reason, both types of categorization are present in the automaton we will describe.

It is important to understand that learning need not necessarily be a factor in recognition although it is often useful. What is required is that a response be associated with a pattern of sensory information corresponding to an object or class of objects in the environment, and that the response be adaptive for the organism. Conventional responses, such as names, can be acquired only through learning, but before we can learn, it is necessary to have categories or, at higher levels, concepts to which the learned responses can be attached. The system we will discuss carries out this more primitive form of pattern recognition that does not involve learning. It incorporates the ability of biological systems to respond to stimuli never encountered before, yet has no program that embodies information about particular stimuli.

To see how this can be done, consider some facts about biological recognizing systems and what they imply. The brain comprises a network of interconnected neurons with apparently a high degree of parallelism

FIGURE 1. Fragment from Maurits C. Escher's woodcut *Metamorphosis II*, illustrating the importance of context in perception. (Reproduced by permission. © M. C. Escher Heirs, c/o V. W. Vermeulen, Prilly, CH.)

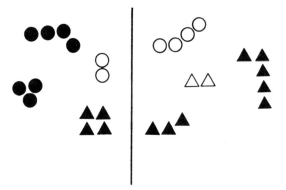

FIGURE 2. Illustration of a polymorphous rule for set membership. Members of the set (left) have any two of the properties roundness, solid color, or bilateral symmetry. Nonmembers (right) have only one of these properties. (After Dennis et al.,[9] with permission from Nature, © 1973 Macmillan Journals Limited.)

in their operations. The speed and dynamic range of these neurons are limited, suggesting that the network cannot carry out algorithmic calculations involving large numbers of steps and high-precision arithmetic. We also know something about the number of neurons and how they are connected. Specialized regions are seen in the brain, consistent with the notion that multiple networks with different functions may need to interact to generate more complex functions. One sees highly overlapping arborizations of individual neurons, with apparently a large degree of variability, even in genetically identical individuals. Such a level of variability in wiring would be a severe nuisance in a digital computer, here one would like to think nature has adopted it as part of the solution to the problem. Finally, no single neuron appears to be indispensible to memory,[3] strongly suggesting that patterns of response in collections of neurons, not individual responses, are what is important.

All of these observations, particularly the necessary presence of variation in the structure of the system and its need to respond adaptively to an unpredictable environment, are the hallmarks of a selective system, the same ingredients that one sees in the working of evolution itself. We suggest that the brain is in fact a selective system operating in somatic time and that selection provides the exquisitely tuned adaptability needed for survival in a hostile environment.

THE NEURONAL GROUP SELECTION THEORY

The conditions needed for a selective system are (1) a collection of variant entities, or repertoire, capable of responding to the environment; (2) sufficient opportunities for those entities actually to encounter the environment; and (3) a mechanism to enhance or amplify differentially the numbers or strengths of those entities whose responses to the environment are in some sense adaptive. All of these elements are present in the neuronal group selection theory[4] (FIGURE 3). The recognizing elements are postulated to be groups of from 50 to 10,000 interconnected neurons. These groups are formed during development, prior to exposure to any sensory stimulation, and their connections, once established, remain stable thereafter. The groups are connected in networks to form repertoires capable of encountering sensory information transmitted along the network connections. When the response of a group

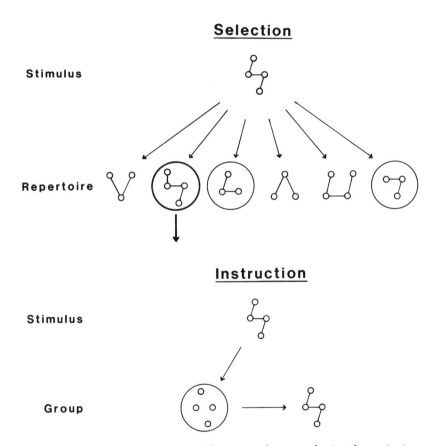

FIGURE 3. Schematic representation of the neuronal group selection theory (top) contrasted with information-processing or instructional theories (bottom). Circles connected with lines represent specific characteristics of stimuli and the matching characteristics of groups that respond to them, not any particular neuroanatomy. Groups whose specificity matches a given stimulus more or less well respond (groups surrounded with larger circles); only those groups that respond best (heavy large circle) are modified for stronger future response (heavy arrow). In instructional theories, groups have no particular initial specificities (group without joining lines, bottom); specificity is dictated by interaction with stimuli.

happens to be adaptive for the organism as a whole, the strengths (transmission efficiencies) of the connections of that group are modified in such a way that the response of the group is faster or stronger to future encounters with the same or similar stimulus patterns.

In such systems there is necessarily a relationship between the number of recognizing groups in a repertoire and the specificities of the individual groups. If recognition is overly specific, there cannot be enough groups in a finite repertoire to recognize all possible stimuli and the system must fail; similarly, if specificity is too broad, similar but significantly different stimuli cannot be distinguished, and again the system must fail. The specificities must therefore be intermediate, but this implies that several groups may respond more or less well to any given stimulus. This phenomenon, which we call degeneracy (FIGURE 4), is critical to an understanding of selective recognition systems. Sufficient degeneracy assures that there will be some response to any conceivable stimulus, and, in fact, that more than one group will respond to any stimulus, assuring the necessary degree of functional redundancy to make the system "fail-safe" against the failure of individual groups.

FIGURE 5 illustrates how a degenerate recognizing system becomes capable of responding to any stimulus, even a novel one, once it becomes sufficiently large. The crucial assumption is that there is a small, but finite, probability that any single group will respond to any given stimulus. This assumption seems reasonable for a network of groups connected so that each of them receives at least some part of the total pattern of sensory input elicited by each stimulus. A change in the recognition specificity serves to shift the entire curve in FIGURE 5 to the

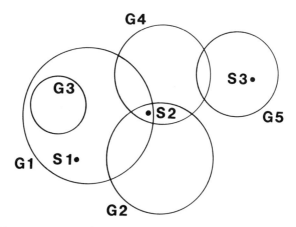

FIGURE 4. Degeneracy. Stimuli are represented by heavy dots labeled S1, S2, etc. Recognizing groups are represented by circles labeled G1, G2, etc. The size of each circle suggests the range of stimuli to which a group can respond. Overlapping circles suggest how multiple groups from a degenerate repertoire can respond more or less well to the same stimulus.

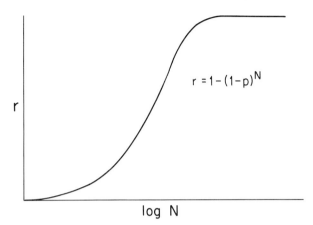

FIGURE 5. Response as a function of repertoire size. Assuming a constant, independent probability p that any one group will respond to any one stimulus, the function r gives the probability that some one or more groups in a repertoire of N groups will respond to any one stimulus.

left or to the right, more groups being needed if the probability of response of each individual group decreases. In practice, the probability of response, p, must be set according to the level of specificity needed to deal with a particular ecological niche, and the required size of the network, N, follows.

This theory is compatible with the biological facts we have summarized and suggests a way that organisms can make use of the unavoidable epigenetic variability in neural nets to recognize and classify stimuli even in the absence of classical reinforced learning. Its relevance to brain function will of course have to be decided by experiment; already evidence in support of the theory is beginning to accumulate.[5] However, independent of its biological applicability, one can, with a computer model, test the consistency of the theory and explore its power to solve real classification problems. Such a model can serve to focus experimental questions for biologists and at the same time point the way to the construction of artificial pattern-recognizing systems employing the same principles. We believe that the model we have constructed, which we call "Darwin II," represents a new kind of pattern-recognizing automaton in that it can function without a program and without forced learning to recognize stimuli, classify them, and form associations between them. The construction of this automaton will be discussed in the next section.

DARWIN II

In devising the Darwin II model, we were guided by a number of ground rules. It was obvious that the system should be a network. The nodes of this network are the recognizing elements of the model, corresponding to the groups of neurons postulated by the theory. We decided to model these groups at the functional level, not at the level of detailed electrophysiological properties. Each group in the model has a state corresponding to its level of activity. A group's state is dependent only on its present inputs and past history. The groups are able to transmit their state variables to other groups along the connections of the network, which are analogous to the synapses in a nervous system. As in the adult central nervous system, the connectivity of the network, once established, is not changed. However, the connections' strengths can change, and it is these changes that provide the mechanism for the amplification of response required by the theory. Finally, one of the most important rules, one that distinguishes Darwin II from systems based on "frames" or "conceptual networks," is that there can be no specific information about particular stimulus objects built into the system. Of course, general information about the kinds of stimuli that will be significant to the system is implicit in the choice of feature-detecting elements we have made—this is akin to the choices built into organisms by their evolutionarily determined programs.

The overall plan of Darwin II is shown in FIGURE 6. At the top is an "input array" where stimuli are presented as patterns of light and dark picture elements on a lattice. (We typically use letters of the alphabet on a 16×16 grid, but any two-dimensional pattern is acceptable.) The system proper is below the input array. It consists of two parallel concatenations of networks, each with several subnetworks or repertoires (indicated by boxes). These operate in parallel, and "speak" to each other to give a function not possessed by either set alone. The two sets of networks are arbitrarily named "Darwin" and "Wallace" after the two main figures in the description of natural selection. The Darwin network (left) is designed to respond uniquely to each individual stimulus pattern, and loosely corresponds to the exemplar approach to categorization. The Wallace network (right), on the other hand, is designed to respond in a similar fashion to objects belonging to a class, and loosely corresponds to the probabilistic matching approach to categorization. Darwin and Wallace have a common level structure. Each has connected to the input array a level that deals with features, and below that an abstracting or transforming level that receives its main input from the first level. Output may be taken from these networks at the bottom.

The first part of Darwin is the **R** or "recognizer" repertoire. It has groups that respond to local features on the input array, such as line segments oriented in certain directions or with certain bends, as suggested by the inset (FIGURE 6). Sets of these feature detectors are connected topographically to the input array so that the patterns of response in **R** spatially resemble the stimulus patterns. Connected to **R** is a transforming network called **R-of-R** ("recognizer-of-recognizers"). Groups in **R-of-R** are connected to multiple **R** groups distributed over the **R** sheet, so that each **R-of-R** group is capable of responding to an entire pattern of response in **R**. In the process, the topographic mapping of **R** is not preserved; as a result **R-of-R** gives an abstract transformation of the original stimulus pattern. (Note that if the stimulus undergoes a change such as a translation to a new position on the input array, the pattern of response in **R-of-R** will be quite different. It is Wallace that deals with this translation problem. **R-of-R** is concerned with *individual* properties of a stimulus, and these include its relation to the background.)

Wallace begins with a tracing mechanism designed to scan the input array, detecting object contours and tracing along them to give correlations of features that reveal the presence of objects as single entities and their continuity properties and that respond to some of their characteris-

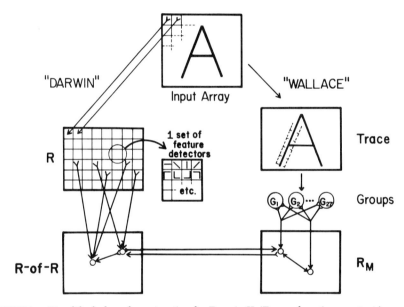

FIGURE 6. Simplified plan of construction for Darwin II. (For explanation, see text.)

tics, such as junctions of various types between lines. In this respect, Wallace works something like the eye does in rapidly scanning a scene to detect the objects present. The result of the trace is that a set of "virtual" groups ($G_1, \ldots, G_{27}$ in FIGURE 6) are excited according to the topology of the input pattern. These groups are called "virtual" because their input does not involve ordinary synaptic connections. The virtual groups are connected in turn to an abstracting network, R_M, which responds to patterns of activity in the trace in much the same way as **R-of-R** responds to patterns of activity in **R**. Because the trace responds to the presence of lines or junctions of lines with only little regard for their lengths and orientations, R_M is insensitive to both rigid and nonrigid transformations of the stimulus object and tends to respond to class characteristics of whole families of related stimuli.

The **R-of-R** and **R$_M$** networks are connected together by the reciprocal cross-connections shown at the bottom center of the figure. These connections are reentrant in that they connect one part of the system to another part of itself rather than to the outside; they provide the mechanism needed for the system to display associative recall by allowing Darwin and Wallace to interact with each other.

All the repertoires of Darwin II are made by connecting together groups that have a common logical structure, summarized in FIGURE 7. There are two classes of input connections. Specific connections (upper left) may come from the input array or from groups in the same or other

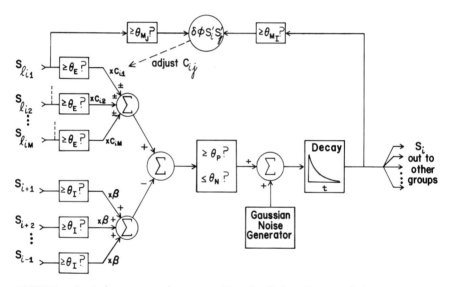

FIGURE 7. Logical structure of a group. (For detailed mathematical description, see Edelman and Reeke, from which this figure is reproduced.)[1]

repertoires. The sources of all these connections are specified by lists, the construction of which differs from one repertoire to another. There are also short-range inhibitory connections (lower left) having a function corresponding to lateral inhibition in neural nets. These connections are geometrically specified and nonspecific. The level of activity at each input connection, if it exceeds a necessary threshold level, is multiplied by a weight corresponding to the strength of its particular synapse. The weight establishes how important the particular input is in determining the overall response of the entire group. The weighted inputs are all combined by adding the contributions from the excitatory inputs and subtracting the contributions from the inhibitory inputs, as suggested in

FIGURE 7. The combined input must exceed a second excitatory or inhibitory threshold to have any effect on the group's activity. If not, the previous level of activity simply undergoes exponential decay. In either case, a varying amount of noise is added to the response of the group by analogy with the noise found in real neuronal networks. The final response obtained by combining all of these terms is made available to whatever other groups may be connected to this one (arrows at right).

To the extent that different groups are constructed with similar input connection lists and connection strengths, repertoires of these groups will have the required degeneracy. The specificities of the groups are implicit in their connection strengths—the best response is obtained when the most active inputs are connected to synapses with high connection strengths. The way these connection strengths are changed during the course of selection is suggested at the top of FIGURE 7 for a typical connection. There are many possible ways to formulate the rules for changing connection strengths. Fairly typical is this one: if a particular group responds strongly, and the input to one of its synapses is simultaneously active, the strength of that synapse should be strengthened so that later applications of the same input will give a still stronger response. Darwin II permits this so-called Hebb rule[6] or any of 80 other possible rules to be chosen for each type of connection. As the figure suggests, these rules have in common that the change in connection strength depends on the activity of either or both of the pre- and postsynaptic activities and on the preexisting value of the connection strength, but not on any other variables. Within limits, it is not too important exactly what rule is used, as long as it is recognized that connections must be able to decrease in strength as well as increase—otherwise, all synapses are eventually driven to maximum strength and the system ceases to show selectivity.

RESULTS

In examining the results obtained with Darwin II, we will be looking for the following criteria of success: in Darwin, the generation of individual representations, that is, unique responses to each different stimulus and the same response to repeated presentations of the same stimulus, but stronger; in Wallace, the generation of class representations, that is, similar responses to different stimuli having common class characteristics. In the complete system, these individual and class representations must interact to give associative recall of different stimuli in a common class.

FIGURE 8 shows the responses of the individual repertoires under conditions in which the cross-connections between Darwin and Wallace are not functioning. It can be seen that the **R** responses are topographic, generally resembling the stimulus letters except for some occasional noise responses. The responses in **R-of-R**, as expected, are individual and

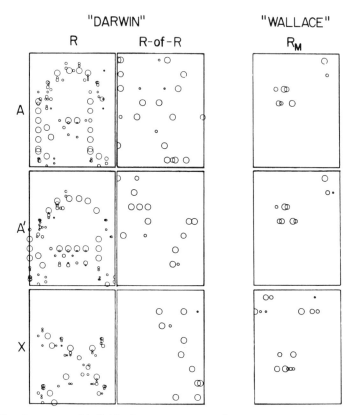

FIGURE 8. Responses of individual repertoires (**R**, **R-of-R**, and **R$_M$**; names at top) to a tall, narrow A (top row), a lower, wider A (middle), and an X (bottom). Circles represent groups responding at 0.5 (small circles) or more of maximum response (large circles). Groups responding at less than half of maximal response are not shown, leaving blank areas in the repertoire plots.

idiosyncratic, and not at all topographic because features from different parts of **R** are being correlated. The responses to the two A's appear to be no more similar than the response to an A is to the response to an X, although statistics do show a somewhat greater degree of similarity, as we shall see. The situation in Wallace is entirely different. The responses in **R$_M$** are very similar for the two stimuli that are in the same class (the two A's) and are not at all sensitive to the idiosyncratic features of each letter. Moreover, the response is independent of any rotation or translation of a letter.

When selection is allowed to occur, in which synaptic strengths are modified in accord with an amplification rule, the responses become more specific, as shown in FIGURE 9. These response frequency histograms show the distribution of responses when a particular stimulus is first presented (a) and again after it has been presented for some time (b).

Initially, most groups respond weakly, but there are a few groups that happen to respond very well. After selection, more good responders have been recruited from among the groups that earlier had been medium-strength responders, but large numbers of nonresponders remain available, possibly to respond to other stimuli not used in this experiment.

This behavior exemplifies *recognition*, that is, an enhanced response to a stimulus after it has been experienced before. If this same type of experiment is done with several different kinds of stimuli, the system displays *classification*. The similarity of the responses of a repertoire to any two letters can be measured by counting the number of groups that respond to both of the letters and dividing it by the number that would have been obtained by chance if the same total number of responding groups were distributed evenly over the repertoire. Classification can be

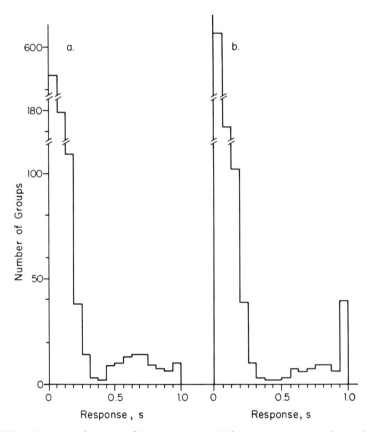

FIGURE 9. Response frequency histograms. (a) Initial response to a novel stimulus. (b) Response to the same stimulus after selection has proceeded for a time. Abscissae: response levels s, expressed as a fraction of maximal response. Ordinates: numbers of groups responding at level s.

assessed by examining ratios in which these similarity measures, obtained for pairs of letters in the same class, are divided by the corresponding similarity measures for pairs of letters in different classes. The class memberships of the different letters used are specified by the experimenter and are not available to Darwin II. In TABLE 1, we present values of this ratio for **R-of-R** and for $\mathbf{R_M}$ at the beginning of a typical experiment and after selection had been allowed to progress for three presentations of each stimulus. It can be seen that for these stimuli, groups in Wallace $(\mathbf{R_M})$ were 91 times more likely to respond to both of two stimuli if they were in the same class than if they were in different classes. The system thus classifies by giving similar responses to different letters of the same kind. As suggested earlier, a minimal amount of classification is also seen in Darwin, as suggested by the 1.21 initial ratio.

TABLE 1. Classification in Darwin II*

	Repertoire	
Time Tested	Darwin (**R-of-R**)	Wallace ($\mathbf{R_M}$)
Initially	1.21	90.93
After selection†	1.41	241.30

*Repertoire sizes: **R**, 3,840 groups; others, 4,096 groups. Total connections: 368,640; no Darwin-Wallace connections. Stimuli used: 16 letters, 4 each of 4 kinds. Quantity shown is ratio of number of groups responding to two stimuli in same class to number of groups responding to two stimuli in different classes, corrected for numbers that would respond in each case by chance alone.

†Each of four stimuli was presented for eight cycles, then the entire set was repeated three times.

After selective modification of the connection strengths, the classification gets better, even though there is no feedback from the environment that would permit the system to "learn" which responses are "correct."

These results can be extended to stimuli not included in the training set (the set presented during selection) to yield *generalization* in both $\mathbf{R_M}$ and **R-of-R**. In $\mathbf{R_M}$, this is a direct consequence of the class-responding characteristics of that repertoire, but in **R-of-R** it is not, and in fact can be obtained only if reentrant connections from $\mathbf{R_M}$ to **R-of-R** and within **R-of-R** are present. These connections permit $\mathbf{R_M}$ to influence the activity of **R-of-R**, supporting common patterns in the responses of disparate stimuli that happen to have similarities in their $\mathbf{R_M}$ responses by virtue of their common class membership. As TABLE 2 shows, in one particular experiment the ratio of similarity of intraclass responses to interclass responses in **R-of-R** for a test set of letters not previously presented was 6.10 after selection based on other letters of the same kind (the training set), whereas it had been only 1.77 initially. The results for a control set of unrelated letters show that this effect is specific, and not due to a general increase in similarity of response to all stimuli.

TABLE 2. Generalization in **R-of-R***

Stimuli	Intraclass Chance	Interclass Chance	Intraclass Interclass
Initially			
Training set	2.09	0.72	2.90
Test set	2.89	1.63	1.77
Control set	—	1.96	—
After selection†			
Test set	6.10	1.00	6.10
Control set	—	1.00	—

*Repertoire sizes: **R**, 3,840 groups; others, 1,024 groups. Connections to each **R-of-R** group: 96 from **R**, 64 from **R-of-R**, 128 from **R$_M$**. Stimuli used: 16 letters, 4 each from 4 classes.
†Each of 16 stimuli was presented for 4 cycles, then entire set was repeated 4 times.

These results indicate that the Darwin and Wallace networks separately fulfill the design criteria we have outlined. A final experiment demonstrates how the reentrant connections between them work to give associative recall of stimuli that the system places in the same class by virtue of similar responses to them in the Wallace network.

The setup of the system for the association experiment is shown in FIGURE 10. Just two stimuli are used, an X and a +, chosen because their responses in **R-of-R** are quite different while their responses in **R$_M$** are very similar (because each consists of a pair of lines crossing near their centers). When the X is first presented (FIGURE 10, left panel), **R** (center left) gives the expected topographic response; **R-of-R** gives a unique pattern characteristic of that stimulus (for clarity, only a single group is

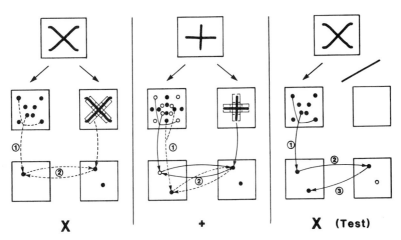

X   +   X (Test)

FIGURE 10. Schematic views of Darwin II showing three stages in an associative recall experiment. Filled circles represent active groups; open circles, inactive groups. Solid lines between groups represent connections selectively strengthened; dashed lines represent connections activated for the first time. Numerals enclosed in circles label pathways that are activated at successive times. (For discussion, see text.)

shown responding in the figure), with stimulation via Pathways 1. At the same time, a trace occurs in Wallace, eliciting an appropriate pattern of response in R_M. Cross-connections are present in both directions between **R-of-R** and R_M; connections that happen to join responding groups in the two repertoires are strengthened by the normal modification procedure (Pathways 2). In the center panel of FIGURE 10, the X is removed and a + is presented. The groups active in the response to the X are now no longer active (open circles), although the connections between them remain strengthened (solid lines). New groups in **R** and **R-of-R** become active in response to the + (filled circles); connections between these groups are strengthened as before (dashed lines, Pathways 1). In Wallace, the trace pattern is the same as for the X, eliciting a response in R_M very similar to that obtained before. Connections between the + responding groups in **R-of-R** and these same responders in R_M are therefore strengthened (Pathways 2). An indirect associative pathway is thus established via R_M between groups involved in the two patterns of response in **R-of-R**.

The third panel in FIGURE 10 shows how the association is tested. The trace mechanism is turned off so that the association will be based entirely on past experience with the stimuli and not on any immediate correlation occurring during the test. When the X is presented under these conditions, **R** and **R-of-R** give responses very similar to those obtained originally with the X. R_M receives input only from **R-of-R** via the previously strengthened Pathways 2, eliciting the common pattern of response appropriate to both the X and the +. Pathways 3 then permit R_M to stimulate in **R-of-R** the pattern originally associated with the second stimulus, the +, even though the + is not then present on the input array. Depending on the time constants chosen, this associated response can occur together with the X response or later.

Results of a typical experiment of this type are shown in FIGURE 11. Responses are plotted as a function of time for a number of individual **R-of-R** groups. On the left (a) are seen the results when the test stimulus was the X. The groups at the top are ones that responded to the X during the first presentation of that letter, and the groups at the bottom are ones that responded to the + during the first presentation of that letter. As expected, these + responders do not respond immediately when the X is presented. After four cycles of stimulation, the **R** repertoire is switched off (arrow) so that it no longer dominates the **R-of-R** response and there is now no outside input to either Darwin or Wallace. Under these conditions, the response of some of the X responders (top) begins to decay away (see, e.g., groups 77, 85, and 91), while some of the + responders now become active as a result of the stimulation they receive through the reentrant connections from R_M (see, e.g., groups 28, 34, and 95). Thus, the system, presented with an X, recalls elements of the response proper to the +; these two stimuli have become associated.

A separate, reciprocal experiment is shown in FIGURE 11b, where the same groups are plotted for the case where the + is the test stimulus. Now it is the + responders (top) that begin responding immediately, but decay

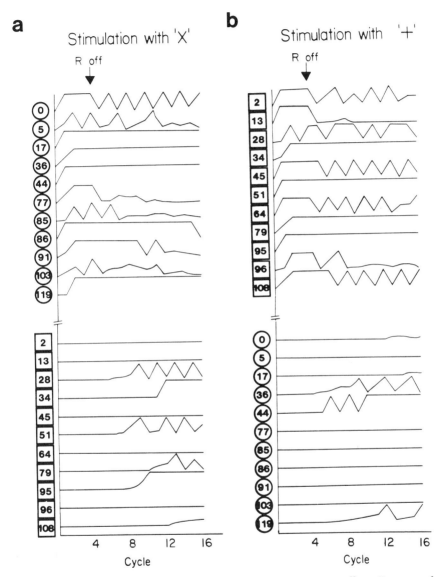

FIGURE 11. Responses of individual **R-of-R** groups in an associative recall test. Response of each group is plotted as a function of time, measured in cycles of the model (scales at bottom). Each group is labeled by its serial number in the repertoire. A serial number is enclosed in a circle if the group responded initially to an X or is enclosed in a box if the group responded initially to a +. Arrows (top) indicate time (after fourth cycle) at which all input to system was cut off. (a) Stimulation with an X. (b) Stimulation with a +.

when **R** is switched off (arrow), and it is the X responders (bottom) that come up in associative recall when the stimulus is removed. Thus, the association is bidirectional—the + is associated with the X and the X is associated with the +. No association occurs if the original stimuli have no common response in Wallace, e.g., an A and an X.

In this experiment, letters are associated in Wallace in a trivial way, because their responses are very similar to begin with. In Darwin, however, their responses are not the same but have individual character. The association obtained in Darwin in this experiment could not have been obtained without Wallace, but at the same time it goes beyond what Wallace could have done alone, because in Darwin the individual character of the responses to the two stimuli is preserved. This example illustrates some of the features we suggested earlier for human perception. It is intended to clarify our assertion that pattern recognition is enhanced by the interaction of two basic methods of category formation, one based on the use of exemplars, the other based on common class features.

SUMMARY

The results we have presented demonstrate that a network based on a selective principle can function in the absence of forced learning or an *a priori* program to give recognition, classification, generalization, and association. While Darwin II is not a model of any actual nervous system, it does set out to solve one of the same problems that evolution had to solve—the need to form categories in a bottom-up manner from information in the environment, without incorporating the assumptions of any particular observer. The key features of the model that make this possible are (1) Darwin II incorporates selective networks whose initial specificities enable them to respond without instruction to unfamiliar stimuli; (2) degeneracy provides multiple possibilities of response to any one stimulus, at the same time providing functional redundancy against component failure; (3) the output of Darwin II is a pattern of response, making use of the simultaneous responses of multiple degenerate groups to avoid the need for very high specificity and the combinatorial disaster that would imply; (4) reentry within individual networks vitiates the limitations described by Minsky and Papert for a class of perceptual automata lacking such connections;[7] and (5) reentry between intercommunicating networks with different functions gives rise to new functions, such as association, that either one alone could not display. The two kinds of network are roughly analogous to the two kinds of category formation that people use:[2] Darwin, corresponding to the exemplar description of categories, and Wallace, corresponding to the probabilistic matching description of categories.

These principles lead to a new class of pattern-recognizing machine of which Darwin II is just an example. There are a number of obvious extensions to this work that we are pursuing. These include giving Darwin II the capability to deal with stimuli that are in motion, an ability that probably precedes the ability of biological organisms to deal with stationary stimuli,[8] giving it the capability to deal with multiple stimulus objects through some form of attentional mechanism, and giving it a means to respond directly and to receive feedback from the world so that it can learn conventionally. Already, however, we have shown that a working pattern-recognition automaton can be built based on a selective principle. This development promises ultimately to show us how to build recognizing machines without programs and to provide a sound basis for the study of both natural and artificial intelligence.

REFERENCES

1. EDELMAN, G. M. & G. N. REEKE, JR. 1982. Selective networks capable of representative transformations, limited generalizations, and associative memory. Proc. Nat. Acad. Sci. USA **79:** 2091–2095.
2. SMITH, E. E. & D. L. MEDIN. 1981. Categories and Concepts. Harvard University Press. Cambridge, Mass.
3. LASHLEY, K. 1950. In search of the engram. In Physiological Mechanisms in Animal Behavior (Society of Experimental Biology Symposium No. 4): 454–482. Academic Press. New York, N.Y.
4. EDELMAN, G. M. 1978. Group selection and phasic reentrant signalling: a theory of higher brain function. In The Mindful Brain. G. M. Edelman & V. B. Mountcastle, Eds.: 51–100. MIT Press. Cambridge, Mass.
5. EDELMAN, G. M. & L. FINKEL. Neuronal group selection in the cerebral cortex. In Dynamic Aspects of Neocortical Function. G. M. Edelman, W. M. Cowan & W. E. Gall, Eds. John Wiley & Sons. New York, N.Y. (In press.)
6. HEBB, D. O. 1949. The Organization of Behavior. John Wiley & Sons. New York, N.Y.
7. MINSKY, M. & S. PAPERT. 1969. Perceptrons: An Introduction to Computational Geometry. MIT Press. Cambridge, Mass.
8. ULLMAN, S. 1979. The Interpretation of Visual Motion. MIT Press. Cambridge, Mass.
9. DENNIS, I., J. A. HAMPTON & S. E. G. LEA. 1973. New problem in concept formation. Nature **243:** 101–102.

DISCUSSION OF THE PAPER

QUESTION: I would like to say, I find that very fascinating. I was wondering—have you presented fields of essentially Gaussian noise following a stimulus to see how long images that you've built up would remain, or whether you have a decay process?

G. N. REEKE: The question is how long it takes for a response to decay?

QUESTION: Right, and whether it's dependent upon the amount of noise that you actually present after that point rather than no image at all.

G. N. REEKE: I didn't show you the details of how the groups work, but in fact there is an exponential decay built in and that's one of the parameters in a given simulation so that the decay time can be controlled more or less independently of the noise.

QUESTION: And do you also notice any kinds of optical illusions beginning to present themselves, I mean responses that don't necessarily tie directly to the original stimulus?

G. N. REEKE: Yes, there are all sorts of interesting pathological behaviors that occur when parameters are set in certain ways. The system can oscillate, lock in on a particular stimulus and not change when a new one is presented, and so on.

QUESTION: As a psychologist I think that your work is very fascinating and I'm struck by the fact that your system seems to be able to take two things that look different but are classified as the same and make a discrimination between them. I'm struck by an example that we often see in child development: a young child growing up sees a dog and learns to classify it as a dog and then, when he ventures out and sees an animal that's about the same size as the dog but that's really a cat, he says, "Look, there goes another dog." Here we have essentially two things that look the same but really are different. Do you think that your system will ultimately have the capability to make those kinds of discriminations?

G. M. EDELMAN: Dr. Reeke, may I intervene to describe an experiment that was performed at Harvard on pigeons? It's a common enough assumption of human beings that we are the grand masters of generalization, but if you present a pigeon with one example of a white oak leaf four times with reward, it will recognize every other genus of oak leaf and reject all other kinds of leaves. If you present it with pictures of fish that it has never seen before in Kodachromes at any scale and within any context, it will perform almost as well. That means that some kind of stimulus generalization of the kind that you have discussed is occurring in a biological system. The linguistic system of course is many steps up higher.

G. N. REEKE: The only comment I'd add to that is that of course in child development there's quite a bootstrapping process going on if one starts with nothing. This perhaps is somewhat analogous to the situation where the specificities of the groups are broad and confusions are made but as time goes on various responses get enhanced, the tuning becomes sharper, and discriminations can be made. Of course long before that I think much more complicated, higher-level things are happening too so it's a bit silly to discuss Darwin II at that level.

QUESTION: Have you formalized your model to the extent that you know where it fits in the formal language hierarchy? For example, do you know if you can recognize regular sets and do you have any kind of measures of the complexity of recognition?

G. N. REEKE: No, there is a great deal of mathematical analysis that one can eventually do after getting some more experience with this system. I would like to make one comment though that I didn't have time for in the talk. If one looks at some of the published analyses of various systems, for example, Minsky and Papert's analysis of perceptrons, one can see that we've built in a lot of things that they have assumed not to be present. In particular the reentrant connections make the analysis so much more difficult that it's very hard to see how one could begin and make those kinds of strong conclusions.

G. M. EDELMAN: There is one other comment that's worth making, which was implied in Dr. Reeke's early mention of polymorphous sets. There's every indication that for an animal, particularly one that doesn't have language, objects that are not stimuli in psychological laboratories do form classes of polymorphous sets. These are sets that are defined by features that are neither singly necessary nor jointly sufficient. Wittgenstein described them when he described games. He said games do not necessarily have anything in common except that they are games. This means that any M out of N possible properties would define one particular game and no single universal description would. Anyone who wants to set up a system that imitates biological systems I think has to pay heed to that.

Taming and Civilizing Computers

ALPHONSE CHAPANIS

Communications Research Laboratory
7402 York Road
Baltimore, Maryland 21204

It is safe to say that technology has advanced more in the last 100 years than it has in all of mankind's history up to that time. In fact, the technological inventions of the last century are so numerous that it would be difficult to count them all. Nonetheless, I am sure many people would agree with me that among all those inventions the automobile and the computer are the two that have most profoundly revolutionized our society, our ways of living, and our ways of working.

Although automobiles do not look much like computers, these two machines have several things in common. First and most important perhaps is that both have given us freedom. The automobile has freed us from the limitations of our human bodies. With it we can almost effortlessly roam at will and over great distances, at speeds that were undreamed of by our forefathers 100 years ago.

The computer has also given us freedom. It has freed us from some limitations of our human minds. We can now store in compact computer memories vast amounts of information, and we can retrieve any or all of it almost instantaneously. We can rearrange, condense, modify, and sort through the stores of information in computer memories so quickly and so flexibly that we can now solve problems that would be insolvable by unaided human intellects. In freeing the human mind from some of its limitations, computers give us the freedom to explore new ideas, to create, to dream, and to enjoy.

There is another important respect in which automobiles and computers resemble each other, and that is in the way they have evolved and are still evolving. When automobiles, or rather horseless carriages, appeared on the scene nearly 90 years ago, they were very crude, clumsy, and uncomfortable vehicles. Although early automobiles were simpler mechanisms than our modern ones, they lacked many of the important features that we take for granted today. As a result, they were difficult machines to operate. There were, for example, no self-starters. To start his first automobile, my father had to get out in front of the vehicle, insert a crank into an opening just below the radiator, and give the crank a vigorous yank. Sometimes he had to repeat this procedure several times before the engine caught. To light the headlights, he had to ignite them with a match. Powered windshield wipers were not available until the 1920s. So in rainy weather, my father manipulated the windshield wiper with one hand while he steered with the other.

Early automobiles were also very uncomfortable. Since heaters and air conditioners were unknown, the driver and passengers froze in winter and boiled in summer. Completely enclosed automobiles did not appear on the scene until many years after cars had first been marketed.

Finally, society did not know quite how to adjust to the automobile. Passable roads were scarce and road signs even scarcer. Traffic regulations, parking lots, and drive-in conveniences were things that people had not thought of. It took many years for society to learn how to live with the automobile. (Of course, some people might say that we still do not know how to live with it.)

Over the years, three things happened. First, automobiles became a lot more complicated, but at the same time they became much easier to operate. Almost anyone can drive these days. The automobile has become everyone's vehicle. Only a small proportion of the people who drive know what goes on underneath the hood of a car, but that is all right. They do not need to know how it works. The important thing is that they can operate it.

The second thing that happened is that automobiles became more comfortable. Contoured and cushioned seats, heating, air conditioning, and carefully designed suspension systems have made vehicles almost as comfortable as one's own living room.

The third thing that has happened is that society has learned how to accommodate the automobile, how to use it, and how to live with it. We have learned how to make the automobile enhance the quality of our human lives. The automobile, in a manner of speaking, was tamed and became civilized.

What has already happened to the automobile is still happening to the computer. In the case of the computer, however, we have not yet fully learned how to tame it, and that is what I want to talk about today. Specifically, I shall talk about making computers easier to use, about making computers more comfortable machines to work with, and then finally, about integrating computers into our ways of working and living.

EASE OF USE

Early computers, like early automobiles, were difficult to operate. Since programming was a skill few people had, computers were largely limited to what are now called data processing, or DP, professionals. The ordinary person who wanted to get a job done had to turn the job over to a DP professional who translated the job into machine language, ran the program, and then delivered the results to the client.

All that has changed in recent years. Computers have moved into small businesses, stores, and homes, and they are being used by the same people who need to get computing jobs done. Computers have become a lot easier to use, as computer salesmen and manufacturers are eager to point out. "Easy to learn," "easy to use," "easy on the eyes," "easy to implement"—these are only a few of the words you can find liberally

sprinkled throughout computer advertisements in newspapers, magazines, and sales brochures everywhere.

Are Computers Easy to Use?

Can we believe what manufacturers and salesmen say? Are computers really easy to use? Well, maybe. There is a kind of curious
ambivalence on this topic of ease of use, even among people who should
know about these things. For example, Carroll, a researcher at the IBM
Thomas J. Watson Research Center, wrote recently:

> Text editors, and other application systems . . . relieve people of having to
> scrawl things on paper—even people who are writing a letter! Once in the
> system, text can be revised, manipulated, or printed out. Repetitive tasks,
> like mass mailing, can be automated by the use of variables: once input,
> forever done. Using a text editor can help a child learn to write more
> fluently and more quickly, and it can make an adult feel more comfortable
> and confident about writing. Moreover, learning to use a text editor is
> easy—at least relative to learning to write or type. Text editing is really only
> a step away from typing and actually reenforces this skill [p. 50].[1]

Carroll then goes on to say, in what I regard as an astonishing denial of
what he has just said:

> But although text editors are potentially "easy" to learn to use, people are
> still having tremendous difficulty learning to use them. In most cases, they
> are learned incompletely and after significant confusion and error. A
> variety of problems beset people who are learning to use contemporary text
> editors . . . these problems are an unpalatable potpourri of troubles [p. 50].[1]

The rest of Carroll's excellent article documents those problems in
some detail.

It is not hard to find other examples of such contradictions. As you
know, a few months ago, the weekly magazine *Time* created quite a stir
by breaking with a long-standing tradition. In its January 3rd issue this
year, it featured not the Man of the Year, but the Machine of the Year, the
computer. In a foreword to that issue, the publisher, John Meyers, quoted
Frederic Golden as saying: "Computers were once regarded as distant,
ominous abstractions, like Big Brother. In 1982 they truly became person-
alized, brought down to scale, so that people could hold, prod and play
with them."[2] But a little later, Meyers says: "For all that computers have
achieved, they can still prove frustrating. In April, Golden's machine
inextricably swallowed the cover story he had written on the Computer
Generation."[2]

Just after I had written the words above, I took time out to have
breakfast and read the morning paper. My eye was caught by an article
on computer clubs, written by Erik Sandberg-Diment for the New York
Times News Service. In his article he says, among other things, "Personal
computer clubs, usually known as user's groups, are probably one of the
best and least painful ways for a beginner to find out what to do with his

computer."[3] Did you notice his choice of words? "Least painful" does not convey to me the impression of something that is easy to use! Perhaps the pain comes from what Johnson-Laird wrote about so bluntly in *Software News* last year: "The computer systems and software we have today are too damn complicated for the end user. There is too much to learn, too many fiddly details, too much jargon, too much said that shouldn't be and not enough said that should be."[4]

Just a couple of months ago, *Software News* published a special feature on office automation. If you sift through all the hoopla and enthusiastic articles in that issue you can find some sobering admissions. Parks, for example, had this to say:

> Data processing still has one ongoing problem to solve: the end user's dissatisfaction with today's systems. The entire industry has been grappling with this problem of ergonomics, or the interface between human and machine. In the case of data processing, ergonomics involves the development of "user-friendly" systems which can be operated by the user at the terminal and which generate results that the user can understand and utilize [p. 23].[5]

These same sentiments were echoed by Lynn:

> Unfortunately, in spite of much improvement, these programs [word processing application packages for personal computers] are not very easy to use. Besides the awkward and rigid commands a user must learn, there are other technical problems [p. 44].[6]

Her article then goes on to enumerate some of those problems, such as small screen size, lack of upper- and lowercase letters, nonstandard keyboards, lack of a unified set of commands, poor documentation, and poor training.

Because cartoons are often witty and satirical mirrors of reality, I would like to share with you a cartoon that I saw in an in-flight magazine earlier this year (FIGURE 1). The message requires no elaboration.

Some Survey Data

To turn to somewhat more quantitative data, Ms. Elizabeth Zoltan and I reported in 1982 the results of a questionnaire survey we had conducted on what professional persons think about computers.[7] Our sample included somewhat over 500 certified public accountants, lawyers, pharmacists, and physicians from the Baltimore area. When the entire set of data was factor analyzed we found six prominent factors. The first factor, that is, the one that accounted for the largest proportion of the variance, could be characterized by a highly positive grouping of adjectives, attesting to the power and productivity of computers. Our respondents felt that computers are efficient, reliable, precise, dependable, trustworthy, effective, systematic, fast, predictable, organized, and cooperative. But the second factor, that is, the factor accounting for the second highest proportion of the variance, was a highly negative one characterized by such adjectives as dehumanizing, depersonalizing, impersonal, cold, and unforgiving. Still another factor had components characterized by the words "difficult, complicated, and language not simple to understand." These views were apparent in responses to questions like: "I would like a computer to accept ordinary English statements" and "I would like a computer to accept the jargon of my profession," both of which our respondents agreed with strongly.

"The computer company says call the software company. The software company says call service. Service says it's not in the contract; read the training manual. And nobody understands the manual."

FIGURE 1. One view of computer "ease of use." (Reprinted by permission.)

Although that study was reported in 1982, the questionnaire had actually been distributed early in 1980 and the cutoff date for the receipt of responses that were included in the tabulations was the 21st of February 1980. Have things changed much in the intervening three years? I do not have exactly comparable data to report, but one of my students, Ms. Kathleen Neumann, conducted another extensive questionnaire survey for a somewhat different purpose just a few months ago. Respondents were invited to add comments of their own. One person replied:

> I have yet to receive a logically sequenced, clear presentation on practical aspects of computer terminology, operations, description of types, etc. The problem that I have experienced is that persons who teach cannot inter-relate computer language to common English. Jargon is difficult to understand.

Another respondent had this to say:

> I have difficulty spelling and have difficulty seting [sic] down at a computer key board.

Comments such as these suggest that users still see ease-of-use problems in the computers they interact with.

Some Difficulties with Computers

What are some difficulties with computers? In preparing my list I have relied heavily on Ledgard, Singer, and Whiteside.[8] Here it is:

- Many languages and systems are too large.
- Documentation and terminology are often incomprehensible.
- Languages are usually difficult to remember.
- Abbreviations are often neither sensible nor consistent.
- Messages are often cryptic.
- It is too easy to make mistakes.
- It is too hard to correct mistakes.
- Users have to learn too much irrelevant information.
- Help features are too often unhelpful.
- Users cannot communicate their difficulties to designers.
- Systems often provide no warning of potentially dangerous actions.
- Many useful tasks that could be automated are not.
- Many systems are too rigid.
- Systems too often provide redundant forms of the same operation.

Let me give you just a few examples of some of these difficulties. I have recently spent some time with IBM's PROFS (Professional Office System), a system that became commercially available a little over a year ago. According to the user's guide, the system is for "those who have little or no experience with computing systems." I got a premonition of what the system is like as soon as I discovered that the guide is divided into "modules," not parts, chapters, or sections. Reading on, I found that days are given as "Julian days." Ask yourself, how many people know what a Julian day is? What is even worse is that what the computer calls Julian days is not correct.

Then I found that documents are identified by 12-digit codes, such as 82252TST0002 or 81231HDC0019, with no dashes, breaks, or slashes. Do you know what the memory span is for an average adult? Seven digits for a young person in his twenties and six digits for a person in his forties! The telephone company discovered years ago that they had to break up long telephone numbers if they wanted to have people use them without too much error.

But I persisted and found abbreviations such as those in TABLE 1, some of which are still mysteries to me because neither the glossary nor the index in the user's guide lists them.

I could go on, but I won't. For some other amusing and not so amusing examples from other systems see Chapanis,[9] and for a perceptive account of one man's difficulties with word processing I recommend Zinsser's highly readable book.[10] These are pervasive problems. Some are easy to solve and require no new breakthroughs in our knowledge. Others are difficult to solve, but solved they must be if computers are really going to be easy to use. I think a substantial part of the explanation of why they

TABLE 1. Some Abbreviations in IBM's PROFS (Professional Office System)

userid	nodeid	CP	CP READ
CONF.	PERS.	PUN	NOHOLD
.SE	.SE EADR	.SE SIG	.SE INITS
.SE COMP	.SE DEPT	.SE TELE	.NL
.CM U5AUTH	.AT text	.CT text	.LF filename
aut$prof	FWD 1/2	BWD 1/2	Alt. PFs
Prev Section	CRON	GETUFIS	REC'D (NO)
.im fn ft (fm)	ar	U	M
D	QNOTE	NEWFILE	XEDIT
HDC	OFS OFSSMCNTL	GOTO n	Nulls off
$SEARCH$	OFSDATA	OFSLOGfl	namesort *

have not been attacked more aggressively is stated in this cogent observation by Carter:

> If the complaints that we hear daily are typical, we need a greater emphasis on human factors that affect team productivity and that affect user system design. We pay lip service to these subjects, but our active involvement in learning and using them seems to stop at learning the latest buzz words or the name of the newest theory.[11]

Measuring Ease of Use

A difficulty with ease of use is that there is no generally accepted standard for it. In fact, there appear to be as many different interpretations of ease of use as there are computers and computer manufacturers. A second difficulty is that as nearly as I can tell no one really measures ease of use scientifically. All the claims we see in advertisements appear to be just that—advertising claims and not much more. As a result, you do not really know when you have it.

Since it involves people, measuring ease of use is not as simple as measuring the number of computations that a computer can do per second. But it can be done. At least four important ingredients need to be taken into account in making such measurements: the user, the tool, the task, and the environment.

Although it is commonly overlooked or ignored, it almost goes without saying that the first, and perhaps the most important, question you need to answer in measuring ease of use is, Ease of use for whom? Words and abbreviations that seem obvious to a college graduate may be completely unintelligible to a high school graduate. Any attempt to measure ease of use must use a representative sample of the population of users for whom the computer was intended.

Next, ease of use is affected by the tools available to the user. It is hard to pound a tack into a wall with a sledge hammer; a tack hammer makes the job much easier. By analogy, some computer programs are unnecessarily complex and difficult, others make the work seem easy.

Any attempt to measure ease of use must also specify the tasks for which ease of use is being measured. Some tasks are relatively easy, others are hard. Finally, ease of use must take the working environment and working conditions into account.

With those requirements in mind, let me propose a standard for ease of use. It is this:

Ease of use is inversely proportional to the time it takes to train a representative sample of users to a level of proficiency such that at least 90% of them can do their work with a computer as fast as, and with no more errors than, they could do the same work without it.

A system that requires two days of training to bring users to a specified level of proficiency is clearly not as easy to use as one that requires only two hours of training. As an absolute standard of when you can truly call a computer easy to use, I would propose the following:

A computer is easy to use if at least 90% of a representative sample of users can be trained to the level specified above in 15 minutes or less.

Let me point out some features of these definitions. First, several parts of the definitions must be sharpened. For example, by "their work" I mean a representative sample of the normal work that a person does. Defining this term, and a few others like it, operationally is no insuperable problem, however.

Second, implicit in my definitions is a distinction between usefulness and usability. A machine may enable a user to do more things than he could have done without it. But that is a reflection on its functionality or usefulness. Usability is a separate dimension. A computer may be useful, that is, it may be able to do a lot of different things, but it may or may not be very usable, that is, it may or may not be very easy to use. My definitions are aimed only at measuring usability, or ease of use.

Third, my definitions apply to a wide variety of machines: word-processing systems, voice-messaging systems, and teleconferencing systems, as well as computers.

Finally, I think my definitions are sensible and reasonable. They define ease of use operationally, that is, in a way that can be measured. And they say that a computer is not usable if it will not let a user do his work at least as well as he can without it.

How do computers, word-processing systems, and other computerized systems measure up against my definition? Not very well, I'm afraid. About the only machines that can be called easy to use, by my definition, are most banking machines, some advanced telephone consoles, and most hand-held electronic calculators. No personal computer, stand-alone computer, word processor, or electronic memory typewriter that I have seen or used meets my standard. Computers are getting better, there is no question of that, but we still have a long way to go!

THE COMPUTER WORKPLACE

Besides ease of use, another major respect in which computers need to be civilized is in the way they are put into workplaces. A workplace includes not only the computer terminal itself, but the desk or table on which it sits, the chair that is provided for the operator, and the general environment in which all these are located. The design of computer workplaces is important because since 1980 the proportion of the total work force in information-handling occupations has exceeded the combined proportion of workers in all other occupations. This shift from a predominantly manufacturing society to an information-handling society has resulted in a movement toward office automation, at the heart of which is a computer with some kind of a visual display terminal (VDT) and keyboard. Something on the order of 10 million office workers in the United States currently use some sort of visual display terminal in their work.

Unfortunately, we are beginning to accumulate a substantial body of information showing that the computer work stations provided office workers are not as good as they could be. For example, in 1979, a consortium of labor unions in the United States presented a series of complaints to the National Institute of Occupational Safety and Health (NIOSH). The general nature of these complaints was that employees using VDTs experienced a variety of symptoms including headaches, general malaise, eyestrain, and other visual and musculoskeletal problems.* In response to those complaints NIOSH conducted an extensive investigation of computer work stations in three companies in the San Francisco Bay area. The study consisted of four phases: (1) radiation

---

*An example of such a complaint is the comment made by a respondent in the questionnaire survey by Ms. Neumann to which I have already referred: "After about 1 hour I get nauseated and have to stop."

measurements, (2) industrial hygiene sampling, (3) a survey of health complaints and psychological mood states, and (4) ergonomics and human factors measurements.

Although radiation from CRTs had long been suspected as a potential health hazard, the NIOSH study conclusively ruled that out. X-Ray, ultraviolet, and radio-frequency radiations in all sites and at all work stations either were not detectable or were well below NIOSH and OSHA occupational safety and health standards. Similar negative conclusions were reached about the chemical environment. Hydrocarbon, carbon monoxide, acetic acid, and formaldehyde levels in and around work stations were not appreciably different from what one would find in an ordinary living environment.[12]

The results of the survey of health complaints were quite different, however.[13] These showed that VDT operators experienced a greater number of health complaints, particularly related to emotional and gastrointestinal problems, than did comparable operators who did not work with VDTs. These findings, according to the NIOSH report, demonstrated a level of stress for the VDT operators that could have potential long-term health consequences. The NIOSH study concluded, however, that it is quite likely that the emotional distress shown by the VDT operators is more related to the type of work activity than to the use of VDTs per se.

The NIOSH study had more concrete things to say about the ergonomic and human factors aspects of the computer workplace than about any other aspect of computer work.[14] Keyboard heights, table and chair designs, viewing distances and viewing angles, lighting, and other aspects of work-station design all came in for criticism. To illustrate just one small feature of these problems, look at the work station in FIGURE 2, which was advertised in a recent catalog of computer equipment and furnishings. I appreciate that this is an advertisement and that it is supposed to look slick so that it will impress customers. Yet I think it is illustrative of what we see in newspapers and magazines all the time. We are evolving into a paperless society, we are told repeatedly, and the implication is that computer workplaces will eventually be as neat, tidy, and uncluttered as the one pictured here. I doubt that I will ever see that in my lifetime. All the real computer workplaces I have seen are surrounded by paper, books, printouts, coffee cups, ash trays, and other paraphernalia, like the one in FIGURE 3. Computer workplaces have to be designed to conform to this reality. They need to fit the ways in which people work and the kind of work they do.

A somewhat different kind of problem is illustrated in FIGURE 4. Here you see an operator facing the computer screen and facing also the glare from a large window directly behind the terminal. This is a situation that almost guarantees that the operator will suffer eye strain or visual fatigue. You might be able to understand this arrangement if it were a temporary or makeshift one, but it is not. It is a working office in the headquarters building of a computer manufacturing firm! And, unfortunately, it is an

FIGURE 2. A computer work station illustrated in a contemporary catalog. (Photo courtesy of Uarco Incorporated.)

FIGURE 3. A real computer workplace.

example of the kind of poorly designed workplace you can find in hundreds of offices.

A recent, thorough review of the literature on these problems by Dainoff summarizes the variables that need to be taken into account to humanize the computer workplace.[15] They are:

1. The user population, particularly their ages and visual abilities.
2. The physical characteristics of the VDT, for example, the type of

FIGURE 4. Another real computer workplace.

    phosphor, refresh rate, interlace characteristics, spot diameter, and character format.
3. The nature of the task.
4. The visual environment, including such things as illumination levels, glare sources, and contrast ratios.

5. The physical environment, including temperature, humidity, noise, and air conditioning.
6. Working postures as determined by relevant dimensions of the furniture and VDT location.
7. Work periods, that is, the average length of time an operator spends using the terminal during a typical working day.

This is a formidable set of variables, but we must deal with them if we are to design computer workplaces that are visually and physically comfortable and satisfying.

LIVING WITH COMPUTERS

I call this last section "living with computers" because computers are here to stay. Our society could not and would not function as it does today without computers. At the same time it is clear that automation in general and computerization in particular have created some serious problems of adjustment for us. These are not merely technical problems, because they involve political, social, legal, and ethical considerations as well. I have already written about some of these problems elsewhere,[16] and several speakers at this conference have addressed a number of them as well.

Even if we restrict ourselves to the ways that computers affect the way we work, we find many reasons for concern. Resistance to change, DP stress,[17] the threat to job security, and the fear of appearing ignorant or stupid[18] are some of the problems associated with job restructuring brought about by automation. However, I want to talk about two particular job-related problems. They are job impoverishment and the computer as Big Brother.

Job Impoverishment

Industrial and organizational psychologists have for a long time recommended job enrichment, or job enlargement, as one way of counteracting the boredom and frustration often experienced by industrial workers. Briefly, job enlargement means the combination of several highly specialized jobs into a single, less specialized, and less monotonous one. The enlarged task creates variety, requires flexibility and increased skill, and is generally more meaningful to workers.

When tasks become computerized, we sometimes see the reverse of job enlargement—job impoverishment. Let me give you an example. Years ago, before computerization, mail sorting was done by sorters who received batches of letters in trays that were distributed to them on a conveyor. A sorter picked up a bunch of envelopes in one hand, decided whether sufficient postage was affixed to the letter, read the address on the envelope, and shoved the envelope into the appropriate pigeonhole. It was slow and it involved a fair amount of physical movement. But that was actually one of the good things about the job. The sorter could change positions, he or she could stand or sit, stretch, yawn, and if he or she sneezed, a letter did not get misdirected.

After computerization, trays of letters are still delivered to an operator but now each letter is positioned in front of an operator mechanically and with unvarying regularity. The operator has merely to read the zip code, key it in, and the letter is whisked away. This modern computerized system is much faster and it eliminates most of the physical activity that was involved in mail sorting years ago. But that is one thing that is wrong with the system. Since the system is machine paced, the operator is almost literally chained to the keyboard and the job is deadly dull and monotonous. The operator cannot change positions very much, and he or she dare not take time out to stretch, yawn, or sneeze because to do so means that letters will be directed into a reject bin. Small wonder that work and rest schedules are common sources of contention between operators and management in the postal system.

Mail sorting is by no means the only kind of job in which operators are subservient to a computer. Dull, menial data-entry work, like entering subscription information into computerized mailing lists, has been on the scene for at least a couple of decades. In such jobs, the computer counts keystrokes and operators are paid according to their productivity in what amounts to an "electronic sweatshop."[19]

Job impoverishment resulting from computerization may have other, more complex effects.[20] Before line testing and repair services were automated in a Bell telephone company, calls came into a central office and the operator would pass the complaints to a skilled line tester. After automation, calls were consolidated for an entire region and new test equipment eliminated the skill needed to test lines. Not only did the line testers feel useless, but operators were no longer in personal touch with the repairmen, they lost some of their discretion in scheduling repairs, and they never learned the outcome of complaints. The result was a sharp drop in morale among both line testers and operators. For descriptions of still other jobs that have been trivialized because of computerization, see Goleman.[21]

People are generally more tolerant about working with automated systems if they have jobs where the pace is determined more by the individual than by the machine, where concentration is required in short bursts rather than continuously, where they can take rest pauses at will, and where the job as a whole is meaningful. They become intolerant, resentful, and dissatisfied when a job is paced by a computer, when intense concentration is required continuously by the system, when there are no opportunities to take rest pauses, when the system is rigidly designed, and when the job is routine.

Computers should enrich human lives, not dehumanize them.

The Computer as Big Brother

From time to time we read about computers that will monitor human behavior, a situation that is sometimes referred to as the computer being Big Brother. Technical people sometimes dismiss such characterizations as uninformed, unreasonable, or hysterical. But are they? Let us consider a couple of situations. Late last year a news sheet of Baltimore Working Women, an organization of women office workers, carried an item called "Fighting the Computer." The point at issue is that since October 1, 1982, federal workers in Maryland have worked "against the computer clock"—that is, a computer tells the worker what to do and how long it

FIGURE 5. A Big Brother view of the computer. (Reprinted by permission of Carla Haag.)

should take. It then measures and scores the worker's productivity. The cartoon that accompanied this article is illustrated in FIGURE 5. The item concludes with the statement "It's hard enough to argue with a supervisor, but how do you talk back to a computer?"

Marcus also describes industrial jobs in which supervisors can monitor the productivity of workers by computers that count keystrokes and record when operators take breaks.[22]

A couple of months ago, Patent No. 4,375,080 was granted to three inventors for an instrument to evaluate teachers and record their classroom activities. From a technical standpoint the device is fairly straightforward. It is essentially a computerized system for doing activity sampling of the kind that human factors specialists have been doing for years. But in a telephone interview, one of the inventors is quoted as saying that the purpose of the invention is to show teachers how much classroom time is nonproductive.

Think about these situations. Would you like a computer to tell you how fast you are supposed to work, decide whether you are engaged in nonproductive work, and tell you or your supervisor how much time you spend in nonproductive activities?

CONCLUSION

Like automobiles, computers are revolutionizing our society, our ways of living, and our ways of working. Although we have learned how to design automobiles so that they enhance our lives, we have a great deal more to do before computers are fully tamed and civilized. In discussions of these and related problems computers are often portrayed as adversaries as though it were "people versus computers." But computers are not our enemies and they are inherently neither good nor bad. After all, computers are designed, built, installed, and operated by people.

If computers are hard to use, if they are uncomfortable to use, or if they seem to make us work in ways that are menial or subservient, it is because some of us made them that way for others of us to use. So what seems to be a computer problem is really a people problem: How can we discover enough about human behavior so that we ourselves can design, build, install, and operate computers that will enhance and enrich our lives? It is a challenging task and one that must be tackled with all the skills, ingenuity, and wisdom that we can bring to bear on it. The one thing we must never forget is that computers are machines and machines exist for only one purpose—to serve people!

REFERENCES

1. CARROLL, J. M. 1982. The adventure of getting to know a computer. Computer 15(11): 49–58.
2. MEYERS, J. A. 1983. A letter from the publisher. Time 121(1): 3.
3. SANDBERG-DIMENT, E. 1983. Computer clubs: getting to know your machine without fear. The Sun (Baltimore, Maryland) 292(84): C3.
4. JOHNSON-LAIRD, A. 1982. Most software more complicated than needed. Software News 2(4): 47.
5. PARKS, M. 1983. Productivity tools enable users to obtain better (not more) code. Software News 3(2): 22–23.

6. LYNN, M. E. 1983. LANs, OA integration gain credence, but . . . Software News **3**(2): 44.
7. ZOLTAN, E. & A. CHAPANIS. 1982. What do professional persons think about computers? Behav. Inf. Technol. **1**(1): 55–68.
8. LEDGARD, H., A. SINGER & J. WHITESIDE. 1981. Directions in Human Factors for Interactive Systems. Springer-Verlag. New York, N.Y.
9. CHAPANIS, A. 1982. Computers and the common man. *In* Information Technology and Psychology: Prospects for the Future. R. A. Kasschau, R. Lachman & K. R. Laughery, Eds.: 106–132. Praeger Publishers. New York, N.Y.
10. ZINSSER, W. 1983. Writing with a Word Processor. Harper and Row. New York, N.Y.
11. CARTER, N. 1983. We must plan to include the users. Software News **3**(3): 19.
12. MURRAY, W. E., C. E. MOSS, W. H. PARR & C. COX. 1981. A radiation and industrial hygiene survey of video display terminal operations. Hum. Factors **23**(4): 413–420.
13. SMITH, M. J., B. G. F. COHEN & L. W. STAMMERJOHN, JR. 1981. An investigation of health complaints and job stress in video display operations. Hum. Factors **23**(4): 387–400.
14. STAMMERJOHN, L. W., JR., M. J. SMITH & B. G. F. COHEN. 1981. Evaluation of work station design factors in VDT operations. Hum. Factors **23**(4): 401–412.
15. DAINOFF, M. J. 1982. Occupational stress factors in visual display terminal (VDT) operation: a review of empirical research. Behav. Inf. Technol. **1**(2): 141–176.
16. CHAPANIS, A. 1979. Quo vadis, ergonomia. Ergonomics **22**(6): 595–605.
17. BEELER, J. 1983. Presently confined to DP pros society seen next victim of DP-induced stress. Computerworld **17**(10): 13.
18. YASIN, R. 1983. Technology of the future to restructure office slots. MIS Week **4**(10): 26.
19. POLLACK, A. 1982. Latest technology may spawn the electronic sweatshop. The New York Times **132**(45,455): 18E.
20. BLUMSTEIN, M. 1982. A marriage of men and machines. The New York Times **132**(45,455): 21F.
21. GOLEMAN, D. 1983. The electronic Rorschach. Psychol. Today **17**(2): 36–43.
22. MARCUS, M. L. 1983. The new office: more than you bargained for. Computerworld OA:Office Automation **17**(8A): 35.

DISCUSSION OF THE PAPER

QUESTION: Since you have the opportunity to speak to large groups of people and correct problems with computers, I would like to suggest that one addition to your talk be that the two groups of people who interface with computers—the computer jocks who write the programs and the people who use them—communicate with each other. Oftentimes in a large company where computers are used frequently and assiduously, the computer jocks are constantly changing the program—so that when you say "hello" to the computer it says "good-by" to you on Tuesday, when on Monday it signed you on. That kind of problem of constantly changing programs means that you are shooting at a moving target—you have a group of people who are expert in the computer and you have other people who have to use it but who are not expert.

A. CHAPANIS: I agree.

Worsening the Knowledge Gap*

The Mystique of Computation Builds
Unnecessary Barriers

DONALD A. NORMAN†

*Department of Psychology and
Institute for Cognitive Science C-015
University of California, San Diego
La Jolla, California 92093*

PROLOGUE

Every so often I have a nightmare. I am trapped, chained to a computer keyboard. All around me are my captors, earnest young folk, all dedicated to their cause, fervent in their beliefs. They come in all sizes, shapes, colors, and sex; bearded, sloppy, neatly trimmed, in suit, tie, dirty tee-shirt, jeans. Each disagreeing with one another about the true way, united only in their opposition to me. A disorganized chant comes from their lips—not entirely in unison:‡

> JCL, grep, compile and load;
> a-dot-out, popstack, format, and code.
> Dimension, declare, goto while true,
> execute, interpret, could-er and queue.
> (Refrain: Foobar, foobar, foobar.)

The nightmare is not entirely without basis. I once was rash enough to criticize a computer operating system, a system favored by one of the highest of the high cults. This system, I said, is fatally flawed, unintelligible for mere users, uncommunicative, and downright unfriendly for all but the expert programmers for whom and by whom it was written. This would be no crime, except that this particular system has been touted as the answer to everyone's dreams, from secretaries to scientists, structured programmers to hackers. It is thought to be the best of all possible operating systems for today's modern computer work station, the joy of the venture capital market.

As a result of my article, I got a chance to be an active participant in

---

*My research into the problems of human-computer interaction is supported by Contract N00014-79-C-0323, NR 667-437 with the Personnel and Training Research Programs of the Office of Naval Research and by a grant from the System Development Foundation.

†Address correspondence to the Institute for Cognitive Science.

‡**Scholarly note.** Spelling is phonetic: the proper spelling for "a-dot-out" and "could-er" is "a.out" and "cdr." "Foobar" derives epistemologically from "fubar," an acronym for the common judgment passed upon incompleted ("undebugged") programs; "fouled up beyond all repair."

yet another cultural breakthrough—national computer networking—whereby close to 400 locations and 8,000 participants daily exchange thoughts, ideas, and off-the-top-of-the-head opinions (the technical term is "flames") on a wide variety of topics. I became the popular subject for the moment, and for nigh unto 30 days and 30 nights I was bombarded with messages, all by computer mail of course, originating from all over the country, enough mail so that every morning when I awoke and went to my home computer terminal, I would spend up to an hour reading and responding to comments on this one topic. In the end I received 30 single-spaced pages of critique—more text than contained in the original article.

Lowering the Barriers

Let me quickly come to my main point; the difficulties that we mortals have with computers are unnecessary. If computers are not understandable, the few will dominate the masses, because the secret language of computation leaves out the uninitiated; those who understand make it hard for those who do not. Today, I fear that computers—machines, software, and systems—are designed for the designer, not the user. They use secret codes, mysterious procedures, with knowledge restricted to those who pass the magic ritual of programminghood. Unless we can demystify, the result will be an increasing gulf between the knowledgeable and the rest, between the doers and the users.

There is a large gap between the knowledge of those who understand computers and those who do not. The gap in knowledge translates into one of power, for those who understand can dominate those who do not. The ones who understand can have access to information, they can control the system, they can take advantage of new styles of communication, decision making, information retrieval. As long as computers are mysterious, forbidding entities, the gap will remain. Moreover, it is only those capable of mastering the abstract and mysterious language of the computer who can cross over the gap, so that if nothing changes save the ever-increasing complexity of computers, the gap will worsen, increasing the separation between those who know and those who do not, increasing the powers of those on the knowledge side of the gap.

To understand computers does not mean to be able to build them; it does not even necessarily mean to be able to program them. What it does mean is to understand something of the nature of computation and of what an information-processing system is, to understand how information can be communicated, interpreted, transmitted, and displayed. It requires knowing something of algorithms, of data structures, and of information processing. None of this knowledge is beyond the ordinary person, with or without a knowledge of science or mathematics, at least not in principle.

Four Levels of Computer Literacy

Computer literacy is a common catch phrase, a popular slogan that whets the appetite of politicians and academics. But what does it mean? How would we produce it? Computer literacy can mean a hundred different things; there is not just a single concept involved, but a large variety of them.

It is important to distinguish among four levels of computer literacy:

1. Understanding general principles of computation.
2. Understanding how to use computers.
3. Understanding how to program computers.
4. Understanding the science of computation.

Level 1. Understanding General Principles of Computation

In my opinion, the most important need is for general education about the basic principles of computation. I speak here of general knowledge, not of expertise. That is, I refer to an understanding of some simple concepts that are at the heart of the use of computers. Here is a sample list:

- Basic concepts. Some simple concepts need to be understood in order to avoid some common fallacies: the terminal is not a computer; hardware must be distinguished from software; most problems with computers result from the ways in which their programs have been written, not problems with the hardware itself; most complaints about computer error or rigidity are really complaints about the lack of foresight by those who wrote the programs.
- Algorithms. The basic nature of an algorithm, how they are developed, and how they are applied in various applications of computers. This should include a basic introduction to the structure of a computer program and procedures, including the role that procedures play in the development of algorithms.
- Machine architecture. What the essential components of a computer are, including the central processor, the various kinds of memory structures and devices, and the role of the terminal. Mainframes and microprocessors, peripheral devices.
- Multiprocessing. How one computer can do many tasks at once. Basic notions of time-sharing and multiprocessing, serial and parallel machines. How security is maintained in a time-shared environment. Why perfect security generally cannot be maintained.
- Data bases. How data are configured, stored, represented. Problems of multiple access to the same data, including problems of synchronization and of security. Encryption.
- Communication links and networks. The communication networks

that link computers together with one another and with their terminals. Local and global networks. Computer mail. Distributed processing and distributed data bases.
- Implications. Changes in work style (distributed offices; work at home). Educational implications. Communication systems. The interrelationship of computers, communication, printing, media, etc.
- Machine intelligence. What it means for a machine to be "intelligent." The enormous nature of the task. How to remain skeptical in the face of exaggerated claims and articles in the media. What advances can legitimately be expected; what things are hard. Robots, both dumb (as we now have them) and intelligent (as science fiction has them).

These points are those that will eventually affect the entire society. I feel it essential that people become educated about them. Note that they do not require extensive technical background; many can be taught without going near a computer and without learning how to program. The literacy of which I speak is for everyone, especially those who are not scientists. Today, such knowledge is difficult to obtain.

Level 2. Understanding How to Use Computers

Experience with computers can help a user understand their powers and limitations. But some experience is more useful than others. Computer users are misled when they can successfully do an application to think they understand the computer. They do not. Still, if one is to understand what computers are about, it is essential to get some experience by using the machine directly, by sitting in front of the terminal and keyboard and doing something useful. Even games are useful. Some skillfully designed games teach useful concepts. Others simply help dispel the common fear of the machine. The danger is that game players—oftentimes very skilled at the game itself—may thereby think they understand the machine; they do not.

Level 3: Understanding How to Program Computers

The third level of understanding is to learn how to write programs, to make the computer do something. I am not convinced that this is a necessary step for the average person, even one who wishes to be "computer literate." In part, this is because contemporary programming languages force the user to work at the wrong level of abstraction, quite far below the problem level. One has to worry about too many tiny details, else the whole program will fail. Learning that this must be done is a useful exercise, for it reveals how limited is the power of the machines and how difficult the task of the programmer. The problem is that it takes a considerable amount of time and effort to become skilled at programming, and although the standard three-month introductory course on programming is informative, the distance between the skills developed in such a course and the skills necessary to write useful programs is so great that it is not clear to me that much benefit is to be gained from the effort.

Knowledge of programming is indeed essential for anyone who wishes to tap the full power of machines, or for anyone who really wishes to understand how things work. Expect to spend considerable time and effort at the task (anything worth doing well requires time and effort, and this is no exception). This level of knowledge is not essential for everyone.

Level 4: Understanding the Science of Computation

This is the most advanced stage. Not everyone need get here. Here is where the professional resides. The important point is simply that not everyone need aspire to full technical knowledge of the computer. I do believe, however, that every educated person should become acquainted with the knowledge of at least one of the other stages.

How Do We Get Out of the Current State?

Computers Manipulate Symbols, Not Numbers

In the beginning, computers were thought to be computational machines, appropriate for doing numerical analyses. Numbers were the primary topic of computation, and mathematicians and electrical engineers the academic carekeepers of the machines. At first, computers were large and clumsy, requiring large teams of skillfully trained personnel to keep them running, fed, and fit. Over the years they have been reduced in size and price, simultaneously increasing in power and reliability. Today they threaten to become as commonplace as the electric motor—that is, so common and so much taken for granted that you will not even realize that they are there. But the computer is unlike an electric motor in that it can be programmed, told what to do, when to do it, and to do its operations through continual interaction with people. The computer is a tool for information processing, and it needs and requires information from people.

The proper domain of the computer is the symbol—characters, words, sounds, and images—and the fact that artists, humanists, and musicians are among the last to use computers in any significant way should be considered a historical accident, for it is precisely the arts and humanities that will be best served by the tools of modern computation. It is possible to make the argument that computers are mismatched for numbers, for in order to deal with them, one must take special pains to provide special methods for accommodating real (continuous) numbers within the discrete representation offered by the computer.

The Computer Should Be a Tool

Computers have the capability to act as tools for us everyday folks, as *knowledge amplifiers*. This means they should help us with our everyday tasks, making it possible to do things we could not do before. Computers are tools, and should be treated as such; they are neither monsters nor savants, simply tools, in the same category as the printing press, the automobile, and the telephone. And like these examples, they have the power to transform our lives.

The Languages of Computation Should Be Changed

Suppose you do wish to take the plunge, to learn how to program. What language should you learn? There is no simple answer. We do not have satisfactory programming languages for many classes of users. The primary languages available to beginning learners are Basic, Pascal, and Logo, all of which were developed, in part, to serve as teaching languages. Basic and Logo were thought to be simple enough that anyone could learn them, Pascal elegant enough that learners would acquire only the proper ideas and perspectives; all were designed to overcome the perceived inadequacies of computer languages in general.§ It is not clear to me that any of these is adequate or necessary. Different people have different needs. Should an artist learn the same things as an engineer? Should a poet learn Pascal? We need a family of application languages, languages constructed so that the users program in the terms and at the level of their substantive problems, but which also provide the full power of a full programming environment. Such languages do exist for scientific applications, but not for the full spectrum of possible uses. Note that any skill, including that of programming, will require time and care to master. By itself, this is perfectly acceptable. My complaint is not that time or effort is required but rather that the existing languages tend to assume a scientific, mathematical background on the part of the user. This is false, and unnecessary. (There is an exception: Logo, to which I turn in a moment.)

Why can we not develop a programming language aimed at the level of the nontechnical user? By this I mean a language that has constructs

---

§Basic was designed for novices, but it is flawed in two ways; first, it is still designed for programmers, not casual users, and it requires knowing low-level concepts of the machine. Second, as a formal programming language it is flawed by the lack of good control structure and decent mnemonics. Pascal is thought by some to be the answer to Basic, but it aims at the purist in programming. The computational structures of Pascal are suited for mathematical-like operations, not for manipulating pictures, sounds, or stories in meaningful units. Pascal is essential to those who would master all facets of computers, but it is badly mismatched to the needs of most ordinary folk.

matched to the needs of the users, not to the formal structure of programs. Why can't we have a language written in a way that is accessible to normal folks? We might very well need several languages (or several variants of a single language) to support physicians, scientists, humanists, musicians, streetwalkers, thirteen-year-olds, and parents, but I see no reason why it could not be done. There will have to be sacrifices, of course; some users will have to forgo the pleasures of learning the distinction between passing arguments by value and by reference, or the joys of opening a file and checking the status bits, or of learning about static and dynamic arrays, but they might instead take joy in composing a poem, or creating a drawing, or even simplifying some mundane household task.

One language that does attempt to cater to the end user—children—is Logo. How successful it will be is yet to be determined, for despite the fact that it is now in its teenage years, it is only within the past year that commercial versions of Logo have been available for use on popular home computers so that large numbers of people could use it. Logo has the virtue of cleanliness and simplicity, combined with elegance and computing power. It is a teaching device, not a real tool, however, and I do not believe that real applications will often be built out of Logo. But Logo is written in the spirit I am recommending, and it is worthy of continued experimentation and evaluation.

Interaction with a Computer Should Be Improved

When we converse with others, we have certain expectations about their behavior. We know roughly what they know, what beliefs they have, and how they are apt to respond to our statements. We expect some feedback, to be told when we are not making sense, and in general, to hold a constructive dialogue between equals. When we use a machine—such as a dishwasher or a kitchen mixer—we have a reasonable understanding of how it works and what it does when we turn it on. Whenever there are deviations in its actions from our expectations, we have some confidence that we can remedy the situation.

A computer is neither as responsive as a conversational partner nor as unresponsive as a dishwasher. Rather, it occupies its own special niche. To the uninitiated, a computer is a mysterious device, endowed with some level of intelligence, working its mysterious ways upon the hapless user. It is as demanding of perfect obedient behavior as the gods of fertility in Hollywood mythology. It mutters its incantations, requires secret passwords, rejects nonconforming inputs in a language intelligible only to the initiated. The problem lies not with the computer, but with those who write its programs.

The problem is to get just the right level of interaction, enough that we understand what is happening, that we get feedback about our actions, and whatever help is needed about our current state, the history of our actions, and our alternatives. Too much feedback or assistance can be as unfriendly and annoying as too little. The system must present a consistent, appropriate *system image*, one that allows the user to construct a *mental model* of what is going on. The task is made the more difficult because different users bring different levels of knowledge and skill to the task, thereby requiring different kinds of assistance and feedback from the computer system. There are other requirements as well, including the proper integration of instructional devices, help mechanisms, and error messages, the ability to "undo" past actions, and the appropriate choice of specification mechanism for commands. Those who would write computer programs must be excellent intuitive psychologists, for they are really designing the machine half of a dialogue that will take place between the user and the machine.¶

This task is more difficult than you might expect because it requires that the designers of computer systems understand the needs of the user far better than they do today. You will find better programs for nontechnical users on home computers than you will find on large, expensive business and scientific computers. I suspect that this is so because the professional programmers work mostly on the larger machines, whereas the everyday user has had more say in the programs developed on the home computers. If you think that I am criticizing the programming profession, you are partially correct: that is why I have that nightmare. But it is not really the fault of programmers; they should not be asked to construct the part of the program that interacts with the users; they do not have the training, the knowledge, and in many cases, the interest to do so.

Programmers are expected to be experts at manipulating the symbols of computer talk, at putting together routines that accomplish the stated goals. They are not expected to be experts at human communicaton or at the needs, desires, and capabilities of people. This being so, we should not be surprised that most computer systems are aimed either at skilled programmers or at the programmer's private beliefs about the end user. These beliefs are not likely to be accurate.

We Need Interface Designers

We should divide up the tasks of programming so that specialists in people and in communications handle the communicative parts of the system, specialists in machines handle the machine parts. Call the first the interface designer, the second the computer programmer. The important point is that they require different talents and should not necessarily be done by the same people.

This means, in computer terms, that we must encapsulate the compu-

¶The appropriate rules for human-machine interaction are not known; research in this area is just beginning. I review some of my thoughts on the matter in Norman, D. A. 1983. Design rules based on analyses of human error. Commun. ACM **26**(4): 254–258.

tational aspects of computers separately from the user interface. We need then to develop some standard internal communicative language to go between the computer program and the interface program. Once this is done, the computer programmer need no longer worry about the user, but only about the technical problem. The program communicates its needs and responses to the user interface, which, in turn, communicates with the user. In this manner, the interface can decide just what to present to the user, and in what manner. Indeed, if things were managed properly, we could radically change the way the program operated without changing the interface, as long as the messages passed between the two were unchanged. More importantly, we could change the interface in radical ways without affecting the operation of the program. This lets us move to the next step in interface design: *the personal interface.*

Toward the Personal Interface

Different people have different needs, understand different things, and have different styles. Why not let the computer interface be tailored for each individual user? If the encapsulation of interface and program were done properly, this would be an obvious end result. And, if standardization of interface systems could occur, all users could carry the specification for their interfaces around in their pockets, in "smart" credit cards, small plastic cards with built in memory. Tailor your home computer to your needs and desires, then walk up to any computer terminal in the world, plug in the card that specified your preferences, and, *voila!*, have the terminal look and act just like the one in your home.

Reasonable Systems Do Exist

The situation is not really quite as bleak as I have described it. There are some reasonable systems, systems designed for the user, with skill, concern, and success. Two prime examples are the *Star* system from Xerox and the *Lisa* from Apple. Some of the modern word-processing systems are quite well done for their intended audience. Spreadsheet programs—starting with *Visicalc*—are dramatic examples of what happens when someone tailors a system to the needs of the person instead of to the needs of the computer. These programs have revolutionized small offices. We bought a microcomputer just so we could use *Visicalc*, despite the fact that my laboratory is well equipped with larger, more expensive computers. I can think of no more damning indictment of the professional programming community than the fact that this most important breakthrough in computer use was first available only on home computers; people whose machines cost in the hundreds of thousands of dollars were denied access to it.

Beware, however, for these are application packages, not full-fledged programming languages. They are made for the end user, to perform the fixed set of tasks provided with the software that comes with the system. The user cannot access the full power of the computer that really lurks beneath the software, at least not without going beneath the smooth, friendly veneer that makes these systems so usable. Yes, one can transform *Lisa, Star,* or word processors into programming environments, but to do so is not unlike transforming the kind Dr. Jekyll into the unfortunate, ill-controlled Mr. Hyde. Having made the transformation, we then revert back to the primitive self, a system requiring a programming language, not suited for the untutored, a system to which all my earlier comments apply.

SUMMARY: ELIMINATING THE KNOWLEDGE GAP

Let me summarize my major points. There is a large gap in knowledge between those who understand computers and those who do not. The gap will worsen unless we do something about it. Everyone will use computers; their benefits are too important to be ignored. But those who do not understand will be at the mercy of those who do. Unless we develop reasonable computer literacy among the users, they will be at the mercy of whatever systems the professionals think is best for them. The users will lose control over their data, they will lose control over the operations that they can do, they will lose control over the end results. They may feel alienated, subject to the mysterious powers of an ill-understood machine.

None of this is necessary. The barriers can come down. However, to break down the barriers we need some effort on everyone's part.

The Everyday Person Must Make Some Effort to Become Computer Literate

Everyone should have some computer literacy, at least to my first level—*understanding general principles of computation.* Ideally, everyone should also gain the second level—*understanding how to use computers.* It is not necessary to go to the third or fourth levels; programming knowledge is not essential.

Do not expect literacy to be easy. Do not expect to become literate about computers in an evening. It takes six months or more to become a skilled driver, six months or more to learn to type. We expect to spend considerable time becoming literate in history, literature, or even simple arithmetic. It will take study and thought to become literate in computers; a year of part-time study, perhaps, will provide a basic beginning. Today it is not easy to do this; there are no established courses, few books. But then again, how would you become literate about literature or poetry? If you can manage one, you can manage the other. It is up to you to take the plunge; others will not do it for you.

We Could Use Computer Languages Tailored for Everyday Needs

I made this point strongly in the paper. Most languages today are expressed at the wrong level, for the wrong audience. We need some good solid development in this area.

We Need More Concern for the Computer User, Less for the Computer

I strongly urge the development of a new profession, that of interface design. We need people who understand people to develop the part of the computer program that interacts with people. This, in turn, requires several things, including the development of standardized encapsulation techniques, standardized message protocols. The end result, however, could be virtuous for all; more pleasurable interfaces for the everyday person, fewer complaints and difficulties for the professional programmer.

There are positive signs. Psychologists and computer scientists are joining together in the study of *human-computer interaction*. There is a new journal and a semipermanent conference series. This is the area that I myself have spent most time in recently, for I have hopes that knowledge gained from the study of cognitive science might yield a kind of cognitive engineering, the applied side of the endeavor. I have expanded upon these ideas elsewhere, so I will not attempt to dwell upon them here. However, the activity gives hope that matters might improve considerably.

Maybe when we can establish the appropriate principles for human-computer interaction, when there is a good body of knowledge and experience, and when we have separated the design of the user interface from the design of the application program, programmers would no longer seek their revenge upon me as I sleep; I could be free of the fear of *foobar*.

ACKNOWLEDGMENTS

I thank Michael Mozer, Allen Cypher, and Bob Glushko for their helpful comments.

DISCUSSION OF THE PAPER

QUESTION: Could you describe, but not in very much detail, a few of these specialized languages? Who would use them and how would they be tailored for the users?

D. A. NORMAN: These languages don't yet exist. But let us consider what they might be like. Suppose we had a language for music that allows us to create music in the way we think about music. Suppose you wanted to create music using contemporary scales: obviously we should be able to use a keyboard or other device to enter the sounds, or to write using standard musical nomenclature. But suppose you want to be a creative musician and break out of the barrier of conventional scales—to get away from nineteenth century or eighteenth century music. We'd like to see if we can invent something new, but now we don't know how to do that. There are a couple of people who are developing computerized music systems, but they don't provide quite the right tools: How would a composer try to specify a new sound never before heard? Today they must specify the sound in terms of physical acoustics, which is not the way a composer should have to think.

I can tell a similar story about creation of art, or a similar story about writing. I would like a language that helps me create a story, that keeps track of where I am, of the outline, and of the stylistic variables.

QUESTION: What is the language psychologists would use? Is LISP an appropriate language for this?

D. A. NORMAN: For what purpose? If I were to simulate how the brain operates I might very well want a specially tailored language that talks about neurons and interconnections, inhibition and activation. Some people are developing such a language. If I wanted to talk about knowledge structures, I might very well use LISP (or some higher-order language perhaps constructed on top of LISP). This would let me do symbolic manipulation. If I want to analyze my data, I'll use FORTRAN or APL. If I want to mimic some other aspect of human thought, I may very well have to develop a special language that gives me the tools I need.

QUESTION: Prof. Norman, you began your speech by talking about the mystique of computers. Then further on, you spoke about Visicalc and the nature of the person who created it; and third, you mentioned how very hard it was to be a computer programmer and the complexities and the time required to really make a contribution to the field. I felt that there was some contradiction there and to me the idea of mystique that you initially suggested is in part enhanced by the idea that being a computer programmer does require enormous years and immense effort and great intelligence to do something useful.

D. A. NORMAN: Not any special intelligence just some time and energy.

It's one thing to understand the machines, to understand how you might go about using them, or even to dream about how they might be used, and quite another thing to be the person who actually pieces together the thousands or millions of details necessary to make them work. Visicalc is a story that fits that pattern.

As I understand what happened, the idea came from someone with a degree in business administration who then found a programmer; the two of them together interacted for about a year, I believe, before they came out with the working version. So it required somebody, the user, with the dream, but who got help and was willing to spend a lot of time and effort to make it come about. The point is that the person with the idea does not have to program.

QUESTION: Dr. Norman, your suggestion about an interface designer was very interesting. The thing that bothers me is that once again we're talking about somebody doing the design for the user rather than involving the user some way in the actual design process itself. We've been doing a study at the Rand Corporation on implementation of office information systems, and we find that one of the factors that's highly predictive of successful implementation is user participation. The problem is that a lot of companies are not quite sure how to facilitate this kind of participation in the process. Do you have any suggestions about how that might be accomplished?

D. A. NORMAN: You're absolutely right; a user or a class of users must be involved in that design. I was emphasizing that the user should not have to do the design. There are 250 million people in the United States, any of whom might eventually use these programs. Each of them should not be involved in design. But when you are trying to do something for a class of users, then some representative of that class must be involved intimately. Moreover, design must be an iterative process, so that as you are evolving the design, it has been used and tested in the real situation and then brought back to be redesigned.

You're also right that most of the companies are not aware of this need and don't understand it. I don't know how to solve that one. Someone at lunch today said, "The marketplace will take care of that because people will buy the good systems and not the bad systems." I don't believe that. The marketplace didn't take care of automobile safety, it didn't take care of drug safety, and I don't think the marketplace will take care of this.

All I can do is go out and cry out into this wilderness and say we must have more people who realize the need to take heed of the users and hope that somebody listens.

QUESTION: Dr. Norman, Dr. Chapanis was talking earlier about the trivialization of jobs such as the post office sorting problem, which has people confined to the desk doing simple repetitive tasks. Would your interface designer or perhaps psychologists have some way to make jobs more physically stimulating and more creative and interesting?

D. A. NORMAN: I wish I could say yes. Unfortunately it could very well be that the interface designer who understands the individual person could make things worse. Machines and people should work in a social setting, within a social environment. This can be liberating, and it can be exciting, and it can increase interperson cooperation—if introduced properly. It can also be dehumanizing, if introduced improperly. I have not addressed myself to those problems. Dr. Chapanis did an excellent job of illustrating the issues and the difficulties.

Computer-Assisted Negotiations

A Case History from the Law of the Sea Negotiations and Speculation Regarding Future Uses

Moderator: DONALD B. STRAUS

Panel Members: T. T. B. KOH, J. D. NYHART,
ELLIOT L. RICHARDSON, AND JAMES K. SEBENIUS

D. B. STRAUS (*Research Institute, American Arbitration Association, New York, N.Y.*): What we're trying to do here is a little different from what has been done before at this conference. Our session has been orchestrated, and we're trying to present a cohesive story.

In previous sessions, we've examined what computers do. Some people have wondered whether or not computers think and, if so, how they do it. There have been forecasts of new levels of artificial intelligence, and there've been talks about computer graphics, about the limits to computation, and about human and psychological factors in computer use.

Here we're going to shift our perspective from the world of artificial intelligence to a real-world case history in which a computer model helped negotiators do a better job of understanding a complex issue and reach some strategies for solving it.

In other words we're moving from the world of artificial intelligence (AI) to intelligence amplification (IA), reversing both the initials and our perspective.

Specifically what we want to do is to share with you some ideas backed by a limited and single experience of how computers may add to the negotiating process more than just their acknowledged ability to handle huge numbers and large quantities of information.

When disputing parties are willing to develop and examine together on computer model the issues that are the subject of their negotiations, there is often movement from adversarial to collaborative attitudes. There can even be new insights and mutual appreciation of each other's goals and values. Additional opportunities for mutually acceptable solutions will be revealed.

As this conference has already demonstrated, the recent technical and hardware developments of computers have been spectacular. The human, or software, developments have lagged behind, especially as they concern the joint use of computers for multiparty deliberations and negotiations.

We on this panel see a need for greater awareness of the potential contribution to international negotiations and a corresponding need for more attention directed to this application of computers, and to more real experience, such as that in the case we will shortly be examining.

Our session is divided into four segments. The first segment will be about the development of the Massachusetts Institute of Technology Deep Ocean Mining Model and its subsequent use in the law of the sea negotiations. In the second segment, we will critique the MIT model and its use in the law of the sea; in the third, very brief segment, there will be a listing of international negotiations where computer assistance might have been used in the past or might be used in the future. And lastly there will be a panel discussion among our speakers on the potential roles of computer-assisted negotiations, or CAN as we have called it, why it is needed, its opportunities, and its limitations. Each speaker will participate in each segment, and as we go along we'll get increasingly less formal.

I wish to remind you at the outset that this is a session on the use of computer-assisted negotiations, not on the law of the sea as a substantive matter itself. The law of the sea (LOS) has been selected as a convenient case history to sharpen our focus. The speakers will not address the important political and substantive issues of the LOS, nor will we entertain questions or discussions on these important and timely questions. We do this, not to restrict free speech, but rather to enhance our free exchange of ideas on this very important topic—the use of computers in negotiations. We do this in the context of the overall theme of this conference—the scientific, intellectual, and social impact of the computer.

Now our first speaker in the first segment, which is on the development and use of the MIT Deep Ocean Mining Model in the law of the sea negotiations, will be Professor Nyhart.

J. D. NYHART (*Alfred P. Sloan School of Management, Massachusetts Institute of Technology, Cambridge, Mass.*): In the fall of 1974, the MIT Department of Ocean Engineering and the Harvard Law School jointly offered an experimental seminar in legal and engineering aspects of ocean uses. The idea was to match a half-class of MIT engineers with a half-class of Harvard law students. The students so mixed were to undertake examination of several projects in order first to analyze both the legal and technical problems involved and then together to create a synthetic problem-solving effort and come up with a joint analysis reflecting both legal and technical training. I was one of the MIT faculty involved. One of the groups was assigned the problem of answering the question, Should the "Mithar Mining Co." invest in deep ocean mining?

Now since the 1860s, it has been known that in parts of the ocean bed, within the first few inches of its surface, are lumps about the size of a fist or a small potato. These "nodules" are created matter that contain in certain parts of the globe what is thought to be commercial quantities of copper, nickel, cobalt, and manganese. Although they were discovered first in the 1860s, it wasn't until the late 1960s that it was thought possible to gather up these nodules and process them in an economically viable way.

No one has yet launched such a mining operation, and today it is generally assumed that the cost would be about $1¼ billion.

The curiosity of one of the MIT students working on the novel project was aroused. Lance Antrim decided to investigate the economic feasibility further, as the topic for his thesis in environmental engineering at the institute. I was his thesis supervisor. Such were the rather humble origins of what was to become known as the MIT Deep Ocean Mining Model.

Basically, the model was and is an engineering costing and sizing effort coupled with a comparatively simple discounted cash flow model. Assumptions are made initially about the desired throughput of three million tons of nodules per year, the location of a United States west coast processing plant, and the location of the mining area southeast of Hawaii. Following these assumptions, the engineering aspects of the study include sizing and cost estimations for the mining collector, the pipestring to carry the nodules from the ocean floor to the ocean mining vessel, the ore ships to transport the nodules to port, the processing plant on shore, and the slurry pipelines for taking the nodules to the processing plants and the waste from the processing plant to tailing ponds to be stored. Unit by unit the equipment believed necessary for these operations was identified and described, and its capital and operating costs estimated.

The model's output summarized both operational and capital costs. It also provided three measures of economic turn on the investment over a 25-year period: the net present value at a range of discount rates, the internal rate of return, and the payback period in terms of years. I should mention that today discounted cash flow programs for a variety of uses are readily available. They are off-the-shelf software. At the time the model was constructed, such programs were far less common. Antrim was soon joined by another graduate student, Arthur Capstaff, who concentrated on the task of putting together such a program.

In good MIT fashion, Lance Antrim and I cast about for money to support his graduate education, while work on his thesis went ahead. A good portion of the costing effort was in hand by the time the new Office of Ocean Minerals of the National Oceanographic and Atmospheric Administration in the Department of Commerce undertook its support. Later, support from NOAA was to be added to by the U.S. Department of State and the Treasury. The Office of Ocean Minerals was looking forward to the day when the federal government would be regulating the mining of the deep seabed by United States consortia. The NOAA administrator's motivation in supporting the development of the model was to provide a creditable and feasible counterpoint in regulatory efforts when dealing with the otherwise superior data base presented by potential regulatees. NOAA wanted to know, as best it could, what the economic impact of different technical options were in the untried and unperfected technology of deep ocean mining. It knew that it would probably have to draw up initial regulations before the technology was tested on the abyssal plains of the ocean. Neither the sponsors nor those of us at MIT envisioned the use of the model we are discussing today, that is, its use in the law of the sea negotiations to assist in the development of acceptable formulas for revenue sharing.

One of the goals in constructing the model was to make it a relatively easy task to introduce new values for its very many variables. This was in the days before the supposed user-friendly programming we have heard reviewed here. So in addition to scouring the current literature and knowledgeable people for the fragments and remnants of cost estimates, an equally important parallel effort was going on to create a model in which the values and basic assumptions could be easily changed. Suppose the processing plant was in Oregon with a 50-foot draft port rather than California with a 35-foot draft channel, and was 700 miles farther from the mine site. The construction of the model grew out of the heavy uncertainties surrounding deep ocean mining in the mid-1970s. Suppose someone thought that the collector at the bottom of the sea would cost $25 million instead of $9.5 million. Suppose the whole project was placed in the Bahamas with no taxes, rather than in the United States, and so on. Although today it can be still characterized as an industry of the future, laden with present uncertainties, at that time still much less was known. Having scouted the literature, performed a reasonable engineering research job, and talked with individual members of the nascent industry, the team completed—by hand—its first set of cost estimates and calculation of the discounted cash flow. These estimates were reviewed in March 1977 at a workshop sponsored by NOAA and attended by representatives of the major industry consortia and scattered knowledgeable academic and government observers of the embryonic ocean mining industry. Their critiques and comments were carefully recorded, and taken one by one into consideration in a reformulation and redrafting of the model. This redrafted report was subsequently circulated to workshop participants, and their comments once again were taken into consideration prior to publication of the report in the spring of 1978. We thus felt that we had had two good reviews by industry of the cost data and other assumptions prior to publication. As will be seen later, these early reviews held us in good stead when the model was actually put to use in the LOS negotiations over a year later.

At this point it might be useful to make three initial observations about the characteristics of the model that were to be important in some later uses.

First, we were persistent and straightforwardly open about the assumptions and the values involved. To the best of our knowledge we tried to set out the assumptions that went into the model, not only any quantitative values, but the process assumptions that we made. Second, we were also persistent about making a continuing offer to put the best data we could get into the model. Repeatedly we said that we had constructed the model so that new data, new values, could be put in as new knowledge was acquired. We said, If you don't like our data, give us yours and we can all see what they look like. Thus the model was not built with results of a particular nature in mind. We recognized that acceptance in any of its uses was to be dependent upon its perceived neutral value. (That phrase, of course, is fraught with difficulty; it may be presumptuous to assume that any value is ever neutral.) Third, as pointed out earlier, the model was not developed with the use in LOS negotiation in mind.

Today, the model has gone through a totally new iteration. Although once the model was seen to be useful and likely to be used, the commentary and critique from the industry increased in volume, it was not until after it had been used for the purposes to be discussed shortly that we began to get anything resembling a flow of data from the consortia. And then it was mostly indirect. The current iteration of the model contains cost estimates that have come basically from the private sector in the United States. But these have also been backed up by a careful, detailed, and somewhat unique engineering effort by my colleague at MIT, Professor Michael Triantafyllou, and several graduate students working under his supervision. My colleague here today, Jim Sebenius, and Lance Antrim (who went to work at the Department of Commerce, joining the United States delegation to the Law of the Sea Conference under Ambassador Richardson) have made a careful study comparing the results of the model we put together in 1976 and the current engineering costing and economic analysis. The two efforts relate in a consistent manner.

The links to the law of the sea negotiations evolved through the imaginative and curious eye of Jim Sebenius. At the time, he was an intern from Stanford University's Engineering and Policy Program working at the Department of Commerce. He was shortly to become, during a transition period between administrations, a critical element in the Department of Commerce's presence at the law of the sea negotiations. We all are fortunate, I think, that he was working for Elliot Richardson. Dr. Sebenius' concept about the need to introduce some quantitative basis for discussion of the thorny problem of seabed mining into the negotiations met with a positive response from the lawyer who would soon head the negotiations committee dealing with these problems, Tommy Koh, Singapore's Ambassador to the United Nations and later president of the conference. I joined Ambassador Koh, Dr. Sebenius, a group of delegates to the conference, U.S. church folk, and foundation people to discuss the problems. As word of completion of the first iteration of the model was made known to this group, the Stanley Foundation made a special supporting effort in the first months of 1978, prior to the next meeting of the conference in March, to provide advance copies of the study to various members of the group of 77, that is, the developing countries, and to personnel of the Department of State and other members of the United States delegation. By that time, Antrim had joined the federal government, so four persons critical to the use of the model in the law of the sea negotiation, Ambassador Richardson, Dr. Sebenius, Ambassador Koh, and Dr. Antrim, were in place. Their story is better told by them.

J. K. SEBENIUS (*John F. Kennedy School of Government, Harvard University, Cambridge, Mass.*): What I'll try to do first is give a sense of how the MIT model came to be used in this long-term global negotiating effort, something about where that effort came from, and then the parts of the negotiation where the model was especially relevant. Then I want to talk a little bit about how the United States delegation used the model and comment on a few aspects of its use within the United States and in the international negotiating effort.

As Dan Nyhart described, these nodules—little conglomerations of copper, cobalt, nickel, and manganese—are located typically in regions that are outside any country's national jurisdiction, so their economic lure needed to be secured by property rights for some exclusive claim to the regions that might be mined. A region for mining is very large, some 40 to 60 thousand square kilometers for a single operation. That's on the order of the size of Switzerland.

Anybody who wanted to mine these nodules needed title to them, and there wasn't any international legal apparatus that people trusted to grant it. The situation at that time regarding the oceans was very complex. There was a dramatic increase in the intensity of use of the oceans for fishing from the early 1950s to about the 1970s, when the catch leveled off and even declined a bit. There was a tremendous increase in the use of the oceans for transport, both in the tonnage and in the size of ships. Energy production was dramatically up from the outer continental shelves, and accompanying this intensity of use were many, many conflicts. Among the most visible were the cod wars over fishing rights between Britain and Iceland.

The right to do scientific research off different coasts was disputed. Many claims of different countries were extended over fish, over oil, for security purposes, for environmental purposes. They promised a world with a great deal of conflict and with feared restrictions on navigation, both commercial and military. A series of these increasing conflicts made the role of international law much more important. But international law regarding the oceans had developed in a haphazard way. The last significant attempt to codify it and grant rights—the Geneva Conventions of 1958—had left many holes. Mineral nodules were hardly part of that agenda, and so certainly this new ocean use needed a better framework in which to proceed.

Not only that, but many nations in the world of the 1970s hadn't existed or were barely independent in the late fifties. The legitimacy of such international laws as there were was called into question by these nations, who wondered why they should be required to abide by laws that they really had no part in formulating. This summary provides only a surface view of these trends, but they led by the early 1970s to a major law of the sea negotiation.

There was an extremely important event in 1970. The General Assembly of the United Nations, without opposition, declared these nodules to be the "common heritage of mankind." That declaration, in combination with some of these other trends, led to these negotiations which had many parts. One—and subsequently the most politically salient—was the attempt to construct a regime for mining these nodules: who would have the rights, under what conditions, with what obligations, environmental, financial, and so forth; how would disputes be settled. A whole set of other questions concerned traditional law-of-the-sea areas like fishing, navigation, the territorial claims, claims to different resources in the oceans as well as the marine environment, and marine and scientific research. It was, in effect, to be a "constitution" for all of the seas.

These negotiations went on actively from 1974 to the end of 1982. The participants there represented well over 150 countries and virtually every conceivable interest and ideology. The divergencies ran in so many directions—North and South, the developed and developing, East and West, the producers of the minerals that would come from the seabed, the consumers of them, and the industrialized, newly industrialized, and less developed countries.

In any case it was an extremely complex process which went on over a long time. As some of you no doubt know, the convention was recently signed in Jamaica by close to 120 countries, the United States notably abstaining. The MIT work was relevant to one particular, very central issue within this constitution-writing effort. The question was how to share any benefits that came from the mining of the deep seabed nodules. With respect to the "common heritage of mankind" notion and trying to arrange a way for broader participation in the mining, there would be two broad issues that this model directly concerned.

The first was the system of payments to the international community, almost like a system of fees, royalties, and profit shares that the company would pay the government. The second was the creation of an international mining entity that itself would mine on behalf of mankind. The model was quite useful at giving insight into both these questions.

What I'd like to do is describe briefly some of the model's uses in the United States delegation and then sketch some of the international uses.

I was working at the Commerce Department, and got an assignment to do some staff work on a bill that was wending its way through the United States Congress to enable the unilateral mining of seabed nodules. I had not heard of these things at all, and so I tried to discover what kind of work had been done to get some notion of what they were and something about their economics. I also encountered somebody in an office of the Commerce Department who said that a group at MIT had been working intensively on this for some time. At the time, the connections to the legislative and the broader international questions that were associated with this issue were unknown to me.

That's how I found the MIT model. I began to use it in doing some of this early staff work to get some understanding of the economic and technical nature of this process of deep seabed mining. It's a long-term capital-intensive project. Studying it from the United States point of view pointed up its incredible uncertainty, uncertainty in the capital costs, operating costs, and revenues. The group at MIT had struggled mightily to get some feeling for it. Studying the model gave a much clearer idea of capital and operating costs and how those would be dependent on energy costs, for example, and chemicals, as well as the metal markets for copper, cobalt, nickel, manganese, and how those things came together in an engineering structure linked to a financial routine. So from the U.S. point of view, we used the model to get a much better sense of what the economics would look like. And, naturally, it was easy to test the effects of various tax proposals—depreciation, tax credits, environmental modifications that might be required, and otherwise.

In the international arena, the model was used in quite a similar sense to understand much more about this international entity that would be created by the negotiations. The staff work that Ambassador Koh presided over in trying to design an effective tax system for this mining involved running many, many different financial proposals, structuring them in a variety of different ways, holding a series of seminars both in tiny groups in the negotiations and in increasingly larger groups up to full plenary sessions where this model and its results could be queried and studied by the delegates, as well as off-the-record sessions and seminars held by such groups as the Quakers and the Methodists away from the negotiation on a kind of neutral ground.

The model became so popular that people would even show up early on Saturday mornings to learn more about what was at that point a very central set of questions in the negotiations.

A number of delegations as well used the model: the European community, the Indian delegation, the Soviet delegation, those of Japan and Argentina were prominent users that borrowed the model to try to get some better sense of what it was that we were negotiating.

E. L. RICHARDSON (*Milbank, Tweed, Hadley & McCloy, Washington, D.C.*): My good friend—until lately, the President of the Law of the Sea Conference—Ambassador Tommy Koh could not possibly have known, in suggesting that I precede him in speaking order, that I was going to deliver what—if this were a National Convention—might be interpreted as a nominating speech. But that is just what I want to do, because it seems to me that at this stage in the exposition, you ought to have some feel for the personalities involved. Without their contribution it is certain that the MIT model, however well constructed and however potentially useful, would not in fact have found the use to which it was put with such remarkable results.

In this story the hero is sitting to the left of our chairman. He is Ambassador Koh. He is a hero in other dimensions as well. Those of you who follow the development of North-South relations and East-West relations generally would have noted in the *New York Times* that

Ambassador Koh, at the recent nonaligned meeting in New Delhi, was the leader and principal tactician of the moderate forces there. He has been a leading force in the United Nations behind the resolutions condemning the Vietnamese occupation of Cambodia and the Soviet occupation of Afghanistan.

In 1978, Ambassador Koh was named chairman of a working group, called Working Group 2, that was charged with trying to resolve the issues under the heading then generally referred to as "financial arrangements." Under this heading were embraced all the issues inherent in figuring out how much should be paid to the International Seabed Authority (ISA) by companies, state owned or private, operating under license of the ISA in the mining of deep seabed manganese nodules.

It was a basic premise, as you've heard from James Sebenius, that these nodules belong to the world as a whole—hence the reference to them as the "common heritage of mankind." But if they belong to the world community as a whole, on the one side, and if, on the other, the costs and risks associated with exploiting them are extremely high, in what amounts, if any, and in what forms of payment, should exercise of the right to mine be required to make some contribution to the ISA? How much should be paid up front in the form of fees or advance payments of some kind? How much would it be reasonable to try to collect in the form of royalties or payments from gross proceeds and how much from net proceeds? To what extent should it make a difference whether or not the investor had recovered his initial investment? Should this affect the rate of contributions from income? How would you go about dealing with the question of what proportion of the net proceeds of deep seabed mining is attributable to operations in the deep ocean as against the proportion attributable to the value added by the extraction of the metals from the manganese nodules in the shore-based processing plant?

All of these questions had to be dealt with, and of course fundamental to them was the relationship between the amount of the investment made by the deep seabed miner and the rate of return, given the risks associated with the enterprise as a whole, that such an investor should be expected to insist upon in order to induce his investment, given the alternative uses to which his capital funds might otherwise be applied. This was the segment of the problem of deep seabed mining committed to the working group chaired by Ambassador Koh.

It happened that the conference also had among its leading participants a man who then held the title of Minister for Law of the Sea in the Cabinet of Norway, Ambassador Jens Evensen—and I might add that one thing Tommy Koh and Jens Evensen had in common is that both had received Master of Law Degrees from Harvard Law School.

Evensen was and is one of the world's leading experts on international law, and particularly ocean law. He had played a prominent role in the earlier stages of the law of the sea negotiations with regard particularly to the traditional areas of international law such as the rights and duties of coastal states, freedom of navigation and overflight, and the like, and he had in 1977 chaired a negotiating group representing all countries in the conference seeking to develop a workable seabed mining text. To deal with the so-called hard-core issues identified in the course of the 1977 negotiations the conference created a series of working groups, including Ambassador Koh's Working Group 2. His charge, as I have said, was to answer the question of what it is reasonable to require in terms of initial fees, royalties, and rates of profit sharing, to define "attributable net proceeds," and so on.

Well, as you've heard, MIT was already developing a computer model, but it probably hadn't yet occurred to its designers that the model would have a central role in the resolution of these questions. The existence of the model created an opportunity, but it was an opportunity that could be exploited only if the model could be endowed with credibility. Fortunately, it was a model developed at an institution whose own stature was widely recognized by participants in the conference. This in itself went a long way toward assuring the model's credibility. But it was also important to find other means of creating the maximum degree of acceptability for the data that it would produce. One was an informal meeting held under the auspices of the Stanley Foundation for members of the conference who would be playing leading roles in these issues. The Stanley Foundation in other connections had already secured for itself the reputation of a neutral forum which offered the opportunity for informal discussion among people from the developing countries as well as representatives of the industrial countries and of the mining companies themselves. This reputation too was a contributor to the development of credibility and trust in the model.

Ambassador Evensen at this stage played a significant role because he began to develop an analysis of his own, to some extent even competitively with Working Group 2. Nevertheless, the fact that he did take this initiative and began to explore possible approaches to the financial arrangement issues also helped to build confidence in the MIT model because he found it increasingly useful in seeking the answers he needed.

Meanwhile Dr. Sebenius was playing a key but low-profile role. He was a member of the United States delegation, but he had by that time achieved such a reputation for total integrity and extraordinary competence that he had come to be used by Ambassador Koh as if he were a member of the Secretariat of the conference itself. And indeed he was actually in the position of having from time to time to tell his colleagues on the staff of Tommy Koh's working group that he could not tell them what had been discussed that day in the United States delegation and later in the day of having to tell me that he couldn't disclose what had been discussed in an executive session of the staff of Tommy Koh's working group that very afternoon. It takes a remarkable person to achieve that kind of status, and I don't think one can easily generalize as to the potential for others to duplicate this role in other situations.

I think it's fair to say that the opportunity to make effective use of what was during this interval becoming an increasingly useful model to a large degree depended on Ambassador Koh's being there, on Evensen's role, on Sebenius' role, and indeed on that of a number of other people, including Inam ul Haq of Pakistan who, although in some respects a militant representative of the group of 77, is also a very bright and very intellectually honest man. Haq will not let himself make an argument that he does not believe to be intellectually valid, and if you give him an effective answer he will not bluster or try to pretend that his original point does not require qualification.

There was Anil Gayan of Mauritius, to some extent perhaps even more militant than Haq, but also very bright and committed like the others to try and find answers. There was Alfredo Boucher of Argentina, who, but for coming from the southern hemisphere and speaking Spanish, could easily have passed for a Covington & Burling tax lawyer. It was this combination that, together with the machine and its calculations, produced a really extraordinary result, a kind of mini–corporate tax code for the future financial aspects of deep seabed mining.

D. B. STRAUS: As you can see, we've set the stage to talk about how the alchemy of men and machines did get together in this particular case. Some of us, from the mediation point of view, which is the one I represent, have been interested in the potential value of computer-negotiator interaction as a means for helping to organize the discussions, and to reduce adversarial attitudes, and to elevate the quality of the decisions eventually reached.

It's a question of helping to manage complexity, of giving a sort of negotiating framework that doesn't exist without this kind of apparatus. In the final analysis, at least from the viewpoint that I represent, the activity of working together to construct and build a model, of participation with previously adversarial persons in trying to do this, is more important than the output of the computer—or at least of equal importance. I think we'll begin to get some flavor of this. Prof. Nyhart will lead us into the second segment.

J. D. NYHART: The question has been put, From the present perspective, how does one evaluate the use of the model in assisting the law of the sea negotiations?

There are pluses and minuses. It is useful to recall that my perspective is not only that of the principal investigator of the project. I was also in the rather unusual and often precarious position of directing model building while being essentially a non–computer person. With that said, there seems to me that there are several good things to be said about the use of a model in the kind of negotiation described.

First, its use provided a way of moving the negotiating parties to become clearer about values and premises. Values of an economic and political nature: What does it take to induce large investments in a novel, uncertain project? How do you best go about estimating costs? And also of a technical nature—Does extrapolation from real-world experience of ore transport, ship costs, or from comparatively primitive sizing estimates provide the best basis for cost estimates? And legal values, too—"When do nodules acquire a market value?" holds an implicit value statement.

The model's use provides an opportunity to link together the requisite components in the system while leaving each component or subcomponent subject to examination. You can take apart a piece of the whole, look at it, negotiate over it, and put it back in place, without losing track of the whole.

Its use provides a way for looking at many different proposals and their impact in a very rapid way. This was critical in the LOS negotiation.

Its use provides a way for different negotiators to "join up." It makes it easier for them to abandon old positions, to assume new positions in the negotiation. Like a good consultant, a computer model can "take the rap."

Perhaps most importantly, its use provides a way for sides both to test and to gain credibility. It can provide the opportunity for negotiators to *gain* credibility through showing and making clear their different assumptions, through showing that they are willing to try different solutions, to experiment with different possible outcomes, through providing the way to show that they are open to change. It provides negotiators an opportunity to *test* the credibility of others through giving them—perhaps mainly the technologically less-advantaged negotiators— an opportunity to learn the language and the base concepts of the technology. The part that the MIT model played as a tool for providing some basic education in the way sophisticated investors look at investments has already been mentioned. It provides a way for negotiators to participate in the process more fully by coming up with their own assumptions, which could then be tested and examined.

All of the above advantages can be erased if computer-assisted models are used as mumbo jumbo to impress, to obfuscate the issues rather than to shed light. But this is a danger that is an old familiar friend in the law. It is the problem of the extra weight given to scientific evidence in trials. The excessive credibility that tends to accompany science in the lay or legal world always has to be guarded against.

Turning to the problems in the model, use of the last issue—the extra weight of science—provides a starting place. The internal rate of return figure of what we called our base case of around 18% became cast in concrete. Among the group of 150 negotiating countries, the fact that a place called MIT had come up with a model with a particular internal rate of return gave that figure far too much credence and power. So the first question in considering the use of computer-assisted negotiations is how to eliminate the quantitative mystique. It is important in the context of multilateral negotiations to recognize up front the power of an accepted model.

Once it was clear that the model was going to be accepted by a large population in the negotiations, the future regulatees—the deep ocean mining industry—became threatened by its use. So a related problem is how to provide safeguards, how to reduce the threat. In fact, Ambassadors Richardson and Koh and Dr. Sebenius used the capability of the model to help generate and communicate a formula that went a long way toward protecting the vital interest of the investing, risk-taking industry while at the same time serving the interests of the nations around the globe.

One way of mitigating the power of the quantitative mystique is to have people focus on one model. As its contents, weaknesses, and strengths become known, people become familiar with it and know its limitations. In the LOS negotiations different parties made an effort to focus on the one model. To this end, MIT licensed the European Economic Commission to use it, in an effort to promote a common language rather than a tower of Babel.

A second major problem was that of data acquisition. Translated more freely, this one becomes a question of how do we know what we are doing. In market economies, most of the critical data are in the hands of the private industrial sector and frequently these data are proprietary. It is a perpetual problem in the United States and similar societies. Our effort in tracking industry data in the first iteration has already been described. In the second round, NOAA hired industry consultants to work with the MIT team in providing data. In fact, these industry consultants have put together their own model and are now operating it. On the other hand, there is the question of checking data from industry. As pointed out, we addressed this problem by providing our own independent engineering workups. These technical assumptions are set forth as an integral part of the second report. They provide a good parallel, independent basis for estimates. It is worth noting that the results of these two paths complemented and supported each other.

Closely related to the question of data acquisition is the very important question of separation of the technological function. Technical data ought, in my opinion at least, to be gathered and assembled and the model built, from a technical point of view, by persons who do not presume the answer to the problem at hand. The answer to the problem, what should be done, necessarily involves value considerations. They are the province of the policy people, the diplomats and politicians, not the technical folk.

That comment raises a related, but distinct, problem in making good use of computer-assisted models, the problem of user participation. How do you get the users aboard early and still get the model built? And, if you bring the users in, how do you keep separate the technology and value considerations just referred to? In our case, in retrospect, working more directly with the different negotiating parties during the intercessions between the law of the sea negotiations would have helped the modeling. However, we had limited capacity, they had limited capacity, and we all had limited funding. I think that ideally we should have had the funding and the time to have transferred the capability of the model to the United Nations, to the Law of the Sea Authority, in addition to our NOAA sponsors. There are problems, huge problems, with transferring the capabilities of such a model, not the least of which are the problems of satisfactory documentation. These problems are made worse when the model-building team is an academic team spread over several different years of graduate students. But that is a different problem.

T. T. B. KOH (*Permanent Mission of Singapore to the United Nations, New York, N.Y.*): I think the best contribution I can make to this discussion is to say something about how the MIT cost model came to have such an important place in the law of the sea negotiations, to talk about what use the negotiators made of the model, why the results of the negotiations would have been different if we did not have the model to use, and what extrapolations one can make from this one successful case to the future.

I'd like to begin by returning to something Dr. Sebenius said in his earlier statement, and this was that the mandate I was given as chairman consisted of two interrelated subjects. I was given a mandate to negotiate an agreement on the tax system that would apply to seabed miners. The tax system would not only include the structure of the system but also numbers, exactly what percentage of royalties the miners would pay to the international community, whether there would be a component of profit sharing, and if so how much of the profits earned by the seabed miners would be taken by the international community.

The other part of my mandate was to get an agreement on how the first mining operation of the Enterprise, the Enterprise being an international public mining company, would be financed.

Very early in my work I came to the conclusion that in order to achieve success in negotiating the first subject, I had to link the first to the second subject for this reason: the industrialized countries were naturally much more interested in getting an agreement on the tax system that would apply to seabed miners; the developing countries, on the other hand, were much more interested in ensuring that the first mining operation of the international enterprise would be financed. So I decided that tactically I had to link these two questions and that I must make simultaneous progress on the two fronts.

Having decided that, I was then confronted in the negotiations on the tax system with what seemed, at first, to be an insuperable intellectual obstacle. The obstacle was that the seabed mining industry does not exist now and did not exist five years ago. We had no reliable estimates of what the capital or development cost for mining operations would be; we didn't know for sure what the annual operating costs would be; we didn't know what the metal prices in the world market in the future would be, and unless we knew that, we could not estimate the profits.

So on all the three parameters—development costs, operating costs, and revenue derived from sale of metals—we were in the dark. It was by a happy accident or serendipity that we had the MIT cost model available to answer a need felt by the delegations in the conference.

However, in order to get the MIT model accepted by the conference we had to overcome many intellectual, political, and psychological obstacles. The fact that it was a study done in the United States generated some political and psychological problems. The fact that the study was financed by a grant from the Department of Commerce was an additional difficulty we had to overcome.

The most important of all was the intellectual burden. Most lawyers, including those who were in the Law of the Sea Conference, had very little knowledge of science and engineering in general and even less of computer science in particular. So the first intellectual hurdle I had to overcome was to hold seminars in order to explain to these lawyers in the conference what a computer model was all about, to explain to them how the MIT team of scholars had built up this cost model, to explain what development costs and operating costs mean, how one arrives at projected profits of a mining project, and then to make them understand what the internal rate of return was, what a payback period was. It was an intellectual burden which took about a year to overcome.

The political and psychological problems we overcame through the help of certain nongovernmental organizations, such as the Stanley Foundation, which Mr. Richardson has referred to, the Quakers, and the United Methodist Church. We were able to hold several weekend conferences and retreats away from the conference, and we were able to invite Professor Nyhart and his colleagues from MIT to come to these meetings to explain how the cost model was built, what was its utility, what were its shortcomings to the delegations. It was a very important encounter because when the suspicious third-world delegates met these American scholars from MIT they were impressed by their objectivity and by their personal integrity. They were persuaded that although the study was financed by the Department of Commerce, the MIT scholars had tried to do an objective piece of work uninfluenced by where the money came from. It was not intended to serve the interests of the American mining industry. This is very important.

The fact that the MIT cost model then came to be criticized by certain representatives of the mining industry and by the European Economic Community reinforced the growing perception on the part of the third-world delegations that it was an objective study and that the scholars were men and women of personal integrity.

Another reason why the MIT model came to be so widely accepted in the conference was because its intrinsic merit was superior to anything else we had to use. The European Economic Community was not satisfied with it, but the rival model which they put forth at the conference was a rather poor thing in comparison to the MIT cost model for this important reason. The MIT cost model was an impressive piece of work because it had disaggregated all the sums down to the component parts of a mining system, a pipe, a ship, whereas the European model used large aggregates but did not disaggregate these global sums and you didn't really know how they arrived at these much larger figures than the MIT team had. Therefore, I was able to convince the conference that when you compared the intrinsic value of the MIT model and the European model, one had to come to the conclusion that the MIT model was the more reliable of the two.

Now I'd like to say something about what use we, the negotiators, and the conference made of the MIT model in our negotiations. I think the most important use we made of the MIT model was to demonstrate and reinforce the element of uncertainty in the economics of this new industry, and the point we were able to communicate to all the delegations from every part of the world was that we are regulating an industry whose economic prospects are very uncertain and that—although the MIT team had done the best job it could to estimate the development costs, the operating costs, and profits of seabed mining—these are, at best, estimates and that any change upward or downward in these three parameters could result in a very significant change in the profitability of the project. So that was a very important element which we got across.

The second utility of the MIT cost model was that I was able, as chairman, to use the MIT cost model to convince delegations that certain proposals they had put forward were financially infeasible. The utility of the MIT cost model was that you could put in all kinds of inputs and variables and the computer would tell you how the internal rate of return of the project would change with these new variables. We were able, for example, to convince the conference that the Indian proposal that every seabed miner should, on signature of the contract, pay a bonus payment of $60 million was such a heavy front-end burden as to make seabed mining projects infeasible.

The third value of the MIT cost model was that I was able to use it to convince the delegations to shift the emphasis in the tax system from a reliance on royalty payments, which are fixed payments, to a greater emphasis on profit sharing. This was a very important achievement which we could not have made without the model.

The last point I want to make is that I was able to use the MIT model to convince delegations that the international community's share of the seabed miners' profits should be pegged to the project's profitability, as measured both on a year-to-year basis and on a project-long basis. In other words, the international community's share of the profits of a mining project would vary from year to year and from project to project depending on the seabed miners' internal rate of return.

Again, this was an agreement that could not have been achieved in the absence of the MIT cost model. My short answer to the question, Would the results have been different if we didn't have the MIT cost model?, would be yes, it would have been very different.

Can the success of the MIT model in the law of the sea negotiations be replicated? We'll come to that in the third segment of the panel, but I just want to end by emphasizing the many happy coincidences that occurred which made this success possible. One was the fact that the negotiation was primarily about numbers and structures of a tax system, and the question I would like to flag now for discussion later is whether or not the computer can play the same kind of helpful role when the negotiations are not primarily about numbers.

My second point was that the MIT model came to play the dominant role it did because of a felt need on the part of the conference for an agreed set of figures and facts, and the model offered this to the conference.

My third point was that the success story could not be replicated in the absence of the critical mass of people who fortuitously came together in this particular negotiation. We had some of the members at MIT who were available to the conference, we had the head of the United States delegation, Elliot Richardson, who was familiar with the MIT model and was willing to allow the conference access to that model. We had, within the conference, a small number of very talented and able men and women both in the secretariat and in the delegations without whom this success story would not have occurred.

J. K. SEBENIUS: Given Ambassador Koh's help in laying out a lot of points that I think are interesting, I'd like to embroider a few. Why did people use the model as much as they did despite the highly politically charged environment where the prospects for using a United States government-financed model, done at a United States institution, for a very important precedent-setting area would have been very dim?

Why did people use the model? I'd underline the disaggregation that Dr. Nyhart insisted on from his graduate students. They identified and documented everything, creating a huge appendix justifying from the ground up how they built the system and where all the estimates came from. That disaggregation was crucial, particularly as against other studies that were aggregated without internal justification. People could look and debate at a very disaggregated level if they wished.

A second important point was that the early apparent implications of the model seemed to cut both ways. When it came to the conference, while many developed countries claimed that virtually no taxes were possible in this highly risky industry, the model seemed to suggest that indeed some more taxes were possible. At the same time, many in the developing world thought that seabed mining would provide an absolute bonanza, a kind of engine of third-world development that itself could fuel a great deal of international progress. But the model suggested that mining would be profitable, but not a bonanza. This, along with the vocal criticism by many of the political advisers to some of the mining companies, somewhat paradoxically added to the model's credibility.

It's interesting that, initially, people latched onto the model since it seemed to offer such a certain projection of the future. People had been swimming around in such uncertainty that the model almost provided an excuse to go forward. Paradoxically, as we went further into the negotiations, the very uncertainty of the estimates around the different parameters became clear and politically relevant. Instead of the numbers that the model contained, its structure was the key—the fact that it used a measure of profitability that was calculated over time. The discounting and the degree of risk that was associated with different tax systems became very clear to the delegates. What ultimately happened, partially as a result of this model, I think, is that the tax structure that was produced in the Law of the Sea Convention is a novel tax structure, much different than you find in most countries. It explicitly takes into account the profitability of an operation over time and in different conditions of risk. It's quite an achievement technically to allow a fair division of revenue without imposing a great deal of additional risk on operations. For example, in third-world countries when mining companies go in, the usual result of too inflexible tax systems is a constant series of painful renegotiations. We had to avoid that, and the model pointed the way for such an achievement.

There is one last point that I would make on the model's use. An example was the case of the Indian proposal for a heavy front-end load. The proposal was made and a lot of political credibility staked on it. But as the negotiations progressed, the model was introduced, and many runs came back and forth, it was quite possible for the Indian delegates to withdraw their proposal in the face of genuine learning. It wasn't a political concession as such to the other side, but instead it was a concession to a more rational look at the problem. And the model was almost like a third party to a number of delegates, so it provided a way to move that didn't involve conceding to another political counterpart. That was quite important, and some delegates went so far I think as to make actual political concessions nominally using the model. It provided an escape route from the frozen positions and deadlocked commitments that are the bane of negotiations. The way the model facilitated such movement was a nontechnical benefit.

E. L. RICHARDSON: I want to make three brief observations which may serve partly to bridge the discussion you've already heard with the discussions to follow with respect to the future international issues where computer-assisted negotiations might be applicable. What I'm about to say isn't really a critique but rather an attempt to highlight points that may be significant when the opportunity arises to apply the lessons to be drawn from this experience.

First of all, although we've been talking about a computer model whose internal calculations take place beyond the reach of human intellectual capacity to follow and which are never articulated but which rather produce their numbers on the basis of the design and the data inputs to the model, it would be a mistake obviously to understate the importance of linguistic lucidity to the potential applicability of any such model.

We have, indeed, using the word model in a slightly different sense, on this dais two models of linguistic lucidity in Ambassador Koh and Dr. Sebenius. I'm sure that in listening to them you can get some sense of what Ambassador Koh was talking about when he referred to his "seminar." And do not lose sight of his comment that it took about a year of such sessions both to create credibility for the model results but also to

educate people to understand the relevance for the issues to be negotiated of the model's findings or projections. And Dr. Sebenius along with
others, but particularly Dr. Sebenius was a very important contributor of
staff support for that purpose. It is not lightly to be assumed that with less
capacity in these respects a successful outcome would have been
reached.

I'm not sure whether it's been mentioned that it was partly on the
strength of Ambassador Koh's performance in this context that, when the
man who had been not only president of the conference from the
beginning but before that Chairman of the United Nations Seabeds
Committee, Hamilton Shirley Amerasinghe, died in 1979, Koh was the
overwhelming choice of the conference to succeed him and served as
president of the conference until its concluding ceremony in Jamaica last
December.

My second observation is that there is needed for any such process to
succeed in a large multilateral conference the judgmental capacity to
assemble a group of people who can negotiate the final resolution of the
issues that have been addressed by the model. As Ambassador Koh told
you, he was charged with not just setting up a system of taxation but also
determining what the tax rates would be and how the question of
attributable net proceeds would be dealt with, and so on.

At that stage he held negotiations in the conference room of the
Singapore Mission here in New York, at which he presided and at which
were represented the individuals I referred to before, Haq of Pakistan,
Gayan of Mauritius, and Boucher of Argentina. I was there representing
all of the western industrial countries. None of us had any authority from
anyone to close any deal, but we did; we filled in all the numbers, and
they remain to this day in the text exactly as they came out of those
negotiations. And this is the one part of the seabed mining regime that the
Reagan administration did not include in its list of things it wanted to
have changed.

How, then, was it possible for five people in these circumstances to
produce such a result? Each of us around that table knew that we couldn't
bind anyone not present. In such an exercise you must know that your
fellow participants have a very high probability, if they go along, of being
able to deliver their colleagues, and if you don't know that, you'd better
not be there. But it is that ultimate process of very intense bargaining—
and only that—that can produce the ultimate negotiated results.

I would just add, as a final point, which really brings us back full
circle, that the MIT model contributed to credible data that, mediated
through the process of negotiation, produced a sensible result. It was a
result that could stand up to the kind of examination it has had since,
especially during the review initiated by the Reagan administration on
the eve of the resumption of negotiations in 1981. And, as I said a moment
ago, it was the one major part of the deep seabed mining regime that
emerged from that review undamaged in the eyes of the Reagan administration itself.

D. B. STRAUS: Before we go on, I would like to address a question raised by someone in the audience: "Does not the equal access to the data by all parties change the very nature of negotiations?" First let me give one answer as a mediator. I think the answer is yes, it does indeed change the nature of negotiations. It can have the effect of moving the adversarial attitude of the parties more towards collaboration, more towards what the academicians call a positive-sum result rather than a zero-sum. One of the newer skills that all of us are going to have to learn as we broaden our skills from dispute resolution to the management of the entire decision cycle is to be sensitive when parties are ready to become more collaborative. In these large-scale and complex issues there are times when the parties can see an opportunity, for their own best interests, not for altruism but for their own best interests, to move towards a collaborative study of a problem rather than withholding information and being purely adversarial. Decision-cycle facilitators must be alert for such opportunities and must be ready to encourage them. Mr. Richardson touched on one aspect of this and so did Ambassador Koh—and this was the *quality* of the agreement that was reached. An agreement, *any* agreement, used to be the only thing that mediators were interested in. But it is increasingly the quality of the agreement that is important as the issues addressed become more complex and far reaching in their impacts. The interactive and joint use of the MIT model indeed changed the nature of negotiations, but it has been suggested that the quality of the eventual agreement was also better than it might have been without it. I think this is an essential point to emphasize.

J. D. NYHART: As we were planning the structure of this session we had the idea that if we compiled and presented a list of upcoming negotiations or treaties, this might stimulate discussion as to future uses of computer modeling in negotiation.

Now when I got to that task, I found that there was no neat list. I was able to group them into major categories: (1) agricultural commodities; (2) arms control; (3) mineral and renewable resources; (4) natural resource exploration and exploitation; (5) pollution liability and compensation; and (6) trade and transnational uses of science and technology.

Arms control does not have some of the characteristics that I want to refer to in a moment. Natural resource exploitation and exploration is what we're talking about this morning. And what I feel is the most important is the last, transnational uses of science and technology.

I looked at the list afterwards and realized that there were some common characteristics. First of all, there is a good deal of uncertainty involved and complexity involved in the science and technology of all of these. Uncertainty in the agricultural products, in the commodity products, in terms of weather, etc.

Secondly, there's economic value—the ability to put numerical values on the subjects of negotiation here. I think that's important. Ambassador Koh expressed the question, "When you aren't dealing with numbers, can you get a useful hold on this kind of modeling?" I'd ask the same question.

I'm not sure you can do much or succeed, or get any leverage if you aren't dealing with some component of these large political questions that is discussable in terms of numbers, in terms of economic values.

D. B. STRAUS: We're now really into the paydirt of our panel discussion. What we are now hearing is that there is a group of users who are of fundamental importance to their governments and to the countries in which we live who are saying: We need help! We are facing too much complexity, too many parties. It is becoming increasingly difficult to understand the nature of the issues that we're up against.

These important users are looking for help—not just from computers. They need access to a whole variety of new tools, a sort of toolshed of procedures that could help at different stages of the decision cycle.

We should now try to be as specific as we can. But first we must examine a threshold question. I either heard, or wanted to hear, because I guess this is my prejudice, that negotiators should be persuaded to collaborate as soon as possible in building a model; in its design, in the selection of the issues and the data, etc. What might have happened if the law of the sea negotiators had collaborated from the start in the design and development of the MIT model? Would that have damaged the process, aided it, or not have made any difference?

J. K. SEBENIUS: It seems to me that a central question for the law of the sea model was why it was accepted. Of course it was useful, but there were lots of models that were proffered and arguably dealt with the same questions. That notion of independence and credibility was so important here that it's hard to go back and reconstruct what would have been the case had apparent advocates gotten to the model much earlier.

On the other hand, there was something else that was very important. Once the model came into general discussion and became part of the LOS conference, it became very clear that it hadn't been designed for the conference's use. For example, the United States tax system was built into the model itself, almost hard wired in a programming sense, and it took a great deal of work to disentangle it so that it could be used for the tax systems of all sorts of other countries or by an international authority.

That made things difficult. But in the process of modifying the model to handle international situations and the particular suggestions of all kinds of individual delegates and countries, those representatives came to have an influence over it and the outputs that they wanted. For example, not only did the model give the rates of return to the contractors and the miners, but it was easily modified to give a rate of payment to the international community under a variety of different people's assumptions and proposals that were structurally quite different. In a sense, the model changed from one that was owned and done only by MIT to one that was susceptible to and modified by lots of input from other people. I think that that cumulative process was important. And it's hard to judge, if that had happened earlier, whether the model would then have been seen as simply an adversary tool.

Another interesting thing that the model did with respect to these measures that I mentioned—the rate of return to individual contractors and payments to the international authority—was that it framed the issue in terms that were quite discussable on the merits. It focused the negotiations and almost provided a language that was much easier to handle than the much larger North-South questions that this issue was a proxy for. So in a sense, the model concentrated and focused and narrowed the discussion a great deal and provided terms for the negotiations that let it go forward in an apparently more rational and productive way than the simple trading of theology back and forth, which often happens.

T. T. B. KOH: I would agree with that. I think it would not have been useful if the users had been on board at the point of model building. But it would have been very useful if, in the review process of the study, prior to publication, representatives not only of the American industry but of the European and Japanese industries and representatives of the third world, mining experts and regulatory experts had some input into the review process. My conclusion is that, in retrospect, the independence of the scholars at MIT was an important element in the credibility of the data. I don't think it would have helped that independence to have made the study subject to the control of the users, although I think the exposure of the earlier version of the study, in the review process, to a wider audience would have been a useful addition.

J. D. NYHART: I'll comment on that too from my perspective. I agree with what Ambassador Koh and Dr. Sebenius said about the independence. There's another aspect regarding management of the project. I don't think we would have got the modeling done. It was difficult enough to get it done under the circumstances, with the funding and time and human resources that we had. I think that if we were dealing at that early stage with much more complexity brought in by many more interests at the beginning, it would have been quite difficult.

I agree with the idea that it would have been very helpful to have had the criticism and input at the early review stage. The other thing I would say is that in the continuation of the modeling, the involvement of the modeling team as its use became significant was very important. The ability of Lance Antrim and Jim Sebenius—who were both on the front line of the negotiations working with Ambassadors Koh and Richardson—to come back up to MIT to give us a sense of what was going on in the negotiations so that we could work to modify the model and make it more useful was absolutely critical.

D. B. STRAUS: It seems at this point that the whole question of the nature and timing of user participation is a matter very much open for further research and development. From my point of view, at the International Institute for Applied Systems Analysis this is a tremendously underrated and underexplored question. Models are being built with very few users actually on the scene. I think this should be emphasized.

Elliot you have a different series of concerns.

E. L. RICHARDSON: They're not so much concerns, as points related to where Dr. Nyhart left off. I want to talk a little bit about the other possible uses that computer models might have for international negotiations. This is going to be a very sketchy indication of some of the considerations that seem to be relevant, but you might be interested to know that there were at least two other uses of computer models in connection with the law of the sea negotiations, neither of which, however, had anything like the practical application that the one you've heard discussed here this morning turned out to have.

One is a computer study of the dynamics of the entire negotiating process in the law of the sea negotiations. You should bear in mind that the seabed mining part of the treaty is part 17, one of 17 parts of the treaty. The issues we're talking about here are a fraction—say a sixth—of the problems dealt with in the seabed mining regime. Quite a lot of work has been done on an effort to feed into a computer the dynamics of the interactions among the attitudes of the various blocs, grouped by issue and national interest and so on, in order to see to what extent the outcomes could be understood in particular areas of negotiation in the light of these variables.

I attended a meeting under the auspices of the Overseas Development Council a few months ago devoted to a discussion of the validity of the analysis heretofore produced and the possible utility it might have in understanding better approaches to future multilateral negotiations. I'm somewhat skeptical on both counts.

I had also made an effort early on in my own role in the negotiations to feed into a computer variables affecting United States negotiating relationships with other participants in the conference. I was soon convinced that this was a worthless exercise, largely because there were no elements of the bilateral relationships between the United States and other countries that could be of any value in the negotiations in the Law of the Sea Conference. It needs to be emphasized in this connection that the United States may be a big strong country, but in a multilateral conference like this, it has very limited negotiating leverage, and none to be derived from threats or promises to individual countries extraneous to the subject of negotiation.

We fed into the computer things like the fact that the United States had a PL-480 program, an AID grant program being phased out, and other such relationships. Well, it became obvious after a little while that I was not about to go to the Secretary of Agriculture and say, Hey, let's squeeze Sierra Leone on PL-480, because they're not going along with us on seabed mining.

Hundreds of negotiations take place in any given year, and we can't arm all our negotiators with the power to apply that kind of pressure. In any event, in a complex negotiation like the law of the sea, you could still apply a sanction or promise or whatever only once. In the course of four or five years you may have a hundred comparable problems at least. As a result, therefore, it has to be understood that the only real leverage the United States has is whatever attaches to the prospect that it won't go along in the end. One of the ironies of the Law of the Sea Conference, as Leigh Ratiner has pointed out, is that the United States may discover that what looked in advance like significant leverage deriving from the fear that we would not go along has turned out to be overinflated because, now that we haven't gone along, nobody will care.

At any rate, coming more directly to the main subject, I'm not sure that I would entirely agree with Dr. Nyhart's formulation of criteria that make a problem appropriate for a computer model in its relationship to multilateral negotiations. Uncertainty was important in the negotiations on this subject because it was important to convince members of the conference that seabed mining was a highly risky operation. It was dramatic to see the impact of a relatively minor adjustment in the prices of copper or nickel in terms of profitability as against that of rather sharp variances in estimates of the investment costs. As you come to see that what is involved is a very high risk enterprise, you begin to absorb the idea that, given these uncertainties, anybody who might be disposed to go into the activity at all would need to have a prospective rate of return significantly better than he could get investing in government bonds.

But in many cases you may be looking for the precise opposite. One of the areas in which computer models can have high relevance to international negotiations concerns environmental issues. There what you're seeking is so far as possible to reduce ranges of uncertainty and to identify variables that are so critical to the equation that it may be important to undertake additional research necessary to narrow those parameters of uncertainty even more. One could easily think of examples in which the application of computer technology would be relevant to that kind of issue, e.g., acid rain and of course nuclear power development. The role of the International Atomic Energy Agency with regard to the nuclear fuel cycle is integrally related to calculations of risk which, as you are well aware, involve very large numbers of variables.

In the context of arms-control negotiations there are a number of relatively easily recognizable opportunities. One of the most significant things about these negotiations is that they are now for the first time addressing the entire range of weapons systems from intercontinental ballistic missiles and submarine launched missiles at one extreme to conventional weapons under MBFR [mutual and balanced force reductions] at the other, with INF in between.

This means, therefore, that we have the potential for the first time of balancing complex and asymmetrical components. I won't elaborate the point, but there are also the uncertainties intrinsic to various combinations of verification devices, etc.

I will just conclude by saying that it occurs to me that one key factor in identifying the potential for the use of computers in negotiations—or at least international negotiations—lies in the recognition that an issue either turns on or is significantly affected by a question of fact whose resolution would contribute to the ability to reach consensus on a given policy result or choice.

A second factor, obviously, is that the problem has to be of a kind that can be handled with a computer, which means that it must have variables capable of quantification, and presumably they must be numerous enough—and the data involved voluminous enough—so that it's worthwhile to do it by computer rather than by some simpler mechanism.

The process of committing a problem to this kind of exercise has the added advantage of insulating it from the more emotional and value-laden factors surrounding other elements of the debate, thereby contributing to a more rational process. I think that this can be a secondary value of the use of computer models in multilateral negotiations. They make it possible on the one side to deal with the rational issues that directly concern the model but also to generate an approach to the resolution of other issues in an atmosphere of rationality and increasing trust.

J. K. SEBENIUS: I would like to address some questions from the audience and related subjects. Some of you must be wondering what the MIT model actually looked like.

The program was written in Fortran-4, it was about several thousand lines of code, and the display capability was absolutely primitive. It was a simple printout, and it was designed much more to answer questions after the fact than it was during the case. A graphics capability would have enhanced it enormously, and today I'm sure that we could have done that much better and gotten real-time responses back and forth from either Geneva or New York to Cambridge and manipulated a lot of the particular variables much more effectively. But that's what the thing looked like and how we did it.

There is a second question relating to the nature of the model, and it's worth making a distinction here between two kinds of models that might be used in negotiation. One is of the negotiation process itself, that is, of the negotiation and its dynamics, the issues, possibly different sides' valuations on the issues, and, as Ambassador Richardson mentioned, possible linkages to other issues. But a model of the negotiation itself is distinct from what this model was, which was of the substantive issue under negotiation. It was a model of the technical and economic issues themselves.

There's a question as to whether early user participation in the development could have effectively been added to this model. My impression in this case is no, although that's a very interesting line of inquiry for research. By and large, such models of negotiations as I've seen that tried to model the negotiation itself tended to be for the tactical use of one side or another.

The second thing is that one tends to model what's specifically and easily quantifiable and chart what's happening in terms of positions on very well defined issues. Sometimes that leads to a creative process. But more often what it tends to do is set up a haggling process back and forth on the position of an indicator, rather than defining the underlying interests and how they might actually be resolved.

There's a third question that relates to this. What happens in a negotiation when both parties have access to the same data and model? Usually one party does not want to let the other have all the information—the one who, say, wants to sell the land does not want the buyer to know the highway is coming through. In a sense the distinction that this question raises is whether negotiation primarily consists of one party getting more while the other party gets less in a situation where the buyer and seller won't see each other anymore.

In cases like seabed mining, the complexity of the issues and the uncertainties among them are such that if an agreement on the correct principles can be hammered out at the political level, then a number of the important scientific, economic, and technical issues underlying them can be elucidated jointly. In many cases, the participants figure out that their interests really don't strictly oppose each other. For example, the early Indian proposal for the law of the sea was that a bonus of a particular size be offered. A standard negotiation scenario might have been, "The Indians wanted it high, the Americans wanted it low, and they went back and forth." Instead, looking at this model, we understood that the time distribution of that payment was all important. It was possible—if the companies had a critical need for it early on and if the international community by and large was concerned with the welfare of future generations and in a much broader perspective—to distribute the payments over time in a way that met both interests. We came to understand the nature of the problem better converting it from this strictly distributive effort.

The second thing I've noticed is how important the sustainability of any agreement like this is. The financial agreements in the law of the sea are linked to a whole lot of other issues in a treaty that will have to work or be renegotiated in 20 years or so if they do not. To trick somebody in the short term in this seems to me very shortsighted and not at all in the spirit of what we want. In a practical sense, it comes right back to haunt you if it isn't sustainable.

T. T. B. KOH: I'd like to move on to a question that we're supposed to discuss in this segment, What other negotiations on the international agenda might make use of a computer model? And somebody from the audience has sent up a question asking, "To what extent can computer-assisted negotiations be useful in the area of the law of space?"

In the law of space, I don't see how a computer-assisted negotiation can be presently applicable because, as Mr. Richardson said in his last statement, the lesson or the generalization I've drawn from the law of the sea negotiations is that a computer-assisted negotiation is most useful when the outcome of the negotiation depends upon an agreement on facts or where the issue or question involved can be reduced to numbers. In the case of the law of space, those two criteria are not present.

Looking at Dr. Nyhart's list, I'm not sure which of the topics he has included satisfy these two criteria. Let's take an example from the area of the international monetary system. As you know the Bretton Woods system of fixed exchange rate has broken down. What we now have is an international monetary system based on floating exchange rates. Some people think that the status quo works reasonably well and there's no reason to be alarmed by the breakdown of the Bretton Woods system. Others take a different view and have called for the convening of a high-level international economic conference in order to arrive at a new agreement based upon more stable exchange rates. And the question I've often asked myself is, Is there any way in which a computer might help us in answering the question whether the world is better off with an international monetary system based on stable exchange rates or is it better off with a system based on floating exchange rates?

The other area where I have been puzzled by disputes that appear, on their face, to be about facts is in the important area of arms control. Is this one area in which the computer can assist us in the negotiations? I'm puzzled for example by the ongoing talks that are taking place in Vienna, between NATO and the Warsaw Pact countries on mutual, balanced force reduction. The facts presented by NATO suggest that in the field of conventional arms the Warsaw Pact countries outnumber NATO on every component of conventional arms.

According to the facts put forward by the Warsaw Pact countries, this is not the case. According to their statements of fact, the conventional forces of the two military blocs appear to be more or less in balance. Is this a case where the issues and questions in dispute are essentially of a factual nature or not? And if they are essentially of a factual nature, would an objective assessment of the facts by a computer be helpful to the two negotiating parties? I'm equally puzzled by the negotiations on strategic issues, because here too there appear to be fundamental disputes about facts. The current negotiations in Geneva on intermediate nuclear forces is a very good illustration of this.

According to the NATO point of view, the Soviet Union has many missiles emplaced in the European part of the Soviet Union targeted on western Europe while NATO does not have any of these intermediate nuclear forces. When you look at the facts presented by the Soviet Union, they are entirely different. According to the Soviet point of view, in this segment, intermediate nuclear weapons as in the intercontinental nuclear forces, the western and eastern numbers appear to be close to parity. I'm very puzzled by this and ask myself repeatedly whether the questions under dispute are essentially questions of fact or disputes about something else dressed up as questions of facts? I think it might be interesting to hear from either the members of the panel or the audience on whether or not computer science could be helpful in the whole area of arms control negotiations both in conventional weapons and nuclear weapons.

D. B. STRAUS: Assuming that the members of this panel wanted to persuade other international negotiators to try computer-assisted negotia-tions, how could we even get them to examine seriously the possibility? Because we have already recognized the various obstacles of distrust, of disinterest in sharing data, of adversarial attitudes. Is there something in Elliot Richardson's earlier suggestion of developing a showcase model of how the negotiations might progress with CAN? Could such a model be used as a selling tool to get the parties hooked, if you will, on this kind of a process?

J. D. NYHART: As I understand this, it's a different kind of a model you're asking about—it sounds like it's more of a process model. I would come back to the criteria that have been thrown out on the table by Ambassador Koh and Mr. Richardson and ask about the numbers. I mean, where do you have something solid in the form of the technology involved? I think that uncertainty is a characteristic of problems of complexity, and yet the goal is to reduce the uncertainty not to enhance it. I would rather take something that had value that was being negotiated about—such as in the Antarctic, for example, the value of either the living resources or the nonliving mineral resources—as a focal point. You know that it's going to come down at some point, as Dr. Sebenius said, to a question of somebody getting more and somebody getting less of resources of economic value. So I'd answer the question in that way.

D. B. STRAUS: Well, let us assume your requirement that the issue should include tangible values and large numbers. Then what would be the best approach to the parties? You've already suggested that a model should first be built by academics before the users get in. But how do you just make that bridge between the construction of a model and its eventual use? This bridge is obviously not being crossed very often because we are talking about almost a single case rather than what I think we are suggesting should be hundreds of cases.

T. T. B. KOH: I'd like to ask you a question, Dr. Nyhart. I'm not sure whether you are saying that arms-control negotiations do not satisfy the two criteria suggested or not. If your answer is that they don't, I would ask you why. Isn't arms-control negotiation preeminently about numbers—about the number of the men under arms, about the numbers of weapons, and the different systems of weaponry?

J. D. NYHART: The element that is missing—and it ought not to be critical, it's just that I don't know the answer to it—is "What do you use as your value?" I mean, survival is the bottom line and of course it's the most critical thing. I would suspect, and again I'm speaking from total ignorance, that both the United States and the Soviet Union have already undertaken some rather sophisticated level of modeling these problems. I hope this is being done, but I just don't know.

J. K. SEBENIUS: I'd like to make another distinction that may help this a little bit. I think that computer modeling is used a great deal in arms-control negotiations, but mostly by one side or by the other side with respect to the suspected or feared capabilities of the other and how the two would fare in this exchange or that contingency. I think what we're mostly talking about here is the models that are of joint use, and I'd add another criterion to those that Ambassador Koh laid out.

There's a distinction between uncertainties that we might think of as natural or technical or economic versus those that we think of as strategic or game theoretic or behavioral, where what you're trying to model is what somebody else actually has done or is doing. I think that models of the former tend to be more useful than those of the latter case for a fair number of reasons. The type of uncertainty is important.

This leads me to think that in arms-control situations, the place where a joint model might be very useful is in a subcategory of those. Say United States and Soviet negotiators were very worried about what to do about a crisis situation that might involve accidents. They very well might get together to try to build a model of a variety of such situations and the possible responses of one side and the other to determine what kind of system they'd like to agree on that would tend to minimize that possibility.

I can imagine a very useful model and a collaborative attempt there, whereas a joint model on what the real intentions of the Soviets or the United States are seems a lot less plausible.

T. T. B. KOH: But if I may say so, the negotiations in Vienna are not about intentions. It seems to me that in Vienna the two military blocs, NATO and the Warsaw Pact, have an agreed objective and the agreed objective is to negotiate mutual balanced force reductions and what is preventing them from making progress in these negotiations is that they proceed from such divergent assertions of fact.

So my simple question is, Why can't we help the two negotiating parties narrow the gap which apparently exists between them about what the facts are? Why can't the Stockholm International Peace Reasearch Institute, for example, build a computer model to help NATO and Warsaw Pact in their talks in Vienna?

Why can't academics from countries in the two military alliances get together and independently see whether or not they are able to build a joint computer model which can be of some utility in comparing the conventional armed forces of the two sides. I mean these are some of the questions I'd like to raise.

E. L. RICHARDSON: Before coming to the question of MBFR, I want to go back to Dr. Nyhart's question about what you might wish to obtain as the end point of your calculations, of what is the equivalent of an answer in the arms-control field to the question of internal rate of return, given certain assumptions, in seabed mining.

The answer is implicit in the title of the negotiations in Vienna, "mutual and balanced force reductions," and it's certainly the understood objective of the START negotiations and the INF negotiations: namely, rough parity or equality under conditions of optimal stability. Some combinations or mixes of weapons on each side are more inherently unstable than others, e.g., a situation in which each side's forces consist predominantly of intercontinental ballistic missiles with a high degree of accuracy and significant vulnerability in their placement. Under that sort of circumstance, each side has a relatively greater incentive to launch a preemptive strike. So the objectives of arms-control negotiations, broadly speaking, are to achieve parity at lower numbers with at least as great stability in the mix on each side as you had to begin with and, if possible, to increase that stability.

Now you can visualize getting out of the computer the optimization of various combinations of weapons mixes, locations, and so on, and you could also feed into a computer calculations designed to answer questions about parity given the asymmetries of the mixes of weapons systems on each side.

You could assign quanta that would equate range, accuracy, vulnerability of the launching site, velocity, and so on, so as to give you answers as to the relative equivalence of mixes of systems in which one side had fewer bombers, more fighters, etc. That is at least theoretically highly possible; I don't know whether it is being done, or has been done. I have been arguing for quite a long time that something like that should be done. And as I said a moment ago, the most important thing about the East-West negotiations now is that for the first time they do address in one form or another the whole range of systems. It's like taking the microphone, a glass, a pad of paper, and a couple of other objects and putting them on one side of a scale and then looking around this dais to find another combination of objects that will balance the other side of the scale. If there are relatively few objects on the table, it may be very difficult to get the two pans of the scale to balance, but if you piled onto the table all kinds of odds and ends, it would be a lot easier for each side then to pick out a number of things that would balance each other.

So in one sense the fact that we now have negotiations across this range is complicating, but in another it could be simplifying. You could, for example, visualize using a computer to determine the equivalents between the mixtures, i.e., what combination of things on one side would balance out a very different combination on the other.

Going directly now to MBFR, I'm afraid, Ambassador Koh, that the problems of fact here don't on their face lend themselves to either involvement of neutral arbiters or the use of a computer. The reasons why the numbers are in disagreement are things like whether or not certain units in a Soviet army corps are to be deemed to be combat troops or not, or whether they're performing roles that in the NATO side are performed by civilians. You thus get counting problems that are essentially definitional; there are also disputes arising over the question of whether or not you count aircraft on a basis that recognizes their downtime while being serviced, and so on. What are the effective combat numbers? And there are questions of when troops are on the line, and part of the problem is that the Soviet forces can of course readily be withdrawn into the Soviet Union and relatively rapidly redeployed on the Polish-German frontier, and so the question then is, How should this affect the balance?

These are the hangups, and the possible involvement of neutrals would raise the question of what the Russians—or for that matter NATO—would let you do in arriving at an independent count. The western numbers, of course, are obtained from satellite and aerial photography, mainly, and by espionage. But even so, whatever may be the relevance of the MBFR example, there is certainly ample room in the field of arms control for the resourceful use of computer technology.

D. B. STRAUS: Mr. Richardson, while you're still close to the microphone, a number of questions have been handed up from the audience. Assuming that computer-assisted negotiations can broaden the arena of discussions in this field, in the arms field, what would be the next practical step? In other words, where should the model be built? Should it be a United Nations initiative, some have asked, or should it be another MIT model, or should a softer approach be made to try and get an agreement among the parties that such a model should be built?

E. L. RICHARDSON: I think the idea of equivalence is a useful one. There are a lot of subjects, by the way, in which it would be useful to do quite a lot of work on quanta. That's where you would have to begin before you could feed anything into a computer and get something useful. There was, of course, one major, crude step taken early on in arms-control negotiations with the evolution of the concept of the "launcher," when it was decided to deal with submarine-launched missiles, ICBM's, and bombers as equivalents: they were all launchers and could thus be traded off for one. Numbers of warheads and throw-weight are less crude measurements. What is needed, I think, is to carry the quantification process much further.

You touched, Ambassador Koh, on the INF problem, and you asked, What's the answer to the point being made by the Soviet Union about so-called forward-based systems on the western side and the weapons that could be launched from naval vessels in European waters? Well, part of the difficulty is that the West is saying that you can't equate these fighter bombers, which are deployed primarily in the event of possible conventional conflict, with weapons that can reach western European cities from Soviet soil, even from east of the Urals, in 7 or 8 minutes. Since these are noncomparable on their face, there's no ready way of dealing with the factual question of equivalence there until you can define terms of equivalence. You'd have to sell the concept before you got to that stage, and if you made significant progress in defining those terms, it would then be relatively easy to wheel out the computers.

The initiatives for this could come from a lot of places. It could come from the United Nations. Indeed, it could be a very useful exercise for the United Nations, and I personally would like to see it come from there for a lot of reasons. I think we are underutilizing the United Nations. The United Nations ought to get off its polemical kick on the politicization of extraneous matters and get at some of these things. Ambassador Koh is just the man to lead such an effort, and I can't think of a better result to come out of this discussion than that he would take that on as his next project.

J. D. NYHART: I'd like to answer some questions from the audience. One is about modeling of values. Yes, it can be done and I think it ought to be done: it was not done in this case. More is known about the problems of separating facts from value, I think, with each passage of each year and it should enter into modeling efforts and I hope they will in the future.

Second, somebody asked about environmental impacts. There has been a really monumental study done called DOMES, the Deep Ocean Mining Environmental Study financed over several years by the Department of Commerce, NOAA, looking at the environmental impacts of deep ocean mining. There was one effort to take these data and to put them into the context of impact on return, or whether it was significant or not in dollar terms. My impression is that the environmental impact of the deep ocean mining by this country, for something that has not come into being yet, has been reasonably well addressed.

Somebody asked if at MIT, the software was available for purchase by industry. We have licensed it to the EEC. As you know universities all over the country are trying to make money from their research projects. We have responded at one time to a potential inquiry by industry saying that we could license it, and would like to get involved with them.

T. T. B. KOH: I think perhaps I would close the discussion on this note, that the experience I've had in the law of the sea negotiations with the use of a computer has awakened me to the importance of this branch of learning and the efficacy of the computer in multinational negotiations. I think we, in the diplomatic community, should be much more aware than we have been in the past of how the computer scientists can help us in our negotiating process. And off the top of my head, I can think of several areas in which the computer may be helpful in our negotiations, arms control being one. The management of marine resources is another; the enactment of environmental legislation both at sea and on land is a third. In the economic negotiations, I can also see a role for computer-assisted negotiations.

So I go away reinforced in my convictions that this is an area where the two cultures ought to get to know each other much better.

The Role of the Computer Metaphor in Understanding the Mind

DANIEL C. DENNETT

Department of Philosophy
Tufts University
Medford, Massachusetts 02155

Professor Sherry Turkle has mentioned that when children look inside a computer toy, they find something utterly inscrutable: a little chip with no moving parts. They cannot make any sense of it at all. The same thing is true, of course, if you take off the top of somebody's skull and look at his brain. Absolute inscrutability. And oddly enough, it does not help if you take out your microscope and look at the details of the brain very closely. You will no more see a thought or an idea or a pain or an intention if you look at the synapses or neurotransmitters than if you look at the hypothalamus or occipital cortex or the other large parts of the brain.

There are several responses to this inscrutability or opacity of the brain. The first, and traditional, response is *dualism:* the ball of stuff we see between the ears could not possibly explain the mind, so the mind must be made of some other stuff altogether, some God-like, nonmechanical stuff. This is a well-known scientific dead end; in fact, it is giving up on science altogether. It amounts to "Let God do it."

Another response that I will say more about shortly is what I call *mysticism about the organic brain:* dualism is false; the mind must be the brain somehow, but it must be essentially mysterious. "I wonder if we will ever understand how!"

The third response is "Roll up your sleeves and dig in." The brain is mysterious, in fact quite inscrutable, but let us just start at the periphery and work our way slowly in, seeing if we can make sense of it. This is often called "bottom-up" as opposed to "top-down" research in the sciences of the mind. "Top down" starts at the mind and mental events and works down, hoping to get someday to the synapses; "bottom up" starts at the synapses and hopes to work up eventually to the mind. This is a responsible and legitimate reaction to inscrutability. We have seen at this conference several good examples of research conducted in this spirit, but it is not the approach I am going to talk about here.

I am going to talk about yet a fourth reaction: the strategy of *theoretical idealization.* As John Searle put it in the panel discussion [Part VII], according to this research strategy, "the brain does not matter"—for the moment! According to this strategy, we should ignore the messy, fine details of the brain for awhile and see if we can find some theoretical idealization that will enable us to begin to get a grip on how the activities and processes of the mind might be organized.

Perhaps the reason I favor this approach is that it is the traditional philosophical approach—and I am a philosopher. The brain does not matter in traditional epistemology: you simply posit a mind, a thinking thing or "res cogitans" as Descartes put it, and then you start theorizing in an a priori fashion about the features and properties of such a knowing subject. Now in traditional epistemology (and I mean by traditional epistemology almost everything before the day before yesterday) this idealization was an *extreme* idealization. Typically the mind was supposed to be infinite or as good as infinite. In Descartes' terms it was explicitly infinite. In the terms of the logical positivists in this century it might just as well have been infinite, since no one was interested in any particular limits there might be on any actual capacities of the mind. But another curious feature of this traditional philosophical idealization of the mind is that the knowing subject was imagined to be a sort of mandarin, a person with no cares in the world, waited on hand and foot, apparently, whose only task was to avoid error at all costs. No difficulties intervened; there was never any time pressure; the goal was not ever to make a mistake. So the theories of the mind that emerged were all designed to describe methods that would permit one always to go from certainty to certainty, and never risk error.

The philosopher Clark Glymour recently said to me that artificial intelligence (AI) is really just "logical positivism carried on by other means." There is a certain amount of truth to that, but as we considered the matter further, several major differences became clear between traditional logical positivism and AI, which Glymour calls "android epistemology"—a good term, I think.

In android epistemology the original overidealized philosophical model is enriched by three constraints:

1. *Mechanism.* Whatever theory is proposed, one must be able to describe (perhaps with a modicum of hand waving) how in principle it could be "realized" in a mechanism. This indirect but important constraint is of course a bulwark against dualism.
2. *Finitude.* The proposed models of mind must all suppose the mind to be finite, to have limited resources.
3. *Time pressure.* The model must be able to find the "right" answers in the real time available in the real world. Life rushes on; the world will not wait for the thinking thing to ponder all possible avenues; it must be able to act intelligently under time pressure. (Professor Rabin, in his talk, brought out in a different way the importance of this constraint. This is a deep, fundamental constraint on any model of an epistemological subject or knower of the world.)

How important are these constraints? Abstract as they are, they make the game of coming up with a top-down theory of the mind deliciously difficult without being impossible—a suitably difficult game so that the theories one comes up with are actually of some interest (unlike most of their predecessors in the over-idealized philosophical tradition). In fact, these three constraints enable one to construct an argument with a conclusion surprisingly close to that of Professor Searle, about the importance of the brain in human thought. The constraints of android epistemology require one to construct a theory that is mechanistically realizable, but couched in very abstract terms—"software" terms, you might say. Such a theory describes what Searle calls a "purely formal system." (We might add, noting our third constraint, a purely formal *but dynamic* system, a system for which time is a critical parameter.) This leads then to a model of the mind or the knower composed in terms of strategies of formal operations and activities. That is in an ancient philosophical tradition, but now enriched with the new constraints. And it leads to a vision of what is important—or "essential"—about minds, vividly expressed by Maria Muldaur in a popular song:

It ain't the meat, it's the motion!

(I am indebted to Richard Sharvy for drawing my attention to this excellent use of Muldaur's song.) This might well be the motto of AI—or of what Searle calls "strong AI." Searle's own position is then succinctly captured:

It's the meat!

Here we have a sharp-edged difference of opinion. But the constraints of AI (or android epistemology) themselves provide the premises for an argument that comes close to resolving this disagreement with a dialectical compromise.

Probably many of you have read Edwin A. Abbott's amusing fantasy, *Flatland: a Romance of Many Dimensions,*[1] which begins in a two-dimensional world—a plane inhabited by intelligent plane figures—triangles and other polygons. Someone—I cannot recall who—objected that this world was impossible (who ever thought otherwise!) because there could not be a two-dimensional intelligent being. In order to get sufficient connectivity in whatever played the role of the creatures' brains, there had to be three dimensions (so that wires could cross each other, in effect). John McCarthy points out to me that this is strictly false; John von Neumann proved years ago that a general automaton—a universal Turing machine—can be realized in two dimensions, but of course such an automaton trades speed for geometrical simplicity. One can vastly increase the speed of operation of a computer (or brain) by folding it back on itself and letting it communicate within itself in three dimensions. So it is no accident that our brains are three-dimensional.

Moreover, one can now see with something approaching certainty that our brains need to be not just three-dimensional, but also organized for *parallel processing*. For many cognitive tasks—especially the pattern-detecting tasks of perception, and some memory-searching tasks—the "machine architecture" of a standard digital computer, a "von Neumann machine" that is organized to operate sequentially, doing just one thing at a time, but doing each thing very fast, simply does not permit the right computations to be executed in the time available. So an intelligent being (a being like us) must have a brain organized for very rich parallel processing—perhaps millions of channels wide. Still, it seems we could build such a device out of silicon chips with scarcely any major advance in technology.

But what if it turns out (as some think) that while the brain's ten billion (or so) neurons are the main *switching* elements of the mind, they do this by making essential use of small information-storing changes in their subcellular organic molecules. It may not be physically possible to mimic the information-handling powers of such collections of molecules with anything other than just such systems of molecules. (An allosteric enzyme molecule capable of considerable information processing weighs in at 10^{-17} grams, and if one tries simulating the behavior of groups of such molecules in other media, one soon creates a very large, very slow model.)[2]

So it may very well turn out that the only way one can achieve the information-handling prowess of a human brain (in real time) is by using—a human brain! So it might turn out after all that the only way to have a mind like ours is to have a brain like ours, composed of the same organic materials, organized in roughly the same way. This leads to an apparent resolution of the disagreement between Searle and the proponents of "strong AI":

Probably, only this meat can give you that motion.

Has the disagreement now been dissolved? Searle, after all, has accused AI of ignoring the causal powers of the brain, and here is an argument, based on AI principles and constraints, showing how important the brain's actual causal powers are. But in fact, not only does this argument not resolve the disagreement, it throws into sharp relief the nature of Searle's curious and mystical view, and AI's reasons for resisting it.

As Professor Dreyfus noted in the panel discussion, Searle concedes that it is possible in principle to build a brainlike device out of silicon chips (or other AI-approved hardware) that perfectly mimics the real time input-output behavior of a human brain! That is, you could throw a person's brain away, replace it with a suitably programmed computer (a "merely formal system" embodied in some inorganic hardware or other), and that person's body would go on behaving *exactly* as it would have gone on behaving had it kept its brain. The control powers of the brain are not the "causal powers" Searle makes so much of: in fact, the causal powers Searle admires are entirely independent of the information-receiving, information-processing, and controlling powers of the brain. A body controlled by a computer rather than a brain might seem to outside observers to be an intelligent person, with a mind like ours (in fact, it would pass the most demanding behavioral tests of intelligence we could devise), but there would not in fact be any mind there at all! Such a computer, being a "purely formal system," would not "produce real intentionality," and hence there would exist not a glimmer of consciousness to associate with this animated (but—according to Searle—inanimate) body.

It has often been pointed out that Searle's view has a curious implication in the area of evolutionary biology. If, as he insists, a mindless ("purely formal") computer brain of this sort is possible, it presumably could have evolved by natural selection. Are we not lucky, then, that our ancestors did not happen to have one of those mindless brains instead of the brains we have! Since such brains would be input-output *equivalent* to ours, from the outside they would be indistinguishable; natural selection could find no leverage for selecting in favor of our conscious sort of brain, full of "intentionality," instead of selecting in favor of the zombie-computer sort of brain (full of the low-priced spread). If it had been our misfortune to have had mindless ancestors of that sort, we would now all be zombies!

Android epistemologists—the defenders of strong AI—declare that this imagined distinction between two sorts of otherwise behaviorally indistinguishable control system is illusory. The illusion is sustained by reflecting on what if anything "it would be like" to be (or have!) such a control system oneself. This insistence by Searle on what he calls the first-person point of view is, simply, a big mistake. It is the last gasp of Cartesian introspective certainty. As John McCarthy said in the panel discussion, the AI community regards its reliance on a *third*-person perspective as "virtuous."

Why should anyone be afraid of the third-person perspective? This idea of bringing the mind into the third-person, objective view of science strikes some people as an esthetically pleasing, promising idea: at last we are beginning to see, however dimly, a path uniting the last great outpost of mystery, the human mind, to the expanding dominion of science. Other people, however, see the idea as profoundly threatening and unsettling. As Professor Turkle has noted, many people exhibit quite strong emotional reactions when confronted with such suggestions.

I am reminded of the reaction that greeted Darwin's theory of evolution by natural selection. As we all know, Darwin's theory hit the world like a bolt of lightning. One of the curious facts about it was that its importance was widely misperceived by the public. People could feel in their bones that this new idea was somehow a terrible threat to their peace of mind, a nightmare dread come true, but in their anxiety, they fixed on the trivial implications of the new theory. Perhaps they were afraid to acknowledge its real force. People said, "He claims we are the cousins of apes!"—as if the presumed embarrassment of having hairy, chattering ancestors in one's family tree were the worst blow to one's self-image that the Darwinian theory could deliver. "He claims the story of creation in the Bible is false!" others charged, and this got closer to the heart of the matter, for it was ultimately the belief in God itself that was effectively undermined by Darwin's theory. Why? Because the most compelling and sophisticated argument for the existence of God, the "argument from design," whose force could be appreciated by the most agnostic scientist, and which owed none of its appeal to faith or revelation or traditional dogmas—that best argument for the existence of God had suddenly lost its credentials. But even here, intelligent people missed, and perhaps chose to miss, the point.

Recall, for instance, the famous Scopes monkey trial, pitting William Jennings Bryan against Clarence Darrow. There was Bryan, the fundamentalist and Populist hero of the farm states, three times unsuccessful Democratic candidate for president, leading the prosecution of Scopes, who dared teach the theory of evolution to his high school students. The trial was one of the first historic events to receive the full attention of the modern media, with armies of reporters telegraphing hundreds of thousands of words about the trial to their newspapers each day. The nation was spellbound. But in all of that intense scrutiny, and in all of the oratory on both sides, the real challenge of Darwin's theory lay all but hidden.

Bryan put on quite a show. With vehement oratory, he laid down a few home truths that any simple man could understand. Any so-called scientist who could not see what any ordinary folk could see was just a fool. He ridiculed the opposition, taking care to find cheapened, oversimplified versions of the views he encouraged everyone to scoff at. We often diminish what we fear, hoping to turn what seems to be a bogeyman into a silly clown we will not have to fear anymore.

Today we see people picking up the jargon of computers and adapting it to popular culture, cheapening and diminishing it, and diverting their anxiety with hackneyed—and implausible—bogeymen. Would you like to marry a robot? Are you a (mere) Turing machine clanking away on a paper tape? Do you know someone who has been "deprogrammed" after being victimized by a religious cult? The fear is evident enough in many manifestations of the computer metaphor. Is it, like the earlier fear of the Darwinian metaphor, a misplaced anxiety? Is there in fact anything to the computer metaphor? Have we made any substantial progress in understanding the mind with the help of the concepts of computer science?

I will describe one very basic, very abstract contribution of computers to the understanding of the mind. There is a well-known purely conceptual problem which I call Hume's problem—not because David Hume solved it, but because he struggled mightily with it. You can find versions of it in recent writings by B. F. Skinner and Gilbert Ryle,[3,4] and in many others. There is a tremendous and plausible theoretical temptation to say that a mind is essentially something containing representations: memories, ideas, thoughts, sensations. Let us call those all mental representations. But a representation does not work, can play no role, unless there is a representation user or representation appreciator to manipulate it and to understand it. So a representation user has to be a mind. But if inside your mind you have representations, and a little representation user using those representations, what is inside that representation user's mind? More representations, with their own inner representation users? Do we get an infinite regress of little men in the brain—"homunculi"—with littler men in their brains and so on? The whole idea of mental representation systems has thus seemed to many to be like the idea of a perpetual motion machine: a strictly impossible mechanism—a miraculous object.

Computer science has changed that. Not just AI but computer science in general, for a computer is, if nothing else, a mindless manipulator of representations. Well, maybe they are not representations, since they do not seem to need inner representation users with minds. Whatever they are, there is no infinite regress, for what is actual is possible, and there sit the computers, honest-to-goodness representation-using mechanisms. Inside these computers are something-or-others—"data structures" and other newfangled entities—that might well be called *self-understanding representations*. They are representations that understand themselves!

Now that might seem like a contradiction in terms, an obviously incoherent joining of concepts. But we should remember that there was a time when the concept of splitting the atom was equally self-contradictory. Atoms were *by definition* unsplittable. We have learned that there are such things as splittable atoms (though now perhaps we should agree that they are misnamed, precisely because they are splittable and do have parts—which their name, in Greek, denies). We have more recently learned that there are such things as self-understanding representations (though there may well be a better name for them). They perform the roles we traditionally assigned to the various dubious sorts of mental representations of earlier theories of the mind. And hence they break the back of the infinite regress argument that sets up Hume's problem.

All this shows, of course, is a certain possibility in principle. It does not establish how or why or in what ways a human mind might be like a computer. All it shows is that in principle we can have a theory of the mind that is mechanistic, finite, operates in real time, and is not a perpetual motion machine. There are still many fundamental conceptual problems (and an excellent survey of them was presented by Professor McCarthy), but progress is being made on them.

Should we, nevertheless, in the light of my earlier conclusion about the probable importance of the brain, abandon "pure" AI in favor of "bottom-up" brain research? No, for a reason that has been very clearly brought out by Professor Michael Rabin. No amount of parallel processing, no matter how many channels wide, and no amount of microminiaturization, even down to the level of organic molecules in individual nerve cells, is going to give one enough computational power to avoid a genuine exponential explosion of computation, a "combinatorial explosion" of information processing. There is only one way of avoiding that sort of frantic paralysis: clever software. Software—"purely formal systems"—is going to be required to make sense of the brain's operations in any case. We are going to have to understand how the *strategies* of representation and representation manipulation have achieved their quite necessary economies, even if we are utilizing the full parallel resources of every neuron and every neuron part.

Some people still may feel the tug of fear at the prospect of taking this third-person perspective on the mind. Some may fear that we will somehow rob each other of what is special and wonderful about us. Some people may thus feel a strong desire to build a moat of some kind around some special part of them—their mind—and keep it forever inviolate and untouchable by science. All I can say to help to assuage that fear is that if you look at the previous great leaps forward in science you will see that far from diminishing our appreciation of the subtlety and wonder and complexity of the phenomena, they have increased it. Our knowledge of the genetic code and its operation, for instance, provides a far more spectacular vista on the nature of procreation than any of the undetailed vitalistic theories that preceded it. I for one have no doubt that if and when we ever do get a good third-person theory of the mind, it will only confirm our most optimistic sense of how extraordinarily complex and beautiful a human mind is.

REFERENCES

1. ABBOTT, E. A. 1962. Flatland: A Romance of Many Dimensions. Blackwell. Oxford, England.
2. MONOD, J. 1971. Chance and Necessity: 69. Vintage/Random House. New York, N.Y.
3. SKINNER, B. F. 1964. Behaviorism at fifty. In Behaviorism and Phenomenology. T. Wann, Ed.: 79–108. University of Chicago Press. Chicago, Ill.
4. RYLE, G. 1949. The Concept of Mind. Hutchinson. London, England.

DISCUSSION OF THE PAPER

QUESTION: There seems to be an assumption in your talk that people out of a sense of dignity and respect for the human mind worry about or are afraid of the computer and seek to maintain our integrity against it, and yet I often see precisely the opposite behavior. I run workshops for computer professionals on computers and human values and I uniformly ask them, Do you believe in the data you process? And they uniformly say, No, we just program the information-processing machines, garbage in, garbage out, but we keep doing it. Managers who don't respect the models around which computer programs are built know there are bad data, and yet the computer says so, so it's easier just to go along with it. And so rather than becoming a something against which we measure ourselves and find ourselves to be greater, it's almost an excuse to stop deep thinking. I wonder how those observations relate to your theory.

D. C. DENNETT: I think you have raised an important problem. Two days ago we heard about expert systems. Expert systems are often very impressive systems and people, including a lot of nonexperts, will soon be interacting with them on a daily basis. There's an amiable but inevitable tendency on the part of human beings to endow these systems with much more intelligence than in fact they have. It is of the utmost social importance, I think, that people become savvy about the limitations of expert systems and learn how to unmask them. They must learn how to find their boundaries and their shortcomings, so that this deep-seated, natural, interpretive tendency (which Professor Turkle has even noted in small children) does not lead us into supposing that these systems are much more reliable and much more worthy of being put in positions of responsibility than in fact they are.

QUESTION: I have a question about the idea of self-understanding representation. I was very excited about the notion. Wouldn't it be a good idea to use already existing philosophical theory, I mean specifically the theory of Ludwig Wittgenstein as formulated in his *Philosophical Investigations*, and use his concept of language games? Wouldn't that be a good starting point?

D. C. DENNETT: I think probably the best answer I could give is yes, it *was* a good starting point. That is, people who have already been thinking about representation in computer systems for some years have probably already benefitted from Wittgenstein's theories on this point. Now it may be that there is much more to be gained from going back to the *Philosophical Investigations* of Wittgenstein, and doing more with the idea of language games. Certainly some of his ideas about family resemblances and both the impossibility and the superfluousness of definitions might play an important role in some part of the artificial intelligence project. I'm not sure.

COMMENT: I don't think the AI community is really aware of the availability of this theory.

D. C. DENNETT: Well it may be that I'm overoptimistic. There are those people in artificial intelligence who are in fact fairly well read and quite sophisticated about philosophy, and then there are those that aren't.

COMMENT: I have no difficulty in understanding your model, because an atom is basically a physical model and of course the physical model can be either divided in parts or it can't. But your second model is a psychological model, but I think maybe you have to be philosopher to understand that you could split a psychological model.

D. C. DENNETT: Once we get away from the idea of an atom as a simple point, and see that it has structure, then we can see how we can split it. The idea of an *idea* as having parts is in fact an ancient one, and can be found in Hume, Locke, Berkeley, and Descartes. Take Locke, for instance, who held that complex ideas are molecules made up out of simple ideas. But that's the wrong way to splitting up psychological processes and states. That leaves all of the understanding on the outside. I think the fundamental insight of computer science is that the decomposition of representation that is needed is of a different sort. It breaks the barrier between the representation and the representation user. But I don't think I can do justice to making that point clear just extemporaneously in a minute.

QUESTION: I wonder whether you would care to give us your opinion on the role of genetic engineering—the revolution that is, next to the computer revolution, probably the most outstanding one since it has helped to create new life forms, organic reproductions, replacements of human parts and is perhaps much more able to give us some highlights in the future of what goes on in what we call the human brain.

D. C. DENNETT: It used to be said that if you made something you understood it. And that used to be true because when we made things we kept our hands on them and we made each part. But we've always known a perfectly good exception to that rule: When you make children, the fact that in one sense you made them does not mean you understand how they work—because you didn't make them in the right way. It wasn't "hands-on" construction involving understanding the principles of all the parts.

Now genetic engineering may be "hands-on" construction of the genes, but development under genetic instruction is still largely a mystery and I don't think myself that from genetic engineering we're going to get any more insight into how the human brain works than we will by simply making more babies in the normal way.

As to the social importance of these two revolutions happening side by side, my own attempt to cut through all of the press agentry and punditry suggests to me that the computer revolution will have an order of magnitude greater social impact than the genetic revolution ever will, but I don't know whether to hope I'm right about that.

Index of Contributors

(Italicized page numbers refer to comments made in discussion.)

Subject Index